EXPLOITING THE LIMITS OF LAW

Exploiting the Limits of Law
Swedish Feminism and the Challenge to Pessimism

Edited by

ÅSA GUNNARSSON
Umeå University, Sweden

EVA-MARIA SVENSSON
University of Gothenburg, Sweden
University of Tromsö, Norway

MARGARET DAVIES
Flinders University, Australia

ASHGATE

Published by
Ashgate Publishing Limited
Gower House
Croft Road
Aldershot
Hampshire GU11 3HR
England

Ashgate Publishing Company
Suite 420
101 Cherry Street
Burlington, VT 05401-4405
USA

Ashgate website: http://www.ashgate.com

British Library Cataloguing in Publication Data
Exploiting the limits of law : Swedish feminism and the
challenge to pessimism
1. Feminist jurisprudence - Sweden 2. Pessimism
I. Davies, Margaret, 1923- II. Gunnarsson, Åsa
III. Svensson, Eva-Maria
340'.082'09485
ISBN-13: 978-0-7546-4935-9

Library of Congress Cataloging-in-Publication Data
Exploiting the limits of law : Swedish feminism and the challenge to pessimism / edited by Åsa Gunnarsson, Eva-Maria Svensson and Margaret Davies.
p. cm.
Includes bibliographical references and index.
ISBN 978-0-7546-4935-9
1. Feminist jurisprudence. 2. Sociological jurisprudence. 3. Law--Social aspects--Sweden. I. Gunnarsson, Åsa. II. Svensson, Eva-Maria. III. Davies, Margaret.

K349.E97 2007
340'.115--dc22

2006100189

ISBN: 978-0-7546-4935-9

Printed and bound in Great Britain by Antony Rowe Ltd, Chippenham, Wiltshire.

Contents

List of Contributors

Monica Burman, LLD, Lecturer in Criminal Law, Umeå University. Formerly, she worked for seven years as an associate judge. She has recently presented her thesis about the Swedish criminal legal constructions relating to men's violence against women. E-mail: monica.burman@jus.umu.se

Catharina Calleman, LLD, Associate Professor in Law, Umeå University. She has published books and articles on labour law from a gender perspective, employment law and anti-discrimination law. She is currently working on a project on domestic work funded by the Institute for Labour Market Evaluation and another project about labour law in the twilight zone between private and public law, funded by the Swedish Council for Working Life and Social Research. E-mail: catharina.calleman@jus.umu.se

Margaret Davies, BA, LLB, MA, DPhil; Professor of Law at Flinders University, South Australia. She has written about legal theory, feminist legal thought, and the philosophy of property. She is currently involved in a project funded by the Australian Research Council on legal pluralism. Email: margaret.davies@flinders.edu.au

Görel Granström, LLD, Senior Lecturer in Law, Umeå University. Her current research project concerns the heteronormativity of law and legal practice. She is the project manager for the research project 'Victims of Crime in the Judicial System' at the Law Department in Umeå. E-mail: gorel.granstrom@jus.umu.se

Åsa Gunnarsson, LLD, Professor of Tax Law, Umeå University. She has written extensively on tax law, social welfare law and legal theory, often from a gender perspective. She is a member of the Board of the National Graduate School of Gender Studies. Currently, she is leading a research project funded by the Swedish Research Council about the legal constructions of social citizenship. E-mail: asa.gunnarsson@jus.umu.se

Päivi Honkatukia, PhD, Senior Researcher, National Research Institute of Legal Policy, Helsinki. She has done research on young girl's relationship to crime as perpetrators, victims and by-standers. She has also studied widely issues related to violence, such as rapes reported to the police in Finland and young people's understandings of violence. Her most recent research projects have concerned multiculturalism and crime in Finnish society: immigrants' victimization to violence and young immigrants' positions in the Finnish criminal justice system as perpetrators of crime. E-mail: paivi.honkatukia@om.fi

Ruth Mannelqvist, LLD, Senior Lecturer in Law, Umeå University. She has published in both social welfare law and victimology. A central topic in her research is victims of crimes' right to compensation from different legal aspects. E-mail: ruth.mannelqvist@jus.umu.se

Johanna Niemi-Kiesiläinen, LLD, Professor of Law, Umeå University, Sweden, Docent of procedural law, University of Helsinki. She has published extensively on procedural law, human rights, violence against women and insolvency law. She has led research projects on violence against women and the legal system and comparative consumer bankruptcy. Her latest book analysed criminal procedure in the context of violence against women. E-mail: johanna.niemi@jus.umu.se

Eva Nilsson, LLD student, Umeå University. The topic for her chapter is a legal study on children in matters concerning residence permits. E-mail: eva.nilsson@jus.umu.se

Åsa Persson, LLD, Senior Lecturer in Law, Umeå University. She has written about the Swedish political parties' views on law and politics, especially the state's use of concealed and coercive measures, legal aid and legislation for the protection of and support to victims of crime. E-mail: asa.persson@jus.umu.se

Minna Ruuskanen, LLD, advocate, Helsinki legal aid office. Her doctoral thesis in criminal law studied claims to self-defence by battered women who had killed their partners. She has coedited with Niemi-Kiesiläinen, Honkatukia and Karma a Finnish book on discourse analysis in legal research. E-mail: minna.ruuskanen@om.fi

Eva-Maria Svensson, LLD, Professor of Legal Science, University of Gothenburg and University of Tromsö. Her main research field is legal philosophy and gender theory and she has written extensively on gender issues in the notion of law and legal scholarship as well as on gender equality law. She is a special commissioner investigating the issue of legislation on gender discriminating commercials. E-mail: eva-maria.svensson@law.gu.se

Lena Wennberg, BA, MA in Social Work, Licentiate in Laws (LLL), Lecturer in Social Welfare Law, Umeå University. She is preparing her thesis on the social constructions of solo mothers in social security law. Her project is part of the research project on the legal constructions of social citizenship, lead by Åsa Gunnarsson. E-mail: lena.wennberg@jus.umu.se

List of Tables

Preface

The academic discipline of law has been changing rapidly in recent years. Legal scholarship has had to come to terms with new practical and conceptual conditions for understanding law. Practically, the internationalization of law and the increasing significance of the European Union, have forced a re-evaluation of the notion that the nation state is the source of all law. Conceptually, new theories of knowledge which emphasize its social and discursive foundations have resulted in a rethinking of the traditional emphasis on legally objective knowledge.

This anthology is a feminist response to some of these recent changes in legal scholarship, focusing especially upon the meeting of feminist thought with the Swedish 'dogmatic approach' to law. It considers in particular how the limits of law may be challenged or extended, or even reinforced, by feminist arguments and strategies. Contributions also reflect upon Swedish and Nordic social, cultural and legal contexts and their effect upon feminist legal studies.

This book is the product of a series of workshops which took place at Umeå University from 2003 to 2005. It follows in the footsteps of two previous works concerning Nordic feminism published by Ashgate. These previous works are *Responsible Selves: Women in the Nordic Legal Cultures* (2001) edited by Kevät Nousiainen, Åsa Gunnarsson, Karin Lundström, and Johanna Niemi-Kiesiläinen and *Nordic Equality at a Crossroads: Feminist Legal Studies Coping with Difference* (2004) edited by Eva-Maria Svensson, Anu Pylkkänen, and Johanna Niemi-Kiesiläinen.

The editors and contributors would like to thank a number of people and organizations for their assistance in the preparation of this book. Andreas Pettersson, lecturer and doctoral student at Umeå University, has undertaken extensive and invaluable work as research assistant over a period of several years. Pat Shrimpton, Director of Studies at the Department of Modern Languages, Umeå University, has undertaken the essential and often challenging task of checking and editing the language. Anna Svedjevik, law student at Umeå University, has made a significant contribution by undertaking the technical and stylistic editing for each chapter. Karin Ågren, Lecturer and President of the Gender Equality Board at Umeå University, has provided many contributors with helpful comments and support. We are also grateful to Frances Olsen, Professor of Law at UCLA, who provided the original inspiration for the topic and title of the book.

Finally, we would like to thank two organizations for funding, without which this project would have been impossible. The Swedish Foundation for International Cooperation in Research and Higher Education (STINT) provided generous funding for research visits to Sweden for Margaret Davies. And the Department of Law at Umeå University has made considerable resources available for hosting the workshops at which the chapters were discussed, as well as for research assistance and editorial support.

Åsa Gunnarsson
Eva-Maria Svensson
Margaret Davies

Chapter 1

Reflecting the Epistemology of Law – Exploiting Boundaries

Åsa Gunnarsson, Eva-Maria Svensson and Margaret Davies

A Changing Discipline

This anthology is a feminist response to some of the contemporary changes in the academic discipline of legal scholarship. The traditional boundaries of legal scholarship are being challenged from a wide variety of different political and theoretical perspectives. Legal scholarship is not only changing, it is also expanding, in keeping with a growing interest in, and need for, critical self-reflection.

There are many reasons for these changes. One is that the primary *object* of legal scholarship – the law as enforced by the nation state – is changing conceptually and practically. The state is no longer the only authoritative source of law. Transnational and supranational organizations are also active as legitimate norm-producers, as are more local customary practices, institutions, or social groupings. There is a growing recognition that 'law' can mean different things in different contexts and that interactions between citizens and law can take a variety of forms (Benda-Beckman *et al.* 2005). Efforts to redefine the boundaries of law take on particular significance within the context of increasing recognition of the pluralistic nature of contemporary law. It is no longer feasible to think of law as a singular entity defined centrally by the operations of state power: the term 'law' extends not only to state law, but also to international law, European law, and trade and security alliances. Moreover, the relationship between 'law' and less formal but nonetheless important unofficial or semi-official normative environments also provides a challenge to the image of law as a separate entity with its own coherence and logic. Even when we consider only such 'objective' systems of norms, the conclusion that we inhabit a legally plural world is unavoidable (Teubner 1997).

A second explanation for the changing nature of legal scholarship is that pluralism also characterizes the social, epistemological and discursive environments of scholarship which have an integral relationship with law. The notion of knowledge has changed radically in recent times and is now seen as social and contextual, at least in most social sciences and in the humanities. The contextual understanding of knowledge encourages reflection about the limits of legal scholarship as an academic discipline and its relationship with other disciplines. It is now regarded as natural to pose questions about the perspective of scholarship – who is studying what and why – since this has an impact upon the questions which are asked as well as the results of scholarship. Sketching out the terrain for legal scholarship is a reflective process, which makes visible paradigmatic concepts that are taken for granted in mainstream research. These concepts are like blind spots as they are given but never questioned. This anthology focuses upon three blind spots which have traditionally influenced the construction of the discipline of legal scholarship, especially in Sweden but also elsewhere. These are the close connection between practical legal knowledge and legal scholarship, the fixation with the 'law' as an object, and the fixation with the idea that the discipline is necessarily limited to the boundaries of its object, current law.

These changes in law and legal scholarship may or may not amount to a transition in paradigm (see generally Santos 2002, 7–20). Our aim is not necessarily to promote such a paradigm shift by arguing in favour of specific or formal changes to the boundaries, or a new 'grand theory' of law and legal scholarship. The critical process in which this anthology takes part emphasizes that law is an inevitable part of the political and social context. At the same time, we wish to work reflectively with (and not against) its changing nature by reference to a pluralistic notion of knowledge, and with the aim of engendering positive outcomes for feminist legal scholarship.

The significance of the title 'exploiting the limits of law' is not perhaps, self-evident. Why have we decided to use the term 'exploit', rather than 'explore' or 'challenge'? It is essentially because one of the ideas behind this anthology is that the question of limits is an extremely important one for feminists and all critical legal scholars. It is not possible to reject those limits completely because they define law in the modern world, but more is needed than investigation or analysis. 'Exploit' has been chosen to express a relationship to the limits of law which encapsulates the ambivalence of practically-oriented critique. To 'exploit' means to take advantage of something or to use it to your own benefit. The term also presumes a prior attempt to explore or critique the limits of law.

As a relationship between two terms, exploitation often also implies a power imbalance whereby the person or thing which is exploited has no choice about the terms of the relationship, and may not even be aware that they are being used to another's advantage. But this is not necessarily the case. The suggestion raised by the title is that, in addition to critiquing law, feminism can take advantage of law's limits for its own benefit. One resonance which the title has is the idea that feminist legal scholars may use law's limits to the advantage of women where this is possible, but also critique and transcend those limits when there is a need (cf. Armstrong 2004). For instance, while feminists are often sceptical of the notion of formal equality or equality as sameness because it excludes the specificity of women's lives, there can be times when the claim to formal equality can still be a very useful strategic position. Thus we exploit the notion of formal equality even as we criticize it.[1]

The challenge to feminism lies in the opportunities which emerge from the exploration, critique and exploitation of the limits of law and legal scholarship (see also Davies this volume). The chapters in this book take different positions on the question of the limits of law and legal scholarship, but all start with the intention to subject these limits to some sort of scrutiny and to use that critique for feminist ends. In this sense, the book is an exercise in applied theory: it takes a theoretical stance

1 A strategy which emerged in the Swedish context in Svensson *et al.* 2004.

towards the question of the limits of law and legal scholarship, and attempts to apply those insights in its analysis of specific areas of law. Another common strand in the chapters is that they take critical and theoretical problems as objects of the studies, instead of merely identifying problems of legal content with the aim of seeking specific solutions (see Kuovo 2004, 71–72). This approach is in line with Carol Bacchi's so-called *What is the problem?* approach and also Margaret Davies' *Asking the law question?* approach (Bacchi 1999; Davies 2002). Such problematization focuses on problem representation of competing social constructions of issues. It opens up a range of questions about what social problems law is supposed to be able to solve and which social issues are not represented in legal solutions. When critical problems are the focus of research, theory and method become interconnected.

Feminist legal scholarship in the Nordic countries has followed a different trajectory to its counterpart in the English-speaking Western world. While the Anglo-American legal feminism of the 1980s and early 1990s was routinely divided into several strands – such as liberal, radical, cultural, and postmodern (Davies 2002) – Nordic feminism has never been characterized by such clear theoretical demarcations. There are several reasons for this. In a Nordic legal setting the state is not regarded with the suspicion which is part of the cultural matrix of the more liberal and neo-liberal societies, and nor can it simply be characterized as patriarchal: most Nordic states have been rather proactive in promoting some quite radical policies in favour of gender justice. Officially-endorsed gender equality policies are based on a radical theory of structural inequality and high ambitions to mainstream gender equality issues within the State. The resulting approach is a mix of liberal anti-discrimination policies and more structural methods of changing the distribution of social power.

This leads to the second point of departure between Anglo-American and Nordic feminism, which is that the focus of Nordic feminism has been on elements of the social infrastructure which materially affect the lives of women. This has meant that Nordic feminism has not easily correlated to the standard taxonomies of legal feminism (where socialist and materialist feminism have never been dominant). In addition, some have commented on the fact that there is a different, less hierarchical, understanding of gender in the Nordic context, meaning that the radical feminist perception of empowerment and disempowerment through one's social position as male and female does not carry the same resonance in Nordic society as it does elsewhere (Pylkkänen 2001). Despite this less hierarchical understanding of gender, there is still gender segregation in both the labour market and the domestic sphere. But these differences are understood as a consequence of social-structural factors, rather than merely through the perspective of the relative power of men and women on an individual level. A final reason for the different trajectory taken by Nordic legal feminism when compared to Anglo-American feminism relates to the lack, until quite recently, of a critical mass of feminist legal scholars in the Nordic countries. Many feminists throughout the world are familiar with the pioneering work of Tove Stang-Dahl in the 1980s (Dahl 1987). However, it was not until the mid-1990s that feminist legal scholarship began to have a really significant institutional presence.

In recent years, two significant edited anthologies about Nordic legal feminism have been published. The first, *Responsible Selves,* focused on the figure of the responsible woman as constructed within Nordic legal culture (Nousiainen *et al.*

2001). It explored the way in which the Nordic model of equality has been linked with the myth of the strong and equal woman within the Nordic cultures – a woman who makes an important and acknowledged social contribution – and a contribution to the 'working-life'. In some respects this myth has obscured the full extent of inequality in Nordic societies, despite a high level of state intervention in some areas.[2] This theme was considered by the contributors in relation to a number of areas of law and policy, including welfare law, labour law, tax law, discrimination law, medical law, and criminal law.

As its title suggests, *Nordic Equality at a Crossroads* continued to examine the idea of equality in the Nordic legal systems, identifying areas where the underlying presumption of equality as sameness was problematic (Svensson *et al.* 2004). The point of departure for this book was a feminist critique of the strong Nordic state's progressive equality politics. A basic strand in the critique is that the strong state regards the citizens as a collective with the same interests. When the state acts as a good state, in the best interests of its citizens, the state also reproduces homogenous ideas about class, ethnicity, gender, sexual identity and so forth. The Nordic equality models of welfare arrangements and labour market policies needs to be adjusted to a more heterogeneous society. However, the need for recognition of greater heterogeneity does not mean that the different contributions in the book argue for a replacement of the equality model in favour of a model mainly based on liberal individual rights. Instead the critical feminist analysis challenges the foundations of the equality model – economic equality, progressive welfare arrangements, general educational policies, equal representation in politics and the equal participation in the labour force – from a comprehensive gender perspective.

Both of these works were the results of extended collaboration across several Nordic countries. In the case of *Responsible Selves*, the collaboration consisted of all five Nordic countries – Denmark, Finland, Iceland, Norway and Sweden – although Norway and Iceland were not represented in the anthology itself. *Nordic Equality at a Crossroads* includes chapters from researchers in Denmark, Finland, Sweden, and Norway. These two works are then, the most significant and recent scholarly collaborations in English by Nordic feminists. There are several other important works written by Nordic feminists in English in the 1980s and 1990s, in addition to many published in the Nordic languages (for English works, see Dahl 1987; Hellum 1993; Petersen 1996; Bentzon *et al.* 1998; Kuovo 2004).

The chapters collected in the current volume are an extension of previous work by Nordic legal feminists, but are more concentrated on the Swedish context. This collection continues the strong tradition in Nordic feminist work of analysing the structural conditions of equality and non-discrimination, as reflected particularly in law regulating social welfare and the labour market in the Nordic welfare state. It also continues the tradition of studies of criminal law and men's violence against women, but with a new approach using social constructionism and discourse analysis

2 For instance, in Sweden policy makers have recognized actual inequality and substantive discrimination, and equality measures have been extensively promoted. When it comes to the end results and the legal application of the equality measures, however, substantive discrimination has certainly not been eliminated.

of the legal texts. Theoretical and methodological issues have always been present in Nordic feminist legal studies. The ambition in this collection is to show how feminist legal thinking applies new concepts, theories and methods to reach new insights into the social dimension of legal contexts. The reasons for choosing a more Swedish centred perspective, are both practical as well as conceptual. Since 1999, it has been mandatory for Swedish legal education to contain a gender perspective. In the process of implementing this legislative directive, a collaboration has arisen between scholars at different academic levels, both in education and pedagogy, as well as in research. What is more, the Swedish concept of *genus* and its relation to equality politics, to legislation and to feminist studies in general as well as in the legal field, creates a specific Swedish understanding of the implications of *thinking about sex/gender*. The genealogy of the concepts sex, gender and *genus* is explored in *Responsible Selves* and in *Nordic Equality at a Crossroads.*

The Limits of Legal Scholarship and Law

The limits of legal scholarship and law are identified and discussed in a number of different ways by the contributors to this volume, and all return to the same basic themes: what are the established limits of legal scholarship and law, what is on the edge of their boundaries, and what is understood as outside the discipline and its object? The contributors largely considered it to be in the interests of women and feminist thought to expand the recognized content of law, and to critique the distinction between the 'outside' and the 'inside' of law. What is more, it is also considered to be in the interests of legal scholarship to reflect on the basic presumptions of the discipline. As indicated above, feminist legal studies is characterized by a double strategy. In some contexts it might be useful to take a purely dogmatic or formalist position, while in other cases it is more useful to challenge legal dogmatism. Both positions are arguably necessary, because of the need to engage pragmatically with an existing legal discourse and also to move beyond it.

The type of limits identified by the contributions that follow are all related to the 'dogmatic' position still present in Swedish legal thought. [3] These limits may be divided into a number of different types. There are limits on the type of scholarship properly regarded as 'legal' as well as boundaries between established and 'challenger' scholarships (that is, between traditional scholarship and new forms of scholarship which challenge its status). Moreover, there are conceptual limits, such as the presumed distinction between descriptive and normative scholarship. In Sweden, the doctrine of legal sources identifies which sources are authoritative as sources of actual law. Together with definitions of law, these sources establish boundaries which exclude politics, culture and other normative discourses. It is a theme of this book that all of these boundaries are not real or absolute limits, but socially and discursively constructed.

---

3 In the civil law tradition the meaning of 'dogmatic' is somewhat similar to the idea of 'black letter law' in common law traditions. For an overview of the Nordic legal culture, see the introductions in Nousiainen *et al.* 2001; Svensson *et al.* 2004.

The Dogmatic Position

The dogmatic approach to law, or legal dogmatics, is the central frame of reference for this book. Legal dogmatics represents knowledge *in* law, and its main purpose is to describe and analyse current law. This approach sees legal scholarship mainly as a support for legal practice: the task of scholarship is to create coherence, consistency and systematic order among rules and principles and various parts of the legal system (see Svensson this volume).

The Swedish dogmatic position has its roots in the German tradition *Rechtsdogmatik* and has much in common with legal positivism. In some senses, it is comparable with 'black letter' and 'formalist' positions in English-speaking jurisprudence, but its effect on the academy in Sweden has arguably been more complete and more long lasting. The dogmatic position is not a theoretical paradigm; it is a doctrine of sources of law. This doctrine identifies what sources are considered as authoritative and what the relations between them are. Sources of knowledge other than the identified legal sources are not authoritative in the process of establishing current law. Legal scholarship is, as already mentioned, considered a source of Swedish law, but not as one of the most important. According to a simplified picture of the normative doctrine, the sources of law in hierarchical order are as follows: written law, preparatory work, cases (in superior courts), custom and legal scholarship (see Svensson this volume). The doctrine of legal sources has been challenged in recent years from different perspectives, but the position of legal scholarship in the hierarchy has not been challenged. It still has a weak position. Preparatory work, on the contrary, is an important source in finding the functional aims of the legislative acts and how they should be interpreted (Nousiainen *et al.* 2001, 20). The intention of 'the legislator' is supposed to be followed and the legal profession is expected to be loyal to the 'will of the legislator'. In the Swedish context, 'legislator' refers to more than a mere member of the institutional body which processes legislation (i.e. the legislature). The 'legislator' is an abstract subject with an explicit will which, in traditional dogmatic legal scholarship, must be identified and respected. Most contributions in this volume refer to the legislator in this sense, in accordance with the Swedish and wider Nordic tradition.

The importance of preparatory work in the Swedish legal culture stands in contrast to the tradition in EU and in common law countries. Despite (or perhaps, because of) the strict boundary between politics and law, the legislative process determines the application of law. The preparatory work is produced during the legislative process and its weight as a source of law depends on where in the process it is produced. For example, a Government Commission comes earlier in the process than a Government Bill, which is the last step before legislation is passed. The earlier the preparatory work, the less important it is as a source. One of the most important statements, for both legal practitioners and scholars, are made by the minister of the department that is responsible for the legal reform, like the minister of finance, the minister of justice and so forth. This means that there are layers of authoritative statements within the preparatory work pertaining to any legislation.

One reason for the influence of the dogmatic position is that in Sweden, the identification of legal scholarship with law itself has been thought to strengthen the role of legal scholarship as a formally recognized primary source of law (see Svensson this volume). In order to enhance the (rather weak, but still acknowledged) position of scholarship as a legal source, a fairly strong culture of exclusion of marginal, secondary, or 'additional' fields of scholarship developed. In contrast, in common law countries, legal scholarship is generally not regarded as a primary, formal, source of law, though it may be regarded as one of many influences on judicial reasoning. Scholarship is used by judges in common law countries on an extremely *ad hoc* basis – while it can have significant and acknowledged influence in the United States, in Britain it has tended to remain more in the background.[4] Moreover, while being cited by a judge may be a source of some prestige to many common law scholars, the potential for influence does not provide a general reason for curtailing the activities of legal scholars (cf. Duxbury 2001, 101–113). It would therefore be possible to speculate that one reason for the relatively loose disciplinary boundaries in common law scholarship is that academic opinion is never *formally* regarded as a primary source of law in common law countries. In contrast, even though scholarship is a weak source of law in Swedish jurisprudence, it does have some formal recognition as such, meaning that calls to strengthen this position by limiting legal scholarship to the object 'law' have some basis in the law itself.

Even though the dogmatic position is the frame of reference for most contributions in this volume, contemporary legal scholarship is more pluralistic than this might indicate. Like scholars in the common law world, Swedish legal scholars have also been influenced by developments in critical epistemology of varying sorts. However, the Swedish legal academy in general has been very protective of the limits of law, leading, as we have indicated, to a preoccupation with the question of whether or not an area of scholarly investigation can truly be characterized as 'legal'. In contrast to the common law tradition where there is a fairly long history of critical, sociological, and policy-based analysis of law, the Swedish preoccupation with the proper nature and content of law is more like an obsession than merely an interesting theoretical question. The question 'is this area of investigation really *law*?' (as opposed to sociology, political science, or some other discipline), is still a question frequently voiced in discussions about non-mainstream legal scholarship.

In relation specifically to law, the dogmatic position has, through an increasing use of framework legislation, become increasingly untenable. The term 'framework legislation' is a direct translation of the Swedish technical legal notion of *ramlag*, a law giving a legal framework but which leaves the filling of the frame to public organs and administrative authorities. Framework legislation can be constructed in different ways with the common denominator that the regulations are not 'complete'; the frame needs to be filled. The legislation only provides the parameters against which the activities could be measured. Such legislation aims to promote material justice, laid down in general statutory objectives, and stands in contrast to the traditional rule of law, which is more suited to a detailed law with a formal notion of justice.

4 Duxbury argues that even though judges do not refer to academic analysis as frequently in England as they do in the United States, this does not necessarily mean that the level of influence is a great deal less – just that it may be manifested differently (not through citations), Duxbury 2001.

A fixation with the limits of the discipline 'law' is known to common law scholars, but transgressions of these limits do not have quite the same resonances or pose the same kind of threat to common law scholars as they do in the Swedish context. Boundaries are clearly of great significance, but common law scholarship and the common law itself have become relatively flexible in their characterization of an issue as 'legal', especially in legal pedagogy and theory, which are not as strongly connected to legal practice (Webber 2004). Over several decades there has been a spread of areas of scholarship and legal practice, so that it is common to speak of fields of knowledge such as law and economics, law and religion and law and literature. The boundaries of law have expanded, so that a greater number and range of normative environments can be included in the study of 'law'. In addition, a more theoretically-oriented critical legal scholarship has been encouraging not only the expansion of boundaries, but also reflection about the metaphysical nature of these boundaries. The focus is sliding over to the nature of knowledge *about* law, or the epistemology of law. This trend is also present in Swedish legal research, however the limits of law and legal scholarship present greater obstacles in the critical process.

Exploiting Limits

The rationality behind the protectiveness of law's limits in legal scholarship is explored in depth by Eva-Maria Svensson in Chapter 2. She has used the concept of boundary-work as a method to make visible the connection between cognitive and social factors with the purpose of analysing how the discipline of legal scholarship is constructed. As Svensson explains, the dogmatic position has been and still is closely connected to practical legal knowledge. This has facilitated a tradition of a non-reflective attitude to theories and methods in Swedish legal consciousness since the 1950s. The conceptual distance between legal scholarship and the object 'law' has been minimal, so that authentic or mainstream legal scholarship has been limited to narrowly-defined doctrinal analysis. Scandinavian realism has unintentionally been a part of this process since the realistic scholarly paradigm left the normative dogmatic position unchallenged in the hands of both practitioners and scholars taking a practical view of law. The dominant paradigm in legal scholarship for many decades continued to be the normative dogmatic position. By using the concept of objectivity, legal scholarship appeared to be 'scientific' in a realistic sense.

One of the important boundaries discussed by the chapters in this volume is that between politics and law, which is often regarded as defining the spheres of the subjective, opinion-driven world of policy-making and the objective, fact-driven world of descriptive legal analysis. Åsa Persson in Chapter 3 describes the limit between law and politics as an 'apparent' and 'diffuse' boundary, that is, a boundary which is constructed within the context of legal culture and legal epistemology, and which 'seems' certain and legitimate but which is 'diffuse' – suggesting that it is in fact open, uncertain, or permeable. In one way or another, all of the chapters identify the uncertainties of law's limits in relation to politics, and suggest ways of challenging or reconstructing those limits. A common strand is to challenge the fixation with a well-defined and demarcated object and instead use an epistemological approach, which opens up new theories and methods.

Critical discourse analysis is one of the methods with which the contextual aspect of legal knowledge can be analysed. This is a way of challenging the taken-for-granted knowledge and the hierarchy of knowledge in the dogmatic position. Chapter 4 by Johanna Niemi-Kiesiläinen, Päivi Honkatukia and Minna Ruuskanen introduces critical discourse analysis and its starting-point in social constructionism as a socio-legal feminist method. Furthermore they show how discourse analysis can be of use for the well-known feminist analysis of how language constructs and interacts with reality. Discourse analysis should be seen as a qualitative improvement of the interpretations of legal texts since it visualizes language as forming our understanding of the world.

Discourse analyses of legislation concerning violence against women shows how patterns of gendered power relations are ignored by the criminal justice system. What is more, gender-related arguments are often met with resistance in this system even when gendered violence has been the specific target of the legislator. Reasons for this reluctance include the alleged social and human character of men's violence against women, and the perception that the legislation is insufficiently precise. In Chapter 5 Monica Burman shows that this ingrained resistance to recognizing gendered violence is reinforced by criminal legal scholarship as well as in the courts, both of which draw strict boundaries around crimes that from a traditional point of view are highly ranked within criminal law. Crimes which demand a contextualized understanding, such as those which punish gendered violence, are understood as atypical and therefore as outside the traditional scope of both legal scholarship and the criminal justice system. According to Burman, however, the separation of criminal law and criminal legal scholarship from discursive environments is a myth: all criminal laws are contextualized and use contextualizing methods even if this is not conscious or reflected upon. Discourse analysis is a method for exploring these aspects of criminal law and criminal legal scholarship.

Several contributions emphasize that power relations in the social constructions of law can be observed by studying what legal discourses exist and how they are used. The regulations of the asylum process, which Eva Nilsson analyses in Chapter 6 is another example of a legal context that is open and policy-driven. In this context, there is widespread use of declarative statements in framework legislation with goal-oriented rules, which contradict the traditional use of legal principles, and preparatory work that provides little specific guidance. This makes it difficult from a formalist dogmatic position to identify a normative coherence in line with authoritative legal sources so that legal certainty can be established. In such a context, from a dogmatic position it is problematic to establish general conclusions about what law *is*, so that similar situations under the law can be treated equally.

The area of social welfare law and policy is absolutely central to Swedish legal feminism because of the importance of the Swedish welfare system in establishing the material conditions of individual existence within society. However a large part of social welfare law falls into this diffuse space between law and politics. One important aspect of the limits between politics and law is the issue of the location and distribution of social power. Ruth Mannelqvist, Lena Wennberg and Åsa Gunnarsson reflect in their contributions on how a comprehensive welfare state like Sweden, with far-reaching egalitarian commitments, still reproduces inequalities between men and women. The gendered dimension of social power within the legal structures of welfare state regulations is an important part of the analysis. In contrast to a dogmatic perspective, this intellectual and empirical standpoint emphasizes that legal research concerns all aspects of legal norms. Wennberg and Gunnarsson in Chapters 10 and 11, examine the contemporary concept of 'social citizenship' as a dynamic challenge to legalistic constructions of equality as sameness. Put simply, social citizenship offers a tool for analysis and reconstruction which is not bound to narrow legal definitions of equality. At the same time, the analysis offered is not simply outside the domain of law, but engages dynamically with legal doctrine in order to establish methods for the state to recognize unpaid care work as well as paid work. The concept of social citizenship is an attempt to formulate a principle of social inclusion which recognizes the plural identities and different forms of contributions made by citizens.

In Chapter 8, Ruth Mannelqvist shows how difficult it is to capture the core of welfare law without a contextual understanding of historical and transformative processes. Welfare law falls under both public law and civil law. Principles of solidarity and redistribution are highly political at the same time as they are a part of the legal constructions of Swedish law, especially in public law where such principles are common within framework legislation. From a dogmatic standpoint these principles can hardly be regarded as 'legal', which means that legal scholarship does not see welfare law as 'purely legal', in contrast to the political sphere. The gendered dimension of welfare law is in turn hard to see without a systematized structure which combines the public and civil welfare legislation. In this case, it seems clear that a gender-based analysis must question the established divisions and limits between law and the political sphere, and between the different spheres of law.

Other examples of structural discrimination occur as a result of the public/private divide and other aspects of social normativity. Catharina Calleman shows in Chapter 9 how the dichotomies of public and private, productive and reproductive, paid and unpaid work are embedded in the legal structure as well as reproduced by it. By emphasizing specific categories such as members of the employer's family and house-workers she shows the gendered dimension of the structure of labour law. At the same time she also illustrates that when the foundations of labour law exclude workers in the private sphere, the law itself becomes a part of the structural discrimination against women. Another example of structural discrimination is explored by Görel Granström in Chapter 7. She shows how conceptions of normality can reproduce inequality, whether it takes a neutral or a specific position in relation to sex and gender. In comparing domestic violence and hate crimes, Granström argues that progressive sex-specific legislation, the law relating to 'gross violations of a woman's integrity', can have unintended gendered effects. She asks whether this piece of legislation, in normalizing women as victims in the private sphere, in fact has made it more difficult for victims of same-sex domestic abuse to become recognized by the criminal justice system.

The Challenge to Pessimism

In Chapter 12, Margaret Davies outlines several sources of feminist pessimism about the project of legal change. One particularly significant source of pessimism in the liberal context is the perception that legal feminism has not achieved a substantially improved social position for women. Despite the improvement in gender-equality rhetoric employed by states and international bodies, there is still a long way to go in terms of reaching gender equality in a wide variety of areas of concern. The optimistic perception of law as a tool for social change, once assumed by feminists, is replaced by a pessimistic view about law reform as insufficient to achieve genuine social change. The political direction of the early liberal feminism and its faith in law reform as a way of obtaining equality has grown into a pessimism that sees the law as an obstacle to justice, rather than its agent. Despite the fact that some legal reforms have an important symbolic function and may change some behaviours, there has been a perception that law reform only scratches the surface and often fails to affect the underlying socio-cultural and structural conditions of gender oppression. The conceptual limits of law are connected to the limits of law reform to have a really substantial impact on social and cultural structures.

In a Swedish context, with a tradition of a strong state allied with the feminist project, gender equality is thought of as a structural issue and reform of both policy and legislation is still seen as an effective method of promoting change. For instance, the latest example of an affirmative gender equality measure is a proposal to apply gender quotas to corporate boards to deal with the unequal power distribution in business. However, problems do arise when policy is transformed into legislation and must be implemented in the legal system. As indicated above, legal professionals can seem to be very confined and protective of the legal dogmatic space. In consequence, there appears to be very significant limitations on how law can be used as a mechanism for change, despite the fact that jurists in the Swedish system are supposed to be loyal towards the legislator. This loyalty seems to be less when it comes to gender equality issues, meaning that laws designed to address an aspect of gender inequality are often less far-reaching than intended. As Burman points out in her chapter, implementing gender-related reforms is difficult. The criminal legal approach meets women-friendly legislation such as 'gross violation of a woman's integrity' with arguments that they are only based on prevention and a wish to solve merely social problems. In the Swedish context, there is a perception that the criminal law must be as restricted as possible, and should not focus on what are regarded as essentially social issues. Thus, the idea of strict legality, i.e. a criminalization anchored in law, is often used as a basis for counteracting gender- or crime-victim related arguments. In Sweden as elsewhere, law and legal scholarship suffer from severe limitations as an instrument for progressive reform, and these limitations flow in part from the doctrinal and disciplinary limits of law within legal scholarship.

One theme of the contributions in this collection is that pessimism generated by the formalist and dogmatic approach to law can be challenged by sustained critical attention to the alleged limits of legal scholarship and that such critique indirectly makes law more capable of meeting gender equality demands. Our method is consequently to focus upon the redefinition of law through legal scholarship and its notion of knowledge. Through challenging the limits of the discipline of legal scholarship, the higher project of gaining equal rights for everybody may proceed but in an epistemological rather than a reformist garment. The question of social power is included inside the boundaries of legal scholarship and once accepted it expands the limits of the discipline.

The presupposition of the chapters in this book is therefore that it is indeed possible to challenge feminist pessimism, but only by ongoing reflection about the limits of legal scholarship and law, and repeated efforts to contest those limits in relation to a multitude of practical concerns. The abstract basis for this view is considered by several of the contributors. For example, Åsa Persson outlines some of the means by which values and normative standpoints are made invisible in legal scholarship and law through the strict separation of politics and the legal arena. This limit acts ideologically and maintains the notion of legal scholarship and law as neutral and objective. Eva-Maria Svensson shows how boundary contests are fought by legal scholars over the nature and limits of their discipline: feminist legal theory is often seen as a threat to the integrity of legal scholarship or, in contrast, is mis-described as not adding anything useful to legal scholarship's core methods. For Svensson, the challenge to pessimism flows from the ability of feminist critique to reveal new sources and methods in legal knowledge, while for Persson, the critique leads directly to a reconsideration of the sources and limits of law. Margaret Davies sees possible challenges to feminist pessimism in a variety of ways and encourages scholars to continue the process of re-thinking the possibilities for achieving 'enduring change'. According to Davies, the heterogeneity of feminist thought, reflecting the demands of a complex and pluralistic social environment, is a cause for optimism.

This beginning of a re-drawing of legal scholarship's limits is the real basis for the challenge to pessimism and for re-drawing the law's limits. A changed perception about the limits of legal scholarship will flow both from new theoretical explanations, but also from new methods in the practice of legal scholarship. Just as important as the theoretical analysis of an issue, is its mobilization in substantive areas of knowledge. It is this task of critiquing, exploring, challenging and exploiting the limits of law in its practical settings which is undertaken by the majority of contributors. These challenges can all be understood as involving a reworking of the fundamental divisions and categorizations of law – for instance its national boundaries, its exclusion of 'social' concepts, its taxonomy in practical areas of law, and its public/private distinction. In each case, the critique of the limits of law leads to a reconceptualization of legal scholarship and even of law, and an opening of new spaces for feminist legal activism to take place. This is the conclusion reached by Eva Nilsson, who argues in favour of methodological pluralism in legal scholarship: the approach adopted by a legal scholar can vary in different contexts and for different purposes. She therefore challenges the law's fundamental presuppositions by 'exploiting the given' in law, that is, its core dichotomies and concepts, a process which can lead to change in the way that law constructs certain categories, in this case children.

In their analyses of welfare law, Åsa Gunnarsson and Lena Wennberg use theoretical concepts, which have previously not been used as *legal* concepts, such as 'social citizenship' and 'solo mothers'. Their purpose is to grasp issues of social power built in and reproduced by the construction of law. Another purpose is to challenge the pessimistic view that legal scholarship does not have the resources to deal with questions of social inequality. This is a distinctive feature of the Swedish feminist approach which has such a strong approach to the structural basis for inequality. What is being done is to bring that understanding of social structure into the law in a distinctive way: with the help of new concepts and new theoretical and practical systems, unequal social power in the legal system can be made visible and open to change. The systematization in the legal system is challenged also in Ruth Mannelqvist's chapter through the use of a 'new' legal discipline in Sweden, welfare law. Welfare law encompasses legislation traditionally belonging to both private law and public law, and characterized by different basic principles. When the limit between private and public law in welfare law issues is dissolved those basic principles are questioned. So are the notions of public law as political and value-based in contrast to the notion of private law as legal and objective.

The structure of the legal system is also the target for Catharina Calleman. The dichotomy between private and public sphere in the legal system is made visible in relation to domestic work and kinship between the employer and the employed. The private sphere of employment law is shown to be less protective towards the weaker party than the public sphere. The challenge in Calleman's chapter is to re-evaluate the exception of protecting work done in the private sphere. With a growing global market for services in the private sphere, this challenge is most important in order to prevent socially unequal distributions of power.

Johanna Niemi-Kiesiläinen, Päivi Honkatukia and Minna Ruuskanen as well as Monica Burman see possibilities for improving theoretical and methodological reflection in legal scholarship and ways of developing the discipline in order to go beyond its constructed boundaries, which prevent criminal law from meeting contemporary social demands. Critical discourse analysis can work as a method to make the discursive aspect of traditional legal thought visible. These two contributions are optimistic about the potential of criminal legal research to open up towards contemporary demands without coming in conflict with basic principles such as legality.

Well-meaning measures for dealing with men's violence towards women may also be problematic and discriminatory. Görel Granström's methodological approach compares different crimes, domestic violence and non-domestic violence motivated by prejudice against homosexual persons, so-called 'homophobic hate crimes'. By this comparative method law's hetero-normative patterns are made visible. Granström challenges the boundaries between different kinds of crimes and questions whether gendered violence ought to be included within the category of hate crimes, an approach which would unmask the misogynistic basis of violence against women.

Taken together, the chapters show new paths for the 'feminist project', which is today defined as a project to deal with unequal social power in a plurality of relationships, not restricted to subordinated (biological) women but to unequal relationships between sexes, gender, ethnicities, classes and so on. As legal scholars, we focus on these relationships as they exist within and intersect with law and legal scholarship. Disciplinary self-reflection, as outlined by Svensson, and theoretical and practical strategies comprising multiple pathways, for which Davies argues, are important tools in the project of feminist legal studies. Discursive change can lead to changes in fundamental conceptions and transformations in institutional arrangements. Utopian visions together with pragmatic engagement in legal scholarship and law are important elements in the feminist and gender equality project.

References

Literature

Armstrong, Susan (2004), 'Is Feminist Law Reform Flawed? Abstentionists vs Sceptics', 20 *The Australian Feminist Law Journal* 2004, 43–63.

Bacchi, Carol Lee (1999), *Women, Policy and Politics: The Constructions of Policy Problems* (London: Sage Publications).

Benda-Beckman, Franz von, Benda-Beckman, Keebet von and Griffiths, Anne (eds) (2005), *Mobile People, Mobile Law: Expanding Legal Relations in a Contracting World* (Aldershot: Ashgate).

Bentzon, Agnete Weis, Hellum, Anne, Stewart, Julie, Ncube, Welshman and Agersnap, Torben (1998), *Pursuing Grounded Theory in Law. South-North Experiences in Building Women's Law* (Oslo: TANO Aschehoug and Zimbabwe: Mond Books).

Dahl, Tove Stang (1987), *Women's law: an introduction to feminist jurisprudence* (Oslo: Norwegian University Press).

Davies, Margaret (2002), *Asking the Law Question: The Dissolution of Legal Theory* 2nd edition (Sydney: Lawbook Co.).

Duxbury, Neil (2001), *Jurists and Judges: An Essay on Influence* (Oxford: Hart).

Hellum, Anne (ed.) (1993), *Birth Law* Scandinavian (Oslo: University Press).

Kuovo, Sari (2004), *Making Just Rights? Mainstreaming Women's Human Rights and a Gender Perspective* (Uppsala: Iustus Förlag).

Nousiainen, Kevät, Gunnarsson, Åsa, Lundström, Karin and Niemi-Kiesiläinen, Johanna (2001), *Responsible Selves: Women in the Nordic Legal Cultures* (Aldershot: Ashgate).

Petersen, Hanne (1996), *Home-Knitted Law: Norms and Values in Gendered Rule-Making* (Netherlands: Springer).

Pylkkänen, Anu (2001), 'The Responsible Self: Relational Gender Construction in the History of Finnish Law', in Nousiainen, Kevät, Gunnarsson, Åsa, Lundström, Karin and Niemi-Kiesiläinen, Johanna (2001), *Responsible Selves: Women in the Nordic Legal Cultures* (Aldershot: Ashgate).

Santos, Boaventura de Sousa (2002), *Toward a New Legal Common Sense*, 2nd edition (London: Butterworths).

Svensson, Eva-Maria, Pylkänen, Anu and Niemi-Kiesiläinen, Johanna (2004), *Nordic Equality at a Crossroads: Feminist Legal Studies Coping with Difference* (Aldershot: Ashgate).

Teubner, Gunther (1997), '"Global Bukowina": Legal Pluralism in the World Society', in Teubner, Gunther (ed.) (1997), *Global Law Without a State* (Aldershot, Ashgate).

Webber, Jeremy (2004), 'Legal Research, the Law Schools and the Profession', in 26 *Sydney Law Review* 2004, 565–586.

Chapter 2

Boundary-Work in Legal Scholarship[1]

Eva-Maria Svensson

Introduction

The boundaries of legal scholarship have been debated for many years and the issue continues to be controversial. The discussion involves both legal scholars and legal practitioners and raises such issues as: what law actually is, whether or not the scholarship is restricted to (current) law, what the purpose of the scholarship is and what kind of knowledge ought or ought not to be included in the academic field of legal scholarship. The differences that emerge vary, but are generally related to a broader scientific and societal context. The term 'legal scholarship' is used to denote the academic field in which legal knowledge is constructed, in both research and in legal education. 'Legal scholars' and 'legal scholarship' are the terms applied to activity within the academic field; practical legal knowledge and practitioners are not included in these categories. Both legal scholarship and practical legal knowledge share the same object, the law, and knowledge concerning it. The differences between them are explored in this chapter as well as the differences between scholars, through debates focusing on the boundaries of legal scholarship and its object – the law.

This chapter falls within a research programme entitled 'Studies of Academic Knowledge', which is a part of the international academic field 'social studies of science and scientific knowledge' in which academic knowledge is studied in a social context (Hallberg 2001).[2] Social studies of science and scientific knowledge represent a shift from non-contextual epistemology towards contextual epistemologies in which knowledge is seen as related to the social context. One pioneering work of importance for this shift was *The Structure of Scientific Revolutions* by Thomas Kuhn, first published in 1962 (Kuhn 1962). According to Kuhn, science moves

---

1 This chapter has been written with contributions from several colleagues. In addition to discussions with the group of scholars collaborating in this volume, I have discussed the text in other international and national seminars. I especially wish to thank the following persons for valuable comments on this chapter: Professor Aleksander Peczenik, Professor Henrik Zahle and Associate Professor Håkan Gustafsson. Two of these scholars, Aleksander Peczenik and Henrik Zahle, I was not able to thank in time before they died, too early and too suddenly.

2 'Science-theory combines philosophic, social and policy studies of research and expert knowledge – producing, legitimating and disseminating capacities in society. It is the domain where the politics and epistemology of science interfoliates.' A definition of the discipline (which in Sweden is called science-theory) by Professor Aant Elzinga. http://www.hum.gu.se/~idewww/

in an oscillation between paradigmatic calm – periods of widespread consensus over what can be known, what is not already known, and how to fill in the puzzle methodologically – and occasional revolutions that turn reality upside down until a new paradigm emerges, which is not commensurate with previously established beliefs.[3] Even though the work of Kuhn focused on the (natural) sciences, his work has had a broader influence. Robert K. Merton's work *The Sociology of Science*, published in 1973, facilitated the taking of a further step in the process called 'the social turn', a widespread change in academic thinking. The social turn has effected not only the pure sciences, but also and even more the social sciences and the humanities. When it comes to legal scholarship in Sweden, the dominant theory of knowledge has been strongly influenced by non-contextual epistemologies, such as empiricism and rationalism, during the 20th century. Influences from an overall social turn in epistemology, i.e. recognition of the importance of the social context, have come to Nordic legal scholarship more recently, in the late 20th and the beginning of the 21st centuries.

Studies in the field of 'social studies of science and scientific knowledge' explore scientific knowledge as an activity rather than the inner logic of knowledge. Several aspects of the context of scientific knowledge are of interest. In the research programme 'Studies of Academic Knowledge' the focus is mainly on the construction of academic knowledge, i.e. the process by which knowledge is discovered, justified, used and communicated. Apart from (natural) science, which is usually the focus in international studies of science and scientific knowledge, Swedish studies of academic knowledge also have an interest in the social sciences and humanities (Hallberg 2001).[4] In this chapter legal scholarship is added to the academic disciplines studied from this perspective.

Legal scholarship and the changes it has undergone in the twentieth century are the focal points of this chapter. In Nordic legal culture the academic discipline has more or less been seen as analogous to its object, the law. As a Finnish legal scholar put it (using the term 'legal science' instead of 'legal scholarship'), 'legal science is not only a scientific but also a legal practice, which participates in the reproduction and modification of the legal order – its own object of research' (Tuori 2002, 285). Legal scholarship has traditionally been understood as one of the sources of law in the application of law, and not as an independent academic activity. However, its influence as a source of law has been weak (Björne 1991, 162). Arguments can only be gathered from inside the system, and the aim of scholarship is to preserve the system (Nousiainen 1999; Nousiainen and Niemi-Kiesiläinen 2001; Peczenik 1995b). From such a perspective, critical analysis of the boundaries of law and its basic presumptions are problematic. However, legal scholarship, like other academic fields, goes through periods of paradigmatic calm supplanted by new thinking, in the wake of revolutions that have varying impacts. Legal philosophy as well as different

3 An apt description is provided by Gieryn 1999, 26.

4 In Swedish the corresponding word for science, *vetenskap*, is used for natural science, social science, humanities and legal scholarship. The meaning of science in Swedish is academic knowledge in general. However, this is a relatively modern interpretation of the word. Cf. the way Tuori uses the term legal science in Tuori 2002, 283.

critical approaches, such as feminist legal studies, have also been challenging the boundaries determined by the current law.[5] The boundaries of legal scholarship are no longer seen as being determined by its inner logic, but by a social context. The purpose of this chapter is to analyse changes in the field of legal scholarship in order to discuss the position of feminist legal studies within legal scholarship. In keeping with the theme of the book, the focus is upon Swedish and Nordic legal scholarship, though many of the changes discussed have also occurred elsewhere.

The Tool

The changes taking place in legal scholarship can be described as a process of delimiting, re-limiting and mapping the legal field. This process is not occurring in isolation. In boundary-work, a concept used and explored by the sociologist of science, Thomas F. Gieryn, the focus is put on the process of establishing boundaries, which denotes the work done by contestants aiming to win credibility contests concerning epistemic authority. Epistemic authority '…is enacted as people debate (and ultimately decide) where to locate the legitimate jurisdiction over natural facts' (Gieryn 1999, 15). In legal scholarship, the issue is not to locate the legitimate jurisdiction over natural facts but over the academic field as such. The boundaries of legal scholarship are the subject of the contests. The boundary-work can be of different kinds, and depends on the nature of the credibility contest, namely whether it concerns expulsion, expansion or protection of autonomy. In legal scholarship epistemic authority cannot be a matter of where to locate the legitimate jurisdiction over natural facts, but is over the academic field itself.

'Expulsion' refers to a contest between rival authorities, each of which claims to be scientific. Real science is demarcated from several other categories such as pseudoscience, amateur science, bad science and popular science (Gieryn 1999, 16). In the context of legal scholarship this type of contest could, for example, be between dogmatic legal scholarship and more 'political' methods of understanding law (see Burman this volume; Persson this volume). Boundary-work becomes a means of social control. 'Scientists' learn how not to transgress the boundaries of legitimacy, and 'science' displays its ability to maintain a monopoly over preferred norms of conduct. Expulsion often pits mainstream science against the fringe; here the fringe science could be 'types' of legal scholarship thought of as being helpful to the 'main or true' legal scholarship (Björne 1991; see Burman this volume). Expulsion can also pit established science against revolutionary science but, according to Gieryn, the issue then in dispute is who and what belongs to which side. In this context, legal scholars and practitioners both make claims about the boundaries of legal scholarship. Neither side wishes to challenge the epistemic authority of the science itself, but rather to deny credibility to the other side. Some expulsionary contests structured as a conflict between established and revolutionary positions are explored

5 Peczenik has challenged this view from within, see for example Peczenik 1989, 42ff, 361ff; Peczenik 2002; Peczenik 1999. According to Peczenik himself the establishment did not appreciate the challenge. See also Tuori 2002.

in this article. Expulsion can be one strategy employed in the work of mapping out a field.

'Expansion' refers to a situation where two or more rival epistemic authorities lay claim to a contested ontological domain. 'Those speaking for science may seek to extend its frontiers, or alternatively, spokespersons for religion, politics, ethics, common sense, or folk knowledge may challenge the exclusive right of science to judge truth.' (Gieryn 1999, 16). The task in this contest is to claim to have the 'right' source of knowledge. Translated to legal scholarship, the contest is about which sources of knowledge are authoritative, which knowledge is relevant, and which theories and methods are legitimate. This kind of boundary-work can be seen in some contests in legal scholarship, for example between feminist legal studies and non-feminist legal studies.

The last kind of boundary-work is 'protection of autonomy' (Gieryn 1999, 17). According to Gieryn, this boundary-work is of a slightly different kind and is a reaction from the inside when outside powers try to exploit science for reasons of their own. Protection of autonomy can be claimed for instance when political or market interests try to use science in order to solve a problem, or to divorce scientific practice from its consequences much further down the road in order to escape responsibility and blame. In the context of boundary-work in legal scholarship, protection of autonomy can be claimed in relation to the politics, to the consequences of legal practice and to scholarship characterized as revolutionary. Contests of this kind will also be problematized in this chapter.

The boundary-work concerning the epistemic authority of legal scholarship must be interpreted in the light of the limited importance of scholarship in the legal field. These contests may constitute efforts to increase its influence as either a valuable legal source or an independent academic activity.

In this chapter all three kinds of boundary-work in legal scholarship will be exemplified through some debates from the 20th century. The contests are structured in a model where the established position is challenged by the revolutionary position. The content of the positions changes; a new established position, emerging from the former contest is challenged by a new revolutionary position. The ongoing process of boundary-work will be related to three epistemological aspects of legal scholarship, namely

- the demarcation of the discipline
- the sources of knowledge that are recognized
- the concept of knowledge.

These three aspects have been chosen because of their importance for the exclusion and inclusion of new perspectives in legal scholarship. The contests and the boundary-work appear to take place around these issues.

Demarcation of Legal Scholarship

As a part of academic legal knowledge, legal scholarship is, and has been throughout its history, characterized by its close connection to the practice of law. Legal knowledge comprises the content of the profession of lawyers and other jurists, one of the classic, pre-industrial status professions (Liedman 1997, 292; Liedman 1998, 11; Burman, Svensson and Ågren 2003). The role of legal scholars has been to train students to become practitioners useful in providing official services. When there have been demands to exclude vocational education from the university (for not being sufficiently academic), legal knowledge has been exempted because, according to Olausson and Liedman, it requires a great amount of learning (Olausson and Liedman 1988, 25).

The relation between practical legal knowledge and academic legal knowledge has frequently been the focus of discussion. Sometimes legal scholarship has been considered to be too removed from practical legal knowledge, sometimes too close. One influential discussion on this issue took place in the 1950s.[6] The legal scholar Per-Olof Ekelöf characterized legal scholarship and the legal method as being in a state of crisis. The crisis concerned the belief that legal scholarship lacked usefulness, i.e. it lacked a practical touch. (The lack of usefulness is still considered a problem by some at the beginning of the 21st century.)[7] The question was whether legal scholarship should be primarily a scientific activity, and therefore not of any use in practice, or an activity aimed at meeting the needs of practical legal life.

On one level the conflict was about the usefulness of legal scholarship. Represented diagrammatically in Table 2.1 below, the contest was between practical legal knowledge on the one side and academic legal scholarship on the other. This was not, as mentioned above, a new question.

Table 2.1 Legal knowledge

Legal knowledge	
Practical legal knowledge	Academic legal scholarship

On another level the contest concerned the epistemological ideal in academic legal scholarship. The opposition was between the 'old' humanist ideal (as in natural law) and the 'new' positivistic scientific ideal with its empirical strain, as in the Uppsalaskolan or the Uppsala School of Scandinavian realism. According to this new positivistic scientific ideal, legal scholarship should not deal with metaphysical issues and values. The desire was to eliminate 'transcendental nonsense', mystique,

6 The discussion took place mainly in the following publications, Ekelöf 1951; Ahlander 1952; Agge 1955. The discussion continued in the 1960s and also referred to publications from the 1940s. See the articles mentioned for further references.

7 See some of the articles in the periodical (2002) 3 Svensk Juristtidning including talks from a seminar in 2001 about the role of legal scholarship.

quasi-religious concepts, and other non-factual elements from the study of law. Law was seen as fact with no inherent relationship to justice, and not representing a general will or will of the sovereign since there is no general will or will of the sovereign (Davies 2002, 142-143). The Uppsalaskolan denies the possibility of establishing the binding force of law and its validity from scientific criteria (Peczenik 1986, 168). Principals such as *pacta sunt servanda* (i.e. promises should be kept) were not seen as natural – as in natural law – but determined by material interests. The scientific ideal in the realistic version was influenced by the tradition of logical empiricism.

In Table 2.2 a distinction is made between two contradictory ways of establishing the boundaries for academic legal scholarship, the established and the revolutionary (Gieryn, 1999). The radical step taken in the middle of the 20th century was from a formerly normative legal scholarship bound by tradition, the established position in Table 2.2, to a descriptive (and realistic) legal scholarship tied more closely to the new political visions, the revolutionary position in Table 2.2.

Table 2.2 Academic legal scholarship

Academic legal scholarship	
Established position 1 – normative	Revolutionary position 1 – realistic

The crisis was a way of mapping the field of legal knowledge as an academic discipline. The discipline changed and new spaces were created in the field. The conflict between the two ideals, law as a normative science and law as a descriptive or empirical science, impacted on what could or should be included in the legal field.

The relationship between various fields of legal scholarship changed. Legal history, legal theory and jurisprudence[8] were losing their importance to current law. They were seen as complementary to or as an aid to current law and not as a part of mainstream legal scholarship. The status of the fields has been, and is still being discussed (Wennström 2003a). Although activities inspired by empirical social science, such as the sociology of law, offered a 'scientific' method by means of which it was possible to describe (value-free) legal phenomena (such as Ross's theory of prognosis), this field too has been defined merely as an aid to current law.

Ivar Agge described the situation in 1955 as a two-directional crossroads, but the divergence is not between the normative and the realistic positions, as one might expect (Agge 1955, 6). The pure realistic position was not an option at all for Agge.

8 There is no strict boundary between legal theory and jurisprudence. In Sweden both are included in the discipline *allmän rättslära* (which is the translation of the German *allgemeine rechtslere*). In English there is, however, a certain distinction. Jurisprudence commonly corresponds to philosophy of law or legal philosophy, (cf. http://www.law.cornell.edu/topics/jurisprudence.html) but it can also be understood as legal scholarship in general. Legal theory seems not to have the same broad meaning but more specifically focuses on theories about law.

Instead he believed that for men of legal scholarship who considered the realistic critique of (normative) ideologically based legal concepts and theses well-founded, but who yet felt dissatisfied with a descriptive, value-free way of thinking about law, two directions were available. The crossroads led either to a pure normative kind of legal knowledge or to a pragmatic kind of legal knowledge.[9] The former (normative) direction excluded empirical knowledge about the social phenomenon, and instead focused on the a priori existing idealistic system of norms and its formal logical structure. The main purpose of the latter (pragmatic) direction was to be of practical use in the application of law, by mapping out the rules, *de lege lata*, and making recommendations, *de lege ferenda*.[10] This pragmatic understanding of legal knowledge is not to be seen as an explicit, pragmatic legal theory, but as a practical knowledge, closely tied to usefulness in the application of law.[11] The tradition is usually called legal dogmatics or the dogmatic perspective. The origin of the dogmatic perspective is the German tradition *Rechtsdogmatik*. This tradition was both normative and conceptual and not as restricted as its current manifestation. Legal dogmatics has been criticized from several points of view especially from a feminist perspective, as not self-reflective. Such a lack of theoretical self-reflectiveness is illustrated by the custom of not exploring the theory and method used in doctoral theses and in other monographs. An extreme example of the absence of theoretical and methodological statements is, *EU & Straffrätten*: *Studier rörande den europeiska integrationens betydelse för den svenska straffrätten*, a book by a Swedish legal scholar (Asp 2002). However, even if this is the dominant paradigm, there are exceptions. Theoretical and reflective legal dogmatics has been explored in Finnish scholarship in the late 20th century. It is usual to distinguish between theoretical and a practical legal dogmatics (Tuori 2002, 284), where the practical is similar to the Swedish dominant tradition.

In the middle of the 20th century, legal dogmatics became the (new) established position in Swedish mainstream legal scholarship, see Table 2.3. Note that this position was not one of the two positions in the original contest (i.e. between the normative and the realistic approaches). It was rather a conflation of or a compromise between the established (normative) and the revolutionary positions (realistic). Mainstream legal knowledge became characterized by its non-theoretical and pragmatic approach, mainly focusing on systematization of the law and descriptions of current law. Taking up the formal-logical direction became the activity of a small circle of jurisprudence scholars, detached from legal knowledge in general (Wennström

9 Agge used the term constructive and not pragmatic, but pragmatic seems to be more accurate. Constructive legal scholarship is used for the tradition developed in Germany during the 19th century, connected with the conceptual tradition of *Begriffsjurisprudenz*. See Björne 2002; Agell 1997.

10 The meaning of the concepts *de lege lata* and *de lege ferenda* is what law is and what law ought to be respectively.

11 The Danish legal scholar Dalberg-Larsen has argued, in a book published in 2001, for a Scandinavian pragmatic legal theory with some characteristics similar to the American pragmatic legal theory and with some specific characteristics, Dalberg-Larsen 2001. When pragmatic is used as a characteristic of one of the directions available in Swedish legal scholarship in the middle of the 20th century, it is more in its linguistic meaning.

2003a; Andreasson 2004).[12] The kind of boundary-work carried out in this situation was a combination of expulsion and protection of autonomy.

Table 2.3 Academic mainstream legal scholarship

Academic mainstream legal scholarship	
Established position 1 – legal dogmatics	No revolutionary position 2

In the dogmatic position legal scholarship is seen as a support for legal practice and as one of several authorized sources of law, though one of lower value than other sources. This goes together with the opinion that jurists in general should be loyal to the legislator and the sources of law and become enforcers of government decisions. Even if the dogmatic position has both descriptive and normative characteristics, its normative side, and the limited space allowed it, make it fragile and open to question as being non-scientific.[13]

The main characteristic of dogmatic legal scholarship is the aspiration to achieve coherence, general or local. The task is to create coherence, consistency and systematic order among rules and principles and various parts of the legal system (Tuori 2002; Peczenik 1995a, 86; Peczenik 1995b, 659; Aarnio 1986, 21; Gustafsson 2002, 91–92). In contemporary scholarship efforts are made to develop the dogmatic position and the inclusion of coherence can refer, for example, to systematization of the legal system, justification of a legal decision, normative statements about the law, and correspondence between a rule and its aim. Stretching its meaning and use, coherence can accompany critical scholarship, but the desire for coherence can also be a hindrance when dealing with problems of inequality and the practical effects of law. Feminist legal studies, as well as other contemporary theories, seem to avoid coherence as an aim and instead see advantages in non-coherence. The critical position here involves a questioning of coherence as a desirable aspiration (Gunnarsson 1995; Svensson 1997a).

The boundaries of the discipline from the dogmatic position are seen as being the same as the object, i.e. the law. The discipline and its object share the same map (Tuori 2002, 285; Kinander 2002, 289; Bernt and Doublet 1998, 205). The discipline is limited to issues and methods used within the system as well as in correspondence with the field of practitioners. No distinction is made between the

12 One example of a Swedish scholar who pursues formal logic with the expectation of serving the jurists is Lars Lindahl, see Lindahl 2000.

13 The conflict is referred to at that time in several articles and monographs. See e.g. Ekelöf 1951; Hägerström 1957, 179 and the preface. Hägerström had as his motto '*Praeterea censeo metaphysicam esse delendam*' (in English, 'Besides, I consider metaphysics should be destroyed'), a paraphrase of the statement (*Delenda est Carthago*) which Cato the Elder is supposed to have said after every speech in the Senate. Cato was obsessed by the military threat posed by the city of Carthage, Bartlett's *Quotations*, http://www.bartleby.com/66/93/11093.html, accessed 30 May 2006.

discipline and the object, as in many other academic disciplines, such as sociology, where society is studied as a varying object requiring varying theories and methods. In the dogmatic position, there is no explicit distinction between the object, the Law, and the academic model of it. One expression for this is the concept of the inner and outer perspective, with the definition of legal dogmatics as the inner perspective and, moreover, as the main activity of legal scholars. Legal scholarship is, from this inner perspective, bound to its object and has little possibility of arguing for something that is not already within the boundaries of law. The possibilities for argumentation are defined by the concepts *de lege lata* and *de lege ferenda*. The meanings of these concepts are descriptions of current law and normative expressions of what law ought to be respectively. Both statements can be made in the dogmatic position but statements *de lege ferenda* should be separate and explicitly stated as normative statements. They have no value as expressions of what law is (the claim to be the 'truth'). A scholar is supposed to deal with *de lege lata* arguments, but can also as an appendix argue *de lege ferenda*. The boundary with politics is, however, fragile and therefore the border is supposed to be strict. The aim of legislation is a political issue and is not seen as a question for legal scholars (Sandström and Peterson 1996). In a period when the strict division between law and politics is being increasingly erased, for example through the wider use of values and aims in legislation, this opinion is hard to maintain.

The role of legal scholarship in the dogmatic position has been weak, and as a low-value legal source it has mainly had indirect importance in the long-term. Practitioners are mainly influenced during their education and lower courts are more influenced than the more independent upper courts. A lot of preparatory work can make legal scholarship more influential as in this case the need for qualified interpretations and normative statements increases (Björne 1991, 161–163). According to Peczenik, the importance of legal scholarship declined under the influence of the Uppsalaskolan or Scandinavian realism, (Peczenik 1986, 229–230). The Uppsalaskolan, as mentioned above, questioned the former normative legal scholarship with reference to logical empiricism as un-scientific. Un-scientific here must be understood in its Nordic meaning, i.e. 'science' as academic knowledge which also includes legal scholarship. In order to 'save' legal scholarship as a scientific (academic) activity, it became either quite formalistic or quite pragmatic. The pragmatic became the dominant tradition with the main purpose of establishing current law out of the doctrine of legal sources (see Persson this volume). This dominant tradition, the Nordic Legal Culture, is described in the introduction to the book *Responsible Selves* by Nousiainen and Niemi-Kiesiläinen (Nousiainen *et al.* 2001, 18–21).

After more than 50 years of discussion about the boundaries between practical and academic legal knowledge and normative and descriptive ideals, the situation has changed. The 'men of legal scholarship' are not the same as they were in the 1950s. Today's scholars are more heterogeneous regarding sex, class, ethnicity and other characteristics. We are also in another world, far from that of the 1950s. Not only has society changed, but also our legal system[14] is more pluralistic, more multi-layered (Sand 1996; Petersen 2002), and what is more, our concept of knowledge has changed. Today, the choice is not only among pure normative, realistic or dogmatic legal knowledge. The social turn, as well as the linguistic turn,[15] in knowledge has changed the epistemological landscape.

Although the effects of the old debate paralyzed legal scholarship for a long time, challenges did develop. New big theories, willing to settle accounts with the old ones, have not yet emerged, but a lot of small stories have. The challenges are located elsewhere than at the crossroads of the normative, realistic and dogmatic jurisprudence. The small stories have also changed the landscape of legal scholarship, even though it is sometimes hard to characterize new stories and to define their place in the field of legal knowledge. Many of the new stories, the revolutionary position in Table 2.2, can be described as critical perspectives, and they have developed out of an interest in law as an object of philosophical and cultural study, i.e. a space in legal knowledge excluded by the realistic approach, not relevant in the constructive approach (described by Agge above) and not normative in the sense of natural law. Margaret Davies' aim in *Delimiting the Law* is to think about the law combining critical theories of law with legal philosophy (Davies 1996). She argues that the law is everywhere and that the limits are constructed and a product of repetitious legal practices. This could also be said about legal scholarship; it is everywhere and it has no fixed limits, at least no fixed limits established in advance. This implies that it is possible to discuss and change the limits (Svensson 1997a). One major purpose of legal scholarship may even be to criticize the limits (Davies 1996). The role of legal scholars is then different from the role of the practitioners. The practitioners use the legal system within its boundaries, but the scholars are not restricted by the boundaries. The limits for legal scholarship can be changed over time, and they are de facto changed (Björne 1991) due to new scholarly practices developing: the object is changed and the theories are also changed. The new stories have influenced legal scholarship and have led to new contests in boundary-work. As Dahl wrote as early as 1985 (Dahl 1985), contemporary legal scholarship is not as dogmatic as before. Nevertheless, she still thought it was useful to make a distinction between legal dogmatics and legal scholarship in a broader scientific sense. It is significant for the latter, the critical position, to search for explanations and connections in a

14 Legal system is used instead of law, not as something essentially different but when the object for legal scholarship is referred to. Law is more generally the object for both legal practical knowledge and legal scholarship.

15 The linguistic turn stands for the epistemological standpoint in social science that language precedes experience and understanding is not possible without language. The world is seen as a mirror for the language. Pioneer work has been done by Charles Sanders Pierce, John L. Austin, Ludwig Wittgenstein, Ferdinand de Saussure, Martin Heidegger, Hans-Georg Gadamer. See the introduction by Mats Rosengren in Perelman 2004; see also Wallén 1996, 36.

wider sense, for example through legal (or other) meta-theory.[16] The positions have different purposes and interests.[17]

The revolutionary position at this stage, the critical position, differs from the dogmatic in several respects. The boundaries for legal scholarship are wider, it is not only understood as one of the sources of law but as an independent activity in relation to law and its context; its field is wider than that of current law and its purpose is different. There are no inner and outer perspectives, since a distinction between inner and outer refers to boundaries of the object (current law). The concepts *de lege lata – de lege ferenda* express a distinction between descriptive (what law is) and normative (what law ought to be) statements. But according to the critical position there is no such 'true' distinction (cf. Kinander 2002, 289). Knowledge is seen as social and contextual.

The critical position follows scientific ideals stating that 'doing science' is a way of acting according to certain (scientific) norms, such as critical thinking as well as systematically and methodologically looking for new knowledge and new ideas. There are several definitions of what 'doing science' is. One well-known definition is that presented by Robert K. Merton in 1942. Merton's acronym CUDOS stands for communism (knowledge is a common good for scientists), universalism (knowledge is independent of time, place and person), disinterestedness (scientists keep the public interest in their sights) and organized scepticism (well-founded theories and methods are used even when the results challenge accepted norms and interests) (Sörlin 1994). This definition, however, seems to be outdated from several points of view. Official definitions of the purpose of academic education and research are expressed in the Higher Education Act (SFS 1992:1434) and Higher Education Ordinance (SFS 1993:100). Important characteristics are the ability to reflect critically and independently, to seek for knowledge and value that knowledge, to solve problems, to follow the development of knowledge and to be able to communicate with people with no expert knowledge in the field.

Periods of normal science in a paradigm are replaced by a new paradigm through revolutions (Kuhn 1962). Seen from a long-term perspective this also includes questioning basic assumptions, both for the study and for the object in focus. Critical legal studies follows the pattern of scientific revolution discussed by Kuhn, insofar as it questions the basic assumptions of legal 'science' and of legal practice. One of the assumptions it challenges is the dogmatic idea that scholarship corresponds to practice. In critical legal studies the purpose of the academic activity is understood as different from the purpose of practical legal knowledge.

---

16 In Svensson 1997a the concept gender-relation is used as a meta-theoretical tool. This means that gender-relation is a theoretical and abstract concept expressing a both-and epistemology instead of an either-or one. 'Meta' is because legal scholarship is analysed from this concept.

17 The process of mapping the field and constructing boundaries is both necessary and problematic. I have discussed this earlier in my thesis, Svensson1997a and in an article Svensson 1997b.

Table 2.4 Academic critical legal scholarship

Academic legal scholarship	
Established position 2 – dogmatic	Revolutionary position 2 – critical

In Table 2.4 the model of boundary-work between the established and the revolutionary positions has been contextualized in late 20th century legal scholarship (from the 1980s and onwards), as the dogmatic position, opposed to the critical. The critical includes several perspectives of criticism, each with different starting points. In his book *Critical Legal Positivism*, Tuori has analysed various critical positions. He argues that critique is directed at unmasking the normative positions of dogmatic scholarship, but points out that such 'unmasking' criticism itself often contains implicit normative elements. Tuori distinguishes criticism based on explicitly normative grounds from criticism, which aims to unmask fundamental presumptions in the law, even if it is more a matter of a difference in degree than a watertight distinction between them (Tuori 2002, 309). The various criticisms share one target; the established position in legal scholarship. Several perspectives in relation to the dogmatic position use tools such as theories, methods and concepts from 'outside' dogmatic legal scholarship. The demarcation of the field and its purpose differentiates between the dogmatic and the critical position, as illustrated in Table 2.5.

Table 2.5 Demarcation of the field (a) and its purpose (b)

Practical legal knowledge	Academic legal scholarship	
	Dogmatic	Critical
a. The object current law b. Uses current law	a. The object current law b. Describes and/or prescribes current law (*de lege lata, de lege ferenda*)	a. Legal systems in a broad context b. Criticizes current law out of its context (unmasking and/or normative)

Table 2.5 represents a way of illustrating the analysis of significant characteristics when demarcating the discipline and its purpose. Practical legal knowledge is included in the table due to its close connection to the dogmatic position in academic legal knowledge. The main distinction in this table is between dogmatic (contemporary established) and critical (contemporary revolutionary) scholarship in academic legal knowledge. Note that the boundaries are neither to be understood as static, nor as descriptions of legal knowledge today. On the contrary the boundaries are constantly under pressure and subjected to boundary-work, i.e. contests about epistemic authority as shown in previous tables.

Dogmatic scholarship follows the tradition in established legal scholarship of staying close to practical legal knowledge. The demarcation of the discipline is the same in practical legal knowledge as in dogmatic scholarship. Current law decides what is and what can be included in the field. Arguments and also solutions are to be found inside the object. The dogmatic position constitutes an inner perspective, a closed room according to Dahl (Dahl 1985, 58). The rules are the starting point for a study. Rules that can be described as concrete and detailed have priority over rules that express goals. If a rule can be interpreted in several ways, a restrictive interpretation is to be preferred. Moreover, argumentation is restricted to an argumentation *de lege lata* and *de lege ferenda* (see Persson this volume). The argumentation *de lege ferenda* offers a possibility of being normative, but that possibility is normally quite restricted. Argumentation *de lege lata* is the main task, even for legal scholarship (and not only for legal practitioners).

In critical scholarship the discipline is not restricted to current law and *de lege lata – de lege ferenda* argumentation. There are no inner and outer perspectives. Issues that are not regulated are seen as potentially of legal interest. According to Dahl, non-regulated issues could be understood as 'law-empty rooms' (Dahl 1985). The fact that an issue is not regulated can be very interesting to study from a feminist point of view. What is not regulated also constitutes a legal standpoint. Areas supposedly ignored by the formal law, can be pervasive as they shape and influence the way we act, even if they are not regulated. This is made visible through feminist studies.[18] For example, the private sphere has historically been the sphere where women have largely lived their lives. This sphere is less regulated than the public sphere and the exploitation of women tends to take place in just this private sphere. The legal system ought to be studied in relation to other norms, such as religious and cultural norms, and to the social context, because other norms and the social context are relevant and influence the everyday life of men and women, in combination with the presence or absence of legal rules.

The purpose of practical legal knowledge is to use current law. The purpose of legal scholarship, according to the dogmatic position, it is to systematize, interpret and define what current law is, in order to preserve and create a coherent legal system free from contradictions to help the practitioners in the application of law, as already mentioned above. A specific legal method, *the* legal method, is the preferred method used in this approach to legal knowledge. The legal method defines what sources are authoritative, in a normative doctrine of sources of law. In the Swedish doctrine of sources of law, the travaux préparatoires have an important role in the interpretation of the laws. They often contain explicit statements about the functional aims of the acts and often also how the acts should be interpreted. Both practitioners and legal scholars are expected to be familiar with these texts and what is more, to be loyal with regard to the legislator (Nousiainen and Niemi-Kiesiläinen 2001).

The purpose of legal scholarship in the critical position is to question the legal system and legal thinking, in accordance with the general scientific ideal

18 Cf. to the discussion above of the limits of law and legal scholarship. See also O'Donovan1985; Davies 1996; Svensson 1997.

of a critical and reflective seeking for knowledge. Such scientific activity can be based on sociological, philosophical or epistemological knowledge. Often it is complemented with argumentation of a normative kind. The distinction is therefore between critical legal scholarship on the one hand and dogmatic scholarship together with practical legal knowledge on the other hand. The activities have different purposes, and in addition to legal knowledge, other cognitive and social knowledge is taken into consideration.

The standpoint chosen impacts on the issues that can be dealt with, the methods that can be used and the fields which may be excluded or included in legal scholarship, as already mentioned. The table above is not to be interpreted as a description of contemporary legal scholarship today, but as a tool and as such it is simplified for the purpose of analysing the boundary-work and the contests that appear in legal scholarship. The boundaries of legal scholarship are constantly changing (Svensson 1997a). Contests and changes in society do in fact move the limits. As Gieryn says, 'science', in this case legal scholarship, does not assume the same shape and content in every contest. New fields have been incorporated at various times and the discipline has changed over time (Gieryn 1999).

Boundary-Work Concerning Feminist Legal Studies

Feminist legal studies is one of several critical perspectives in legal scholarship with different stories told out of an interest for equality and justice. The name (feminist legal studies) using the plural form shows that there is not just one but several perspectives with varying starting points, using different theories and methods, focusing on several fields within the legal system. Yet, feminist legal studies can also be seen as one research field defined by its cognitive content, the use of theories with concepts, methods and explanations and, finally, by the existence of a research network and its institutionalization in academia. There are only a few professorships in the Nordic countries (Norway and Finland) in the field. Even though feminist legal scholars mostly have their titles and posts in other fields, such as tax law, civil law or legal science, there are conferences and research funding for feminist legal studies. Since 1999 it has been compulsory in legal education in Sweden to produce gender sensitive legal knowledge, according to the Higher Education Ordinance (SFS 1993:100). Feminist legal studies are taught both in the form separate courses and integrated into other courses (Burman *et al.* 2003).

Table 2.6 Different critical positions

Academic legal scholarship		
Dogmatic	Gender-sensitive critical positions	Gender-insensitive critical positions
a. The object current law b. Describe and/or prescribe current law (*de lege lata, de lege ferenda*)	a. Legal systems in a broad context b. Criticize current law in relation to its context c. Gender is one important factor in legal scholarship and its analyses of law	a. Legal systems in a broad context b. Criticize current law in relation to its context

Tuori makes a distinction between different types of criticism of the law, unmasking and normative, which can both in turn target legal practice or law as norms. He seems to have a problem defining feminist criticism. He sees it as targeting both legal practices and law as norms, but as normative criticism and not as unmasking. He does however put a physical question mark in the text (Tuori 2002, 310). Whether the question mark means that he is uncertain as to whether or not it ought to be defined as unmasking or normative is not made explicit. He does not explore the issue.

The reason that Tuori defines feminist criticism as normative criticism is probably the explicit political aim, often associated with feminism as a research field, to promote gender equality and women's situation. This political starting-point does not necessarily have anything to do with the epistemological starting-point. If that were so Critical Legal Studies (CLS) could be defined as normative criticism and not as unmasking, in Tuori's scheme. I would say feminist legal studies primarily has an unmasking aim, in the sense of trying to show the hidden power relations in legal doctrines and policies. But again, feminist legal studies is not easy to place into a scheme like the one Tuori uses, because the unmasking and the normative critiques are linked within feminist legal studies. Moreover, feminist legal studies is as pluralistic as many other perspectives and encompasses different epistemological standpoints. Tuori's scheme is insensitive to gender as an important factor not only for law and legal practice but also for the tools scholars use. The very foundations of knowledge differ, and feminist legal studies is, using Kuhn's concept, incommensurable with Tuori's scheme.

As shown in Table 2.6, feminist legal scholars have to do boundary-work on two frontiers at the same time, against the dogmatic position and against the (other) critical positions. Arguments used to exclude feminist legal studies from a dogmatic position can take the view that the theoretical approach does not bring anything more to the issue (Nycander 2001/02). From a critical, but not gender-sensitive position, it has been argued that the tools used in feminist legal studies are (already) common (at least broadly) in mainstream legal scholarship (Dalberg-Larsen 1986; Doublet 1989). Non-gender sensitive legal scholarship has acted in varying ways when deciding whether or not feminist legal studies is a specific field, and whether it has any legitimate claims to exist or to be a part of legal scholarship and legal education. The boundary-work here has been concerned with expulsion, where the dogmatic position is held to be the 'real science'. According to this dogmatic position, theoretical approaches, including feminist legal studies, have nothing to contribute to legal scholarship. Expansion is the kind of boundary-work exemplified by the critical non-gender sensitive position. What feminist legal studies offers is nothing new, it is relevant, but it is not new. Mainstream legal scholars already do what feminist legal scholars say they themselves do in contrast to mainstream scholarship.

Protection of autonomy can be seen as a reaction on the part of non-feminist legal scholars in order to exclude feminist legal scholars. The inclusion of feminist legal studies in legal scholarship has not been unproblematic. Christensen wrote in 1986 that women's law was criticized and excluded from legal scholarship (Christensen 1986). In a review of one women's law edition (Nordborg 1995), feminist legal studies were described as being about 'special interests' (Nuotio 1997). Another article paints the picture of a (mainstream) legal scholarship still suspicious of feminist legal studies (Wennström 2003b). Some of the scholars in the field of feminist legal studies have personal experience of being criticized and/or prevented from doing such research.[19] Nuotio points out that it is desirable that feminist legal studies establish contact with other legal research and that some of the issues go beyond its own 'special interests'. From such comments, the detachment of feminist scholarship from other legal scholarship seems to be voluntary and driven by the 'selected few'. Gustafsson, in contrast, sees it as being non-voluntary (Gustafsson 1998). Feminist legal scholars do not have entry tickets to the male, legal, scientific world, he says. They have been marginalized, not by themselves, but by the men. Regarding the 'special interests' criticism, Gustafsson argues that this evaluation is based on the presumption that there is a common interest in non-feminist scholarship. However, the definition of common interest is determined by scholars with epistemological authority; it is a matter of power. Issues about women are often described as special interests, despite the fact that women constitute quite a large group in society – as large as that of men. Men's interests are seldom described as special interests.

In Sweden, most feminist legal studies projects are financed through external funding and not from (ordinary) faculty funding. Whether or not the field is accepted can be investigated through institutional analysis of the academic organization. Is it possible to qualify for academic posts, are there any academic posts in the field and how is the competence valued? Christensen demonstrated both the open and the implicit critique of women's law by using the example of the process whereby the women's law forerunner Tove Stang Dahl was not considered competent for a professorship in Social Law (Christensen 1986). According to Christensen, the reason was that the discipline of women's law was considered to be insufficiently scientific or legal.

19 Simply being a woman was a problem earlier, cf. the tragic history of Elsa Eschelsson, the first LLD in Sweden. See Eschelsson 1997; Silius 1995; Widerberg 1995.

In 1999, as mentioned above, it was made compulsory to include gender-related knowledge in legal education in Sweden. Taking all this together, the field does exist as a special field, even if not as one of the most established, in legal scholarship and in education but not to the same extent in the organization.

There have also been discussions about whether feminist legal studies is a specific field, different from 'other' legal scholarship. There are arguments for both specificity and its opposite. The early scholarship aimed at mapping a specific field, different in its purpose, its starting-point in a specific group, its theories and methods (Kvinderet 1979; Dahl 1985; Dahl 1988). Furthermore, Christensen claimed that feminist legal studies is the 'good-science' (to use Gieryn's words related to expulsion boundary-work). Women's law is consistent with the tradition in legal scholarship, she wrote, while the narrow dogmatic scholarship is not (Christensen 1986). The latter had, according to her, reached a dead end and she saw women's law as a way out of the dilemma.

Dalberg-Larsen, in contrast, was concerned with showing that there was nothing special about the discipline of women's law. In a discussion about whether women's law could be characterized as dogmatic or critical in the mid-1980s, Dalberg-Larsen thought that dogmatic scholarship was a long way from the narrow practical activity described by Dahl and Christensen. Using an extensive definition there is not such a great difference between a dogmatic and a critical position, in his opinion. As an academic activity, Dalberg-Larsen wrote, legal dogmatics not only has to, but also does follow scientific principles (Dalberg-Larsen 1986).

Dahl considered that the distinction between the dogmatic and the critical position was useful, even if legal dogmatics could be defined in both a narrow and an extensive way (Dahl 1988). But why does Dahl consider it worth upholding the distinction between the dogmatic and critical positions, if not simply to map out a special field for women's law? Was it perhaps difficult to gain acceptance for women's law in legal scholarship at that time? Could it only be legitimized through its specificity or were there attempts to exclude it from other fields? Was it a protection of autonomy?

The answer probably involves two factors. First, as shown in Table 2.6, extensive dogmatic scholarship and critical scholarship also lack the sensitiveness of gender. There is no guarantee that the critique of narrow legal scholarship accepts gender as an important issue. Second, not only cognitive but also social factors are important. Without any recognition of social factors it is hard to understand Dahl's strategy. The social factors are connected with the legitimacy and careers of the scholars and with the acceptance of a specific knowledge and competence called feminist knowledge. This knowledge differs from non-feminist knowledge, but it also has similarities with other legal knowledge. Feminist legal studies have features of both positions, the dogmatic and the critical, but at the same time criticize the lack of awareness of the importance of gender both cognitively and socially, in both the critical and the dogmatic paradigms.

Feminist legal studies needs tools obviously not available in mainstream legal scholarship in order to carry out gender analyses, but clearly, the field also uses the same tools as are used in other fields of legal scholarship. Basically, the boundaries are not restricted to the object current law. Feminists see the legal system as pluralistic, multi-layered, contradictory, constructed and an expression of power relations. This means that the law and its practitioners cannot be impartial, merely as non-partial as possible. The law always takes a position. Not only what is regulated, but also what is not, becomes an issue for feminist legal scholars. The boundaries between law and not-law are seen as constructed and not at all self-evident. The role of legal scholars is therefore to make visible, through critique, the impact of the system in a specific context, which includes both philosophical and sociological concerns. Knowledge about current law as well as the methods used in dogmatics is necessary. Arguments may often be found from a position inside the legal system, such as argumentation based on the principle of equality. The purpose however, is often to make visible hidden contradictory values and the lack of coherence in the law according to normative values. Legal principles expressed as certain aims may be impossible to achieve within the current law. Conflicting interests, as well as non-regulation, can counteract the legal aims. Argumentation to deal with this requires both dogmatic and critical tools. A legal scholarship with strict boundaries, which remains loyal to both legislation and to the legal system, and which takes legal principles seriously, might be an obstacle to such scholarship.

What is more, feminist legal studies is often meta-theoretical and meta-methodological. It is also both theoretical and oriented towards the legal norms. The field is not mapped out in the same way as other legal disciplines defined according to specific rules, such as labour law, social law and tax law, but cuts across these boundaries. This is quite normal for theoretical perspectives, but norm-oriented feminist legal studies also tend to study law in an interdisciplinary way. This characteristic is shared with other disciplines such as children's rights and indigenous rights.

In legal dogmatics it is permissible to use arguments touching on politics and morality only within narrow boundaries. But issues about the relation between law and sex/gender touch on both political and ethical issues that can hardly be answered within the paradigm of 'current law'. There has been a connection between politics and 'the friendly state' on the one hand and feminist legal studies on the other. Nevertheless, feminist legal studies has also criticized sex-equality politics (Svensson 2001), arguing that a focus on the public sphere is not sufficient; the private sphere must also be included in the project. Moreover, much of what is important for women and the relationship between men and women is defined in a manner that is closer to ethics than to politics and law (Nousiainen 2001).

To conclude, feminist legal studies as a discipline in the Nordic context, is partly dogmatic, partly critical and has similarities to as well as differences from those positions in legal scholarship. There are no obvious reasons to exclude it from legal scholarship. There are some reasons for preserving it as a specific field of legal scholarship and there are some reasons for mainstreaming it in other fields. Today, we can see attempts to do both. In legal education, the official strategy is to mainstream, but in practice it is mostly a specific field with its own courses (Burman *et al.* 2003). In scholarship, it is a specific knowledge field comprising not only cognitive but also social issues. In doing boundary-work, feminist legal scholars are not only mapping a cognitive field, but also a way of conducting oneself towards academic scholarship and moreover, a social field. Irrespective of whether feminist legal studies is dogmatic or critical, the specific field still has its meaning.

Sources of Knowledge

The authoritative sources of legal knowledge are sources of law according to a doctrine of sources of law (Strömholm 1996, 311). The doctrine is quite normative and considered legitimate in both practical legal knowledge and legal scholarship. Usually no significant difference is made. Legal scholarship, moreover, is considered to be one of the sources of law but, as such, is not highly valued. However, critical legal scholarship may have a divergent understanding: legal scholarship has a more independent status and the sources of law are not the only sources of knowledge, as shown in Table 2.7.

Table 2.7 Sources of knowledge

Practical legal knowledge	Academic legal scholarship	
	Dogmatic	Critical
Hierarchy of legal (acknowledged) sources	Hierarchy of legal (acknowledged) sources, legal scholarship is one of the sources	Relevant sources of knowledge, including sources of law

Three questions are relevant here. First, what is the status of legal scholarship? Second, what are the sources of law? Third, does legal scholarship have different sources of knowledge from practical legal knowledge and correspondingly, does dogmatic scholarship have different sources from critical scholarship?

In the previous section I mentioned briefly the distinction between the dogmatic and the critical positions when it comes to sources of law and the view of legal scholarship. Is legal scholarship to be regarded as one of the sources of law or is it, in relation to the doctrine of the sources of law, an independent activity? It is of great importance which opinion is held on this issue. If it is one of the sources of law, the purpose of legal scholarship is not to break the boundaries of the field, but to consolidate the established position, as in the periods of paradigmatic calm according to Kuhn. What is more, as a part of the hierarchical doctrine of the sources of law, legal scholarship has a very low status. A typical expression of this is a statement that appears in a textbook on practical legal method. To receive authority, legal scholarship has to be of practical value and propose good solutions to legal problems. It does not need to be of high academic (scientific) quality, on the contrary, that may, according to Lehrberg, be a disadvantage if it involves presenting new and original ideas (Lehrberg 2001).

There is not, however, consensus about the sources of law and their relative positions. A historical study shows that the doctrine of sources of law in Nordic countries varies over time and among scholars (Björne 1991). Neither the traditional doctrine, nor the modern one (which is usually considered to begin with the work of Alf Ross in the 1930s) is unambiguous.[20] The doctrine of sources of law can, according to Björne, be divided into three parts, the philosophy of sources of law, a normative and practical doctrine and finally, descriptive information about sources of law (Björne 1991). The second one seems to be the major part of the doctrine of sources of law and it is according to this part that the statements of authoritative sources of law are posed.

So what are the authoritative sources of law according to different Swedish scholars? Lehrberg mentions four (in order of importance – written law, preparatory work, cases and legal scholarship); Strömholm seven (in hierarchical order – written law, preparatory work, cases in superior courts, custom, legal scholarship, non-specific legal considerations and contract) (Strömholm 1996). Peczenik makes a distinction between sources which must be considered (in hierarchical order – written law of varying value, customary law, trade custom and contract, the two latter when it is so stated in the law), those which ought to be considered (cases in superior court, preparatory work, authoritative opinions about custom, international conventions) and finally, those that may be considered (directives from official authorities, cases and decisions from authorities and courts, preparatory work of a more general character, proposed bills, obsolete laws, utterances in superior court, legal scholarship, various kinds of arguments) (Peczenik 1995b, 214–218). Note that legal scholarship is accorded a low value as a legal source in all three of these constructions of hierarchies.

Peczenik is normative in his way of defining the sources of law. He clearly declares what sources must be considered and what sources may be considered. This is in opposition to the influential realistic approach, which aims at describing the sources (of different kinds) that jurists used in their legal decisions. The role of legal scholarship was not to prescribe what sources ought to be used and how, but to describe on what grounds decisions were made. The realists made a distinction between legal scholarship and legal practice in order to make legal scholarship scientific at a time when 'scientific' was considered to be descriptive and absolutely not normative. This absolute distinction was not dominant, as mentioned above. The constructivist approach is more one of a pragmatic, useful scholarship.

The distinction between different tasks for legal scholarship and legal practice can have more far-reaching consequences than the difference between normative and descriptive. The sources of knowledge which may be used, may also differ. Lehrberg may have good reasons for defining the sources of law mentioned as the only acceptable ones, because he addresses the practical application of law. His receiver is not the legal scholar, but the lawyer. Using Björne's definition, Lehrberg talks about the normative and practical doctrines, as do Strömholm and Peczenik, even if their compilations are more nuanced. This is typical of legal knowledge in general since as a field of knowledge and as a discipline it is mainly practical,

20 Sometimes the doctrine includes hermeneutics or the doctrine of interpretation, sometimes not. Stuer Lauridsen for instance, suggests a distinction between the doctrine of sources of law and the doctrine of interpretation, Stuer Lauridsen 1977, 348.

normative and professional. The legal field of knowledge has, for a period, not been primarily academic (Burman, Svensson and Ågren 2003).

One way of explaining these discrepancies between different normative doctrines about legal sources is that practical legal knowledge and legal scholarship require different sources of knowledge. If questions about legal sources are interpreted as questions about sources of knowledge, it is possible to problematize which sources are relevant or not relevant from an academic point of view and not only from the view of legal current law (Gustafsson 2002, 73-76). Practical legal knowledge and academic legal knowledge do not always share the same interests, as I explain below.

The status of legal scholarship will change if it comes to be seen as an academic activity with no (formal) restrictions concerning sources of knowledge, theories and methods. Legal scholarship would be able to interact with practical legal knowledge on a more equal basis and not just be viewed as a low-value legal source. It could also make more independent analyses of legal knowledge so that it becomes more considered and better able to reflect democratically determined objectives. This view is close to that which Björne labelled the philosophy of sources of law, which allows a reflection on its own assumptions and boundaries.

The sources of knowledge used in the field of feminist legal studies are, of course, the sources of law mentioned above. But feminist legal studies also uses other kinds of sources such as empirical and statistical knowledge (Schömer 1999; Fransson 2000), which are accepted in legal scholarship today, but were problematic 20–25 years ago. Studying patterns in lower court cases was not totally accepted as a methodology earlier, but it is today. When it comes to sources of law, feminist legal studies together with other critical perspectives, have contributed to a wider definition of the sources of law (Petersen 1995; Schömer 1999; Lundström 1999). This is also true of combining different fields within the legal system and their sources (Gunnarsson 2003). Previous divisions, for example between private law and public law, have been dissolved in feminist legal studies and conflicting principles and interests become visible when different sources of law are analysed together. What is more, feminist legal studies (again like other critical perspectives) also uses other kinds of knowledge when analysing the legal system (Svensson 1997a; Lundström 1999). Knowledge from other disciplines, theories, methods and concepts developed in contexts other than the legal are frequently used in order to understand, reflect on and analyse why current law is interpreted and used in a certain way.

To conclude, the sources of knowledge may differ between practical legal knowledge and legal scholarship. The purposes of the two activities are divergent and legal scholarship has a wider task than simply to be of practical use as one of the sources for practitioners. Feminist legal studies and other critical perspectives have contributed to a less strict doctrine of legitimate sources of law. They are also sources of knowledge, in addition to others.

The Concept of Knowledge

Is there a true foundation for knowledge or not? Is there an ultimate foundation, a point that it is possible to reach where it can be said that something is true or not?

Or if not, how is it possible to rely on something called knowledge? The question of the foundation of knowledge has occupied academic thinkers for many years. The desire for a foundation is easy to understand, but is it possible to know whether or not there is such a foundation?

Table 2.8 Foundation for knowledge

Practical legal knowledge	Academic legal scholarship	
	Dogmatic	Critical (not gender-sensitive and gender-sensitive)
Experience Contextual	Reason Non-contextual	Experience and reason Non-contextual or Contextual

In an epistemology based on the statement that there is a true foundation of knowledge, the two main bases are experience and reason, as shown in Table 2.8. Empiricism is the tradition, which holds experience to be the bedrock of true knowledge, and for a rationalistic epistemology it is reason. Both traditions believe in true knowledge. The question of exactly what the law is (and accordingly, what legal scholarship is) has been answered in various ways. The law has been seen as the will of God, the will of the king, the will of the state or as a system based on rational criteria following its own inner logic (Svensson 1997a). The question remains alive; Peczenik tries to answer it in a book with the ambiguous title of *Vad är rätt?* [What is law?] (Peczenik 1995b). The question in Swedish can mean both what is the law and what is just, and may be understood as an example of an established understanding. Jurists often act as if legal knowledge has a true foundation in legal knowledge (see for example Vindeløv 1997). The foundation for legal knowledge from a dogmatic perspective is the law and the sources of law described above.

The belief in a true knowledge was challenged and questioned in science during the 20th century with the context of knowledge attracting increasing interest. Contemporary academic thinking has partly abandoned the search for the foundation of true knowledge and instead understands knowledge as something contextual and constructed as well as dependent on language (these understandings are referred to as the social turn and the linguistic turn, respectively, see above). The epistemology here is based on the foundation that knowledge is social and contextual. Different variants of constructivism are frequent and have the common standpoint that there is no true foundation of knowledge. The interesting question is not to ask what something is, but rather how, why and what does it mean.

Both the social and the linguistic turns may have an impact on legal knowledge. Critical perspectives, such as feminist legal studies, have been influenced by both the social and the linguistic turns. Here the law is understood to be constructed by human beings and influenced by social conditions, such as power relations. Structural explanations are added to the individual perspective, common in legal scholarship. Feminist legal studies has also questioned the individualistic approach in the legal system. The context in the Nordic countries has generally emphasized substantial social equality and redistribution of wealth and power. The legal system deals with inequalities through a balance of power to a certain extent but when it comes to gender equality, the main focus in the system remains on individuals, in contrast to political ideas based on a structural understanding (Svensson 2001). The focus on the individual in the legal system means that the system is inadequate when it comes to dealing with matters of systemic inequality and discrimination (Svensson and Pylkkänen 2004). A structural understanding of gender as hierarchical and the idea of a male norm (Dahl 1985; Smart 1989) are difficult to combine with a dogmatic perspective (Nousiainen 2002).

The task for legal scholarship according to feminist legal studies is to make such conditions visible in order to enable the aims claimed in the law or the values accepted in society to be realized. Legal scholarship has to adjust to changes in the legal system and in society. Aims, theories, methods and sources of knowledge must be open in order to meet the challenges of the contemporary situation.

Other issues that go together with a social, contextual epistemology are to make visible the kind of knowledge that is sought, the relation between knowledge and human interest, how and where the problems are formulated and choice of theory and method.

Table 2.9 Knowledge sought for

Practical legal knowledge	Academic legal scholarship	
	Dogmatic	Critical
Prediction and statement	Prediction and interpretation, statement and recommendation	Critique Emancipatory – aiming at changes

The knowledge sought in practical legal knowledge is (see Table 2.9) prediction, statements about current law and what the possibilities of using it are. What arguments and what style of argumentation will be successful in a given situation? From a dogmatic perspective of legal scholarship predictions and statements are also the main form of knowledge, but the field of interpretations and recommendations is wider than in practical legal knowledge. Legal scholarship has a creative element that practical legal knowledge lacks. For feminist and other critical scholarship the critique is often fundamental to the emancipatory project, which is to change law for the better.

Table 2.10 Knowledge and interest

Practical legal knowledge	Academic legal scholarship	
	Dogmatic	Critical
Technical, to find the 'best' legal solution within the system, defines what is applicable law	Technical and hermeneutic, to find the 'best' legal solution within the system, define what is applicable law, systematize, preserve	Hermeneutic and emancipatory, to find the 'best' legal solution according to values, rights, demands from society etc., not restricted to the system, to question, to challenge the evident

The knowledge sought is connected with the relation between knowledge and interest. According to Habermas' theory of knowledge and human interests, dating from 1965, there are three different knowledge-constitutive interests, the technical, the practical and the emancipatory (Habermas 1978)[21] as shown in Table 2.10. For practical legal knowledge technical interest predominates, for legal scholarship from a dogmatic perspective the practical (here called hermeneutical-practical) and the technical seem to be most important and, finally, for critical scholarship the emancipatory and the hermeneutic-practical interests are most relevant. Which knowledge-constitutive interest a perspective has as a starting-point, impacts on the questions that are posed and the tools that are used. Feminist legal studies generally have an emancipatory interest, but this also includes knowledge of a technical and hermeneutic-practical kind. The latter in particular has often been focused on. Dahl has argued that legal scholarship needs to adopt external methodological assistance when analysing its own scientific character (Dahl 1985; Dahl 1988). This argumentation was met with scepticism by Doublet who considered that legal scholarship already contained methods enabling such self-reflection. Women's law did not contribute to legal scholarship in this respect, according to Doublet (Doublet 1989). Dalberg-Larsen has followed the same line, writing that if a dogmatic position is seen as not only an activity for practitioners but also as an academic activity, this position would include contextual studies as well as the construction of new concepts and explanations (Dalberg-Larsen 1986).

Table 2.11 Starting-point

Practical legal knowledge	Academic legal scholarship	
	Dogmatic	Critical
Practical problems	Rule oriented	Problem oriented

21 An article was first published in 1965 in *Merkur*, in 1968 as an appendix in the book *Erkenntnis und Interesse*.

A distinction commonly used in legal scholarship is (see Table 2.11) whether a study is rule-oriented or problem-oriented (Westberg 1992). The rule-oriented study starts in the law and is typical of a dogmatic scholarship. Feminist legal studies, as well as other critical perspectives, are often problem-oriented. When identifying problems, empirical knowledge is used as a source for studies on the impact law had on the living conditions of women, the so-called 'life-long conditions' perspective. The use of this kind of knowledge has sometimes been controversial in legal scholarship.

Feminist legal studies has a base in the values of equality and justice. The aim in the field has been to achieve these values and the way to do that has been to explore inequalities and injustices. Values were excluded from legal scholarship for a long period but women's law included them, as well as arguments about justness.

Feminist legal studies is sometimes described as transformative (Wennström 2003b). This can be interpreted both positively and negatively, but if it is understood to mean open to changes in the object, it seems to be a fitting aim for all research. Feminist legal studies is a very expansive field, open in relation to concepts, theories and methods. The field is sensitive to changes in the legal system. For instance, the principal of material neutrality (gender equality), which implies both sex neutral and sex specific regulation, has become one of the main legal principles in both national and international law as well as a prioritized political goal. This means that today the objective of the early women's law has become a binding legal norm. It is obviously important to take such a change into account even in a theory. The field is also sensitive to changes in society and in academic knowledge. It has been influenced by the social turn as well as the linguistic turn and it shares this influence with postmodernism, constructivism and other contemporary theories.

Table 2.12 Methods (a) and theories (b)

Practical legal knowledge	Academic legal scholarship	
	Dogmatic	Critical
a. Legal method; doctrine of sources of law, doctrine of interpretation b. Dogmatic	a. Legal method; doctrine of sources of law, doctrine of interpretation b. Dogmatic	a. Critical reflection and analysis of legal method and its limits b. Varying social and contextual theories

The question of theory and method in legal scholarship is interesting. Yet, legal education is a vocational education and contains little or no element of preparation for scholarly research. The dogmatic position remains dominant. The authoritative doctrine of sources of law is supposed to be the same for practitioners as for legal scholars and, as we have seen, legal scholarship has only a weak position. The method preferred is a specific legal method. This method however is not just one method and it is not obvious exactly what is meant when the method is referred to

(Strömholm 1996, 411–420). Nevertheless, it is quite common for questions about method and theory to be problematic in dissertations and in other research projects. See for an illustration of the problem Table 2.12.

The problem with an academic field, not explicitly with regard to theory and method, is that it is difficult not only to know what the scholarly norm is, but also to know when the norm is being challenged. It is through other scholars' reactions that one becomes aware of what the norm is and when it is broken. It is not always possible to understand and argue rationally in relation to a discipline that is not explicit in its boundaries.

One example of this tacit scepticism towards theoretical and methodological reflection is the reaction in a review by Nycander of three dissertations on gender discrimination (Nycander 2001/02). The relevance of the feminist theory used in two of these dissertations was questioned. On the one hand, the question posed is whether there are any differences at all between the two dissertations explicitly using feminist theory and the one using the (implicit) legal method. Nycander's answer seems to be that the explicit feminist theory is not of any value, it does not add anything valuable to the analysis. On the other hand, he points out a difference between the dissertations, characterized as a difference in objectivity. The authors using feminist theory are criticized for not being objective. The explicit feminist theoretical and methodological standpoint is seen as supposed to be in contrast to the legal method, which only describes current law and is therefore objective, according to Nycander. In making this judgement, he refers to a comment by the author of the dissertation using the legal method. The latter writes that, first it is necessary to clarify what gender discrimination is according to current law, and then it is possible to adopt a gender perspective towards the legal system (Lerwall 2001). This statement is a striking, though unconscious, example of a non-contextual epistemology.

What both the author of the review and the author using the legal method miss are the differences in purpose and the relation between the research and the object, as well as the fact that this has consequences for the knowledge that is produced. When using feminist theory it is possible to dissolve the connection between the object, the legal system, and the study of it. In fact, this is essential in order to correlate the research better to its aim, namely dealing with gender discrimination in practice. In legal dogmatics there is a close connection between the object and the study, and therefore the study will maintain the legal system. The study has no intention of asking whether the legal system can adequately deal with a problem, it is rather to explain the legal system and its boundaries. Therefore, it is no surprise that in the conclusion of the 'legal method' dissertation, negative treatment of part-time employees cannot automatically be seen as discrimination. The reason, according to the author, is that the direct connection is between special treatment and part-time work and not between special treatment and gender. This is surely a statement aimed at preserving the system. It discounts the problem that the special treatment is in fact, if not automatically in law, connected to gender. It is women who work part-time. The explanation using the legal method is a formal one, correct from a dogmatic perspective, but inadequate from a critical perspective (Kouvo 2002).

Feminist legal studies use various methods as well as theories. The problem determines which theories and methods are suitable and often several theories and methods are used together (Svensson 1997a). This approach often implies that methodological and theoretical issues are intertwined and this is frequently made explicit. Critical reflection requires tools from outside the legal dogmatic field. Explanations from outside the legal system have not been usual from a dogmatic perspective. In feminist legal studies explanations from outside legal scholarship are often used. This also applies to theories and tools, such as concepts and methods. The dogmatic perspective has not been able to produce tools suitable for explaining and answering questions posed in women's law and feminist legal studies. Legal scholarship, in its more external or critical fields, has relied on theories from other disciplines within the social sciences and the humanities. Legal tools are, still, either dogmatic (and not explicit) or taken from other disciplines (and then explicit). There are some broader legal tools, such as alternative jurisprudence, sociology of law, anthropology of law and some legal theories such as reflexive law, system theories and pluralistic theories. There are also theories and methods developed within the feminist legal tradition suitable for use in critical reflection (Nousiainen 2002). The theories and methods are sometimes adopted from other disciplines, sometimes developed as feminist legal tools. One characteristic is the openness and the searching for tools, which can help with the asking of questions. To question how instead of answering what, is not only an issue when it comes to the understanding of sex/gender, it is also a general methodological approach that characterizes feminist legal studies (Bacchi 1999; Davies 1996; Svensson 1997a).

Conclusion

The boundaries for legal scholarship are constantly under negotiation in contests among participants from the legal field (see Table 2.13). The concrete questions in focus may differ from time to time. This chapter has focused on the demarcation of legal scholarship using Gieryn's concept of boundary-work where established and revolutionary positions come into conflict. In order to make the boundary-work understandable, I have considered some issues about which there have been discussions. The issues chosen were the demarcation of legal scholarship, the sources of knowledge and the concept of knowledge. I have a special interest in contests that are important for feminist legal studies.

Table 2.13 Spheres studied for boundary-work

<table>
<tr><td rowspan="2">Practical legal knowledge</td><td colspan="2">Academic legal scholarship</td></tr>
<tr><td>Established x</td><td>Revolutionary x</td></tr>
</table>

The distinction between practical and academic legal knowledge on the one hand and between established and revolutionary legal scholarship within academic knowledge on the other, are the main borders contested in legal knowledge. Traditionally in Sweden there has been a close relationship between practical legal knowledge and academic legal knowledge. The purpose of legal knowledge, even as an academic activity, is mainly to educate jurists. Therefore it is not surprising that academic legal knowledge has had a practical character. But legal scholarship may also have other tasks to fulfil than simply being of practical importance. As a part of academic society it has obligations to be critical and reflective and not bound to current law, but serve as a guarantee of ideals connected with science and 'free' academic reflective knowledge. The contest between practical legal knowledge and academic legal knowledge is about the practical impact of legal scholarship. This contest was current in the 1950s and is still so today at the beginning of the 21st century. My conclusion is that practical legal knowledge on one side and academic legal knowledge on the other, have different spheres, interests in knowledge and concepts of knowledge. For me this does not exclude practical usefulness. In the long term critical reflection may well be useful in practical life, but the main purpose of legal scholarship cannot be restricted to practical usefulness alone. If it is, legal scholarship is not an academic activity but a vocational training.

The contest between established and revolutionary scholarship has been the main focus in this chapter rather than the contest between practical and academic legal knowledge. Contests change the academic field and move the limits for established scholarship and also, indirectly, for practical legal knowledge. Every contest may lead to new established and revolutionary positions. The process is continuous while the contesting parties may vary. Contests can be seen as conditions for change, no matter whether they can be described in terms of expulsion, expansion or protection of autonomy. Contests are not only, and perhaps not even primarily, about knowledge itself, but about the credibility of scholars. The social context is important for the academic field. A study of the social context of legal scholars occupying contesting positions would be of great interest. Perhaps such a study could explain why the boundary-work concerning feminist legal studies and its relation to established scholarship has seldom been explicit or consistent. It is only recently that established scholarship has started to adopt feminist legal knowledge. This is also partly true when it comes to critical scholarship. Credibility contests between feminist legal scholars and others seem to be non-existent, invisible, or hidden behind other contests. Scholars critical of the established position have defined feminist critique sometimes as controversial, sometimes as self-evident or uninteresting. The (former) lack of interest in feminist legal studies on the part of established scholarship is obvious. In the worst case, the non-apparent contests have been an obstacle not only to the development of the established and the revolutionary non-gender-sensitive field, but also to the development of feminist critical scholarship. At best, the non-apparent contests have offered a plurality of (new or not so new) positions the chance to grow.

Some concluding comments can be made from the study presented in this chapter. Legal scholarship in general is quite unreflective about theory and method. The close relationship to practical legal knowledge and the pragmatic-dogmatic influence in the middle of the 20th century, together with a strict formal-logical direction in legal theory, led to a reduced interest in theoretical reflections in general. One symptom of this is the former lack of theoretical and methodological courses in doctoral studies. The revolutionary position contesting the established dogmatic position has been quite theoretical and, due to the practical direction in legal knowledge, not influential either within practical legal knowledge or legal education. The separation between (critical) scholarship and other legal knowledge (both practical and academic) has been strong.

The feminist critical, revolutionary position has contested both the established position and the critical (non-gender-sensitive) position, through both theory and practice. The contests have only recently become influential. Feminist legal studies is not easy to place in opposition to the other positions as it both shares and does not share characteristics with the others. Feminist legal studies raises several questions that are important for legal knowledge to deal with. The contest today seems to be about what role legal scholarship may have as an independent academic activity and which knowledge interests it may have. If legal scholarship is to be critical, it cannot be restricted to certain sources bound to a specific time and context in the same way that practical legal knowledge is. It may well have as its object the current law, but there must be a free choice of the knowledge, tools, theories for understanding and analysis of the object that are to be used.

References

Literature

Aarnio, Aulis (1986), 'Inledning', in Peczenik, Aleksander. *Rätten och förnuftet* (Stockholm: Norstedts Juridik).

Agell, Anders (1997), 'Rättsdogmatik eller konstruktiv rättsvetenskap', i *Festskrift till Stig Strömholm*, (Uppsala: Iustus Förlag).

Agge, Ivar (1955), 'Till frågan om rättsvetenskapens gränser', *Festskrift tillägnad Nils Herlitz*. (Stockholm: Kungl. Boktryckeriet P.A. Norstedt & Söner).

Ahlander, Björn (1952), *Om rätt och rättstillämpning: studier i juridikens idéhistoria och rättstillämpningens teori* (Stockholm: Almqvist & Wiksell).

Andreasson, Reidar (2004), *Att beskriva rätten, En kommentar till försök att ge en generell beskrivning av rätten* (Uppsala: Uppsala University).

Asp, Petter (2002), *EU & Straffrätten: Studier rörande den europeiska integrationens betydelse för den svenska straffrätten* (Uppsala: Iustus Förlag).

Bacchi, Carol Lee (1999), *Women, policy and politics: the construction of policy problems* (London: Sage).

Bernt, Jan Fridthjof and Doublet, David R. (1998), *Vitenskapsfilosofi for jurister – en innføring* (Bergen-Sandviken: Fagbokforlaget).

Björne, Lars (1991), *Nordisk rättskällelära: studier i rättskälleläran på 1800-talet* (Stockholm: Institutet för rättshistorisk forskning, Nordiska bokh. Distributör).

Björne, Lars (2002), *Den nordiska rättsvetenskapens historia* (Stockholm: Institutet för rättshistorisk forskning: Rönnells antikvariat distributör).

Burman, Monica, Svensson, Eva-Maria and Ågren, Karin (2003), 'Kunskapsbildning inom juristutbildningen: exemplet könsrelaterad kunskap', *2 Retfaerd: Nordic Journal of Law and Justice* 2003, 20–38.

Christensen, Anna (1986), 'Kvinnorätten och lagpositivismen', *33 Retfaerd: Nordic Journal of Law and Justice* 1986, 88–96.

Dahl, Tove Stang (1985), *Kvinnerett I* (Oslo: Universitetsforlaget).

Dahl, Tove Stang (1988), 'Mot en fortolkende rettsteori – det kvinnerettslige argument', *Tidskrift for rettsvitenskap* 1988, 54–70.

Dalberg-Larsen, Jørgen (1986), 'Har kvinderetten fundet sin endelige form?', *34 Retfaerd: Nordic Journal of Law and Justice* 1986, 86–98.

Dalberg-Larsen, Jørgen (2001), *Pragmatisk retsteori* (København: Jurist- og Økonomforbundets Förlag).

Davies, Margaret (1996), *Delimiting the Law: 'Postmodernism' and the Politics of Law* (London: Pluto Press).

Davies, Margaret (2002), *Asking the Law Question. The Dissolution of Legal Theory* 2nd Edition. (Sydney: Lawbook Co.).

Doublet, David R. (1989), 'Hermeneutikken of rettsvitenskapen', *Tidskrift for rettsvitenskap* 1989, 589–612.

Ekelöf, Per Olof (1951), *Är den juridiska doktrinen en teknik eller en vetenskap?* (Lund: C. W. K. Gleerup).

Eschelsson, Elsa (1997), *ad studium et ad laborem incitavit*, in Jareborg, Nils (ed.) (1997) (Uppsala: Iustus Förlag AB).

Fransson, Susanne (2000), *Lönediskriminering: en arbetsrättslig studie av könsdiskriminerande löneskillnader och konflikten mellan kollektivavtal och lag* (Uppsala: Iustus Förlag AB).

Gieryn, Thomas F (1999), *Cultural Boundaries of Science: Credibility on the Line* (Chicago: University of Chicago Press).

Gunnarsson, Åsa (1995), *Skatterättvisa* (Uppsala: Iustus Förlag AB).

Gunnarsson, Åsa (2003), *Fördelningen av familjens skatter och sociala förmåner* (Uppsala: Iustus Förlag AB).

Gustafsson, Håkan (1998), 'Från axiom till paradox? Om kön: rätt och makt', *82 Retfaerd: Nordic Journal of Law and Justice* 1998, 51–78.

Gustafsson, Håkan (2002), *Rättens polyvalens: en rättsvetenskaplig studie av sociala rättigheter och rättssäkerhet* (Lund: Lunds Universitet, Sociologiska Institutionen).

Habermas, Jürgen (1978), *Knowledge and Human Interests* (London: Heinemann Educational Books Ltd).

Hägerström, Axel (1957), *Filosofi och vetenskap* (Örebro).

Hallberg, Margareta (2001), *Etnologisk koreografi: Att följa ett ämne i rörelse* (Nora: Nya Doxa).

Kinander, Morten (2002), 'Skaper Høyesterett ny rett? Spenninger I norsk rettskildelære', in *Nybrott og odling, Festskrift til Nils Nygaard på 70-årsdagen, 3 April 2002* (Bergen: Fagbokforlaget).

Kouvo, Sari (2002), 'Lotta Lerwall: Könsdiskriminering. En analys av nationell och internationell rätt', *3 Europarättslig tidskrift* 2002, 613–618.

Kuhn, Thomas (1962), *The Structure of Scientific Revolutions* (Chicago: Chicago University Press).

Kvinderet (1979), Special issue, *10 Retfaerd: Nordic Journal of Law and Justice 1979.*

Lehrberg, Bert (2001), *Praktisk juridisk metod* (Stockholm: Iustus).

Lerwall, Lotta (2001), *Könsdiskriminering: en analys av nationell och internationell rätt* (Uppsala: Iustus Förlag AB).

Liedman, Sven-Eric (1997), *I skuggan av framtiden: Modernitetens idéhistoria* (Stockholm: Bonnier Alba).

Liedman, Sven-Eric (1998), *Mellan det triviala och det outsägliga; blad ur humanioras och samhällsvetenskapernas historia* (Göteborg: Daidalos).

Lindahl, Lars (2000), 'Deskription och normativitet: de juridiska begreppens janusansikte', in Henning (ed.) *Normativa perspektiv* (Lund: Juristförlaget).

Lundström, Karin (1999), *Jämlikhet mellan kvinnor och män i EG-rätten: en feministisk analys* (Uppsala: Iustus Förlag AB).

Merton, Robert K. (1973), 'The sociology of science: theoretical and empirical investigations' (Chicago: University of Chigago Press).

Nordborg, Gudrun (1995) (ed.), *13 kvinnoperspektiv på rätten* (Uppsala: Iustus Förlag AB).

Nousiainen, Kevät (1999), 'Equalizing Images? Gendered Imagery in Criminal Law', *24 Suomen Antropologi,* 1999, 7–24.

Nousiainen, Kevät (2001), 'Transformative Nordice Welfarism: Liberal and Communitarian Trends in Family and |Market Law', in Nousiainen, Kevät, Gunnarsson, Åsa, Lundström Karin and Niemi-Kiesiläinen, Johanna (eds), *Responsible Sevles: Women in the Nordic Legal Culture* (Aldershot: Ashgate Publishing).

Nousiainen, Kevät and Niemi-Kiesiläinen, Johanna (2001), 'Introductory Remarks on Nordic Law and Gender Identities', in Nousiainen, Kevät, Gunnarsson, Åsa, Lundström, Karin and Niemi-Kiesiläinen, Johanna (eds), *Responsible Selves: Women in the Nordic Legal Culture* (Aldershot: Ashgate Publishing).

Nuotio, Kimmo (1997), Nordborg, Gudrun. (ed.): 13 kvinnoperspektiv på rätten, *76 Retfaerd: Nordic Journal of Law and Justice 1997*, 85–92.

Nycander, Svante (2001/02), Karin Lundström, Jämlikhet mellan kvinnor och män i EG-rätten. En feministisk analys. Ak. Avh. Iustus Förlag. Uppsala 1999. 461 s. Susanne Fransson, Lönediskriminering. En arbetsrättslig studieav könsdiskriminerande löneskillnader och konflikten mellan kollektivavtal och lag. Ak.avh. Iustus Förlag. Uppsala 2000. 530 s. Lotta Lerwall, Könsdiskriminering. En analys av nationell och internationell rätt. Ak. Avh. Iustus Förlag. Uppsala 2001. 471 s. *3 Juridisk Tidskrift* 3 2001 (Uppsala: Iustus Förlag), 687–693.

O'Donovan, Katherine (1985), *Sexual divisions in law* (London: Weidenfeld and Nicolson).

Olausson, Lennart and Liedman, Sven-Eric (1988), *Ideologi och institution: Om forskning och högre utbildning 1880–2000* (Stockholm: Carlsson).

Peczenik, Aleksander (1986), *Rätten och förnuftet: en lärobok i allmän rättslära* (Stockholm: Norstedts Juridik).

Peczenik, Aleksander (1989), *On Law and Reason* (Dordrecht: Kluwer Academic Publishers).

Peczenik, Aleksander (1995a), *Juridikens teori och metod* (Stockholm: Norstedts).

Peczenik, Aleksander (1995b), *Vad är rätt? Om demokrati, rättssäkerhet, etik och juridisk argumentation* (Stockholm: Norstedts Juridik).

Peczenik, Aleksander (1999), 'The Passion for Reason', in Wintgens, Luc (ed.) *The Law in Philosophical Perspectives*: my Philosophy of Law (Boston, Mass.: Kluwer Academic Publishers).

Peczenik, Aleksander (2002), 'Legal Doctrine and Value Pluralism' in *Associations* 6/2002.

Perelman, Chaim (2004), *Retorikens imperium* (Stockholm: Symposion).

Petersen, Hanne (1995), 'Reclaiming "Juridical Tact"? Observations and Reflections on Customs and Informal Law as (pluralist) Sources of Polycentric Law', in Petersen, Hanne and Zahle, Henrik (eds), *Legal Polycentricity: Consequences of Pluralism in Law* (Aldershot: Dartmouth).

Petersen, Hanne (2002), *Globaliseringer, ret og retsfilosofi* (København: Jurist- og økonomforbundet).

Rosengren, Mats (2004), 'Introduction to Perelman', *Retorikens imperium* (Stockholm: Symposion).

Sand, Inger-Johanne (1996), *Styring av kompleksitet: rettslige former for statlig rammestyring og desentralisert statsforvaltning* (Bergen-Sandviken: Fagbokforlaget).

Sandström, Marie and Peterson, Claes (1996), 'Lex lata – lex ferenda. Fakta eller fiktion?', in Rosén (ed.) *Lex Ferenda: Rättsvetenskapliga studier av forskare vid Stockholms universitet* (Stockholm: Skrifter utgivna av Juridiska fakulteten Stockholms Universitet), 159–177.

Schömer, Eva (1999), *Konstruktion av genus i rätten och samhället: en tvärvetenskaplig studie av svenska kvinnors rätt till jämställdhet i ett formellt jämlikt rättssystem* (Uppsala: Iustus Förlag AB).

Silius, Harriet (1995), 'Att vara kvinna och jurist', in Nordborg, Gudrun (ed.) *13 kvinnoperspektiv på rätten* (Uppsala: Iustus Förlag AB).

Smart, Carol (1989), *Feminism and the power of law* (London: Routledge).

Strömholm, Stig (1996), *Rätt, rättskällor och rättstillämpning: en lärobok i allmän rättslära* (Stockholm: Norstedts Juridik).

Stuer Lauridsen (1977), *Retslaeren: trykt som manuskript* (København: Akademisk Förlag).

Svensson, Eva-Maria (1997a), *Genus och rätt: En problematisering av föreställningen om rätten* (Uppsala: Iustus Förlag AB).

Svensson, Eva-Maria (1997b), 'Avskiljandets logik – en nödvändighet och en begränsning', in Hydén H. and Thoor A. (eds.), *Rätt i förändring: Om kristendenser i svensk rätt* (Lund: Sociologiska Institutionen Lunds Universitet).

Svensson, Eva-Maria (2001), 'Sex Equality: Changes in Politics, Jurisprudence and Feminist Legal Studies', in Nousiainen, Kevät, Gunnarsson, Åsa, Lundström, Karin and Niemi-Kiesiläinen, Johanna. (eds) *Responsible Selves: Women in the Nordic legal culture* (Aldershot: Ashgate-Dartmouth).

Svensson, Eva-Maria and Pylkkänen, Anu (2004), 'Contemporary challenges for Nordic feminist legal studies', in Svensson, Eva-Maria ,Pylkkänen, Anu and Niemi-Kiesiläinen, Johanna (eds), *Nordic Equality at a Crossroads. Feminist legal studies coping with difference* (Aldershot: Ashgate).

Sörlin, Sverker (1994), 'Inledning', in Sigbrit Franke-Wikberg *et al.* (eds) *Vetandets vägar: Perspektiv på universitet, vetenskap och utbildning* (Lund: Studentlitteratur).

Tuori, Kaarlo (2002), *Critical legal positivism* (Aldershot: Ashgate Publishing).

Wallén, Göran (1996), *Vetenskapsteori och forskningsmetodik* (Lund: Studentlitteratur).

Wennström, Bo (2003a), *Bör den allmänna rättsläran omorienteras?* (Stockholm: Elanders).

Wennström, Bo (2003b), 'Allmän rättslära och feministisk rättsteori', in Fogelkou, Anders and Spaak, Torben (eds), *Festskrift till Åke Frändberg* (Uppsala: Iustus Förlag AB).

Westberg, Peter (1992), 'Avhandlingsskrivande val av forskningsansats – en idé om rättsvetenskaplig öppenhet', in *Festskrift till Per-Olof Bolding* (Stockholm: Juristförlaget), 421–446.

Widerberg, Karin (1995), *Kunskapens kön: Minnen, reflektioner och teori* (Stockholm: Norstedts Förlag AB).

Vindeløv, Vibeke (1997), *Konflikt, tvist og mægling: konfliktløsning ved forhandling* (København: Akademisk Förlag).

Internet-Based References

Bartlett's *Quotations*, <http://www.bartleby.com/66/93/11093.html> (home page), accessed 30 May 2006.

Nousiainen, Kevät (2002), *Kvinnorättens betydelse i Norden*, <http://www.congrex.fi/njm2002/indexs.htm. 479> (home page), Det 36 Nordiska juristmötet I Helsingfors, 15–17 August 2002, accessed 30 May 2006.

<http://www.hum.gu.se/~idewww/> (home page), accessed 30 May 2006.

<http://www.law.cornell.edu/topics/jurisprudence.html> (home page), accessed 30 May 2006.

Chapter 3

An Apparent Boundary Between Law and Politics

Åsa Persson

In the Nordic context legal scholarship usually raises questions other than those concerning the relationship between law and politics. Theoretically law is usually understood to be current law, or law 'as it is'. Current law is considered to be the core of the academic discipline of legal scholarship and is also a common object of study.[1] In legal scholarship law is often seen as an empirical object. When regarded as an object, law simply lies before us, ready for us to use and explore. Assuming this dogmatic position (see Svensson this volume) the fundamental premises for the legal system are unquestioningly taken for granted. One in-built premise of law is the powerful and tenacious idea that law is free from subjectivity.

The idea of law as an object finds expression in the drawing up of a boundary between law and politics, which is important both theoretically and methodologically. Such a concept sets limits for argumentation in law and guides legal action since it suggests what is, and what is not, to be regarded as legally relevant. It also governs the issues that may legitimately be dealt with in legal scholarship. A judicial issue is regarded as being of legal relevance, while a political issue is seen as being of non-legal relevance. However, it is not clear why some matters are to be considered as either judicial or political.

In this chapter I argue that the boundary between law and politics is an 'apparent' boundary, meaning that there is a *conception* of a limit separating law and politics in legislation, adjudication and legal scholarship. This conception has an influence on actions and decisions in these areas since judgements and decisions are made as if there is a real boundary. Even if the boundary is merely fictional it influences what is to be regarded as of legal and non-legal relevance. The apparent boundary also seems to be moveable, i.e. an issue considered as political in nature can suddenly be considered as judicial. The basis for such a change is, however, often unclear. Both the apparent boundary itself and its flexibility are conducive to a diffuse, rather than a clear, meaning of the differences between what is regarded as being of legal or non-legal relevance. Sustaining an apparent boundary between law and politics, facilitates the exclusion of certain spheres from both legal regulation and adjudication. Understanding law as a set of normative considerations characterized by objectivity

1 Current law is quite a complex concept impossible to cover in a short chapter. For instance Strömholm deals with the concept over several hundred pages. See Strömholm 1996 and also Peczenik 1995.

while politics is regarded as subjective may also nourish an understanding of law and politics as existing in totally different worlds. Thus, one way of understanding the relationship between law and politics is as a separating concept of great influence. An alternative and equally conceivable way of understanding them is in terms of an intersection concept, where it is not theoretically possible to separate law and politics.

In this chapter I focus on the relation of law to politics. First, I describe established definitions of law and politics, and recapitulate common Swedish debates on the relationship between legal scholars and political scientists. From the starting point of widely accepted definitions of politics used in political science, I confront law and its limits as seen from the dogmatic position in legal scholarship. My aim, however, is not to find fault with any definition of politics but rather to use the definitions in order to challenge the concept which separates law and politics. I provide some examples where the concept of separation plays a part in legislation and adjudication when decisions are made about whether an issue or a circumstance is to be regarded as judicial or political. Issues or circumstances regarded from the dogmatic position as political are simultaneously seen as having no legal relevance. Finally, I argue for a reconceptualized comprehension of the relationship between law and politics where they are not seen as theoretically distinct phenomena. I will start by describing the construction of an apparent boundary separating law and politics.

The Construction of a Boundary Between Law and Politics

Within legal scholarship law and politics are often dealt with as if a clear-cut line separates them. While law is often seen as devoid of value judgements, politics, as the stuff of political science, is regarded as being emotionally charged. Law and politics are constructed as distinct and this distinction is manifested and maintained in legislation, in the motives preceding legislation, in adjudication and also in the scholarly view of law. The examples provided below have at least one starting point in common, namely the concept that law and politics are separate: they assume the premise of a clear-cut line separating law and politics. The common outcome of such a constructed separation is that issues or circumstances characterized as being of a political nature are explicitly excluded from a legal context. The separation between law and politics, and the subsequent exclusion of certain issues, cannot be seen as the result of any reasoned criteria or logical principles. Yet it works by excluding some issues regarded as being of no legal relevance, which are then often accorded the attribute 'political'. Before illustrating the separation, I will present some common definitions of law and politics. My aim is not to definitively state the meaning of these terms. I will simply give them some substance, and also point out what I mean when I use them below.

The meaning of law cannot be covered in a few sentences but consideration of some different understandings can clarify, to a certain extent, what is commonly understood by the term. In a widely used Swedish judicial textbook, law is defined as the doctrine of the rule of law combined with the practice of adjudication. Sometimes law is depicted only as the specific methods used to describe current law.[2] Another common way to view law is to describe it according to its functions. In principle law is described, on the one hand, as attached to intrinsic values such as the protection of human rights and on the other as an instrument to be used by the government and the parliament to achieve stipulated goals (Algotsson 1987, 105 and 1993, 391). Apart from its instrumental usage, law has several other functions, such as solving problems which frequently arise in society, maintaining political order, counteracting undesired behaviour by criminalizing certain acts, and maintaining the intrinsic values of law (Hydén 1999, 17 and 2002, 134; Strömholm 1996, 153; Peczenik 1995, 520). Law is consequently used as a means to preserve and consolidate, but it is also used as means to bring about changes in society.

Sometimes law is described as a process of standardization and administrative long-term planning to solve problems that frequently arise in society. To a great extent law could be seen as 'standardized politics' (Hydén 1999, 17 and 2002, 134, my translation), with completed solutions in readiness (Strömholm 1996, 153). Determining values in a society is also considered to be a function of law (Henricson *et al.* 1976, 9).

In recent years there has been a tendency to use legislation on a more frequent basis as a means of achieving political goals in connection with more varied social issues, even though legislation is not necessarily the only way to achieve a social goal. One explanation that has been offered for the increasing use of legislation in relation to social and political objectives is that EU Member States are forced to legislate in accordance with EC directives (von Eyben 1991, 3). This development emphasizes an understanding of law as being instrumental because of its considerable efficiency.

In a common definition used in political science, politics refers to 'the process by which groups take, or fail to make, collective decisions.' (Hague *et al.* 20). The definition is wide as it has a bearing on behaviour in all human interaction in both the private and public spheres. In another definition, which is both classical and diligently used in national as well as international political science, politics is described as a process which authoritatively determines values within society (Easton 1965, 50). This definition is wide but not to the same extent as that mentioned above. The main difference between the two is the emphasis on *authoritative* decisions and policies, such as parliamentary decisions, in the latter definition.

The scholarly research tradition in Swedish political science has emphasized institutional conditions in general and what is understood as the state in particular. The discipline is united by an interest in political activity, and especially the institutional features of politics (Ruin 1990, 1).

The mixture of law and politics in issues which, at first instance, may be regarded as being of either a judicial or political nature, and consequently of legal or non-legal relevance, can be illustrated by some examples. The first one refers to matters concerning aliens. Before March 2006 applications for asylum, residence permits and other immigration matters were dealt with by the Migration Board and the

2 This theoretical description of law is rather common, see, for instance, Sandgren 1999–2000, p. 868.

Aliens Board. The Swedish government wanted to make it possible to appeal against decisions made by the Migration Board.[3] This proposal was referred to the Council on Legislation, consisting of a handful of either Justices of the Supreme Court or Justices of the Supreme Administrative Court, for a pronouncement. Their task was to carry out a judicial preview.[4] The Council's standpoint was that settlement of these issues embraces the general bases of Sweden's migration policy, and involves judgement of appropriateness or even discretionary considerations, which the Council considered to be political and should not therefore be settled by courts.[5] However, after some adaptations, the proposal was approved and alien matters are now decided by courts. This issue, which was at first considered to be political in nature and non-legal, subsequently became the subject of legislation. Thus the separating line changed and the issue became legal rather than political.

In another example the Supreme Court rejected an application for legal aid citing the need for extreme loyalty to the legislator.[6] The legal case being decided was a child custody dispute, in which the Supreme Court rejected the mother's application for legal aid. This rejection was based on a prior pronouncement by the Government: in the preparatory work for the legal aid legislation the Government cited saving money for the state as the reason for restrictions on the legal aid system. No other direction was given about the administration of justice.[7] Such an extremely loyal attitude to the legislator is usually seen as judicial rather than political, as if the separating line between law and politics were clear.

Additional examples also show attitudes to law and politics that assume the two are separated by some kind of boundary. In an article in a Swedish law periodical a Justice of the Supreme Court stated that the most important thing for the administration of justice is to seek and judge according to the legislator's intentions as expressed in preparatory work. This should be the case even if such pronouncements are in conflict with the law (Vängby 1996, 892). This standpoint has been criticized since it gives support to an understanding of law where judges should be loyal to politicians rather than individual citizens, the law and legal principles (Nergelius 1997, 430).

In contrast, there is sometimes a reluctant attitude towards the will of the legislator. One example refers to sexual violence and abuse. In the preparatory work for the Penal Code it is said that judgements concerning rape should be made independently of both the relationship between the parties and also of circumstances preceding sexual violence and abuse.[8] Yet discourse analysis of the criminal legal protection against rape and other sexual abuse shows that the perpetrator's violence is often seen as related to the victim's expression of will. The absence of resistance

3 Government Proposal Bill 2004/05:170 A new order for court hierarchy and procedures in matters concerning aliens and citizenship, p. 105.

4 Judicial preview refers to the process by which the Council of Legislation, among other things, examines the constitutionality of legislation usually proposed by the Government. See 8:18 RF and the Act (2003:333) relating to the Council on Legislation.

5 Extract from the report of the proceedings in session 2005-05-09, p. 4.

6 See Lind 1996/97, p. 357, where the Justice of the Supreme Court is arguing for extreme loyalty to the legislator.

7 NJA 2000, p. 390.

8 Government Proposal Bill 1983/84:105, p. 21 and bet. JuU 1983/84:25.

or other protests against the assault constructs a victim who is available to others. The focus is not on the perpetrator's violence: rather the limits of the victim's body are determined in the discourse by the victim's expression of will (Andersson 2004, 264). It is well-known that, for instance, the relationship between the victim, usually a woman, and the perpetrator is given legal relevance through consideration of whether she was provocatively dressed at the time, her behaviour and whether she was under the influence of alcohol. These kinds of circumstances tend to reduce the victim's credibility while simultaneously strengthening the perpetrator's argument that he did not realize she did not consent to sexual activities (Wennstam 2002).[9] Such attitudes contradict the stated intentions of the legislator, and since loyalty to the legislator is usually seen as judicial in nature it would seem logical that a reluctant attitude would therefore be regarded as political and hence excluded from legal consideration, but it is not. Directions about the administration of justice are lacking but the attitude is still seen as judicial. When it comes to sexual violence and abuse the separating line between law and politics has obviously changed, though the justification for such a change is unclear.

There are also examples within legal scholarship where the separating concept finds expression, for instance, in the context of parliamentary decision-making. In the Swedish legal tradition it is often necessary to consult preparatory works, containing the intentions of the legislator, when analysing current law. The legislator is also thought of as an essential actor by legal practitioners (Peczenik 1999, 12). Legislative decision-makers are seen as an anonymous, and thus neutral, legislator. Both Swedish legal scholars and legal practitioners close their eyes to the interests behind the legislator.

Another example is the very familiar academic distinction between what the law is, or rather prescribes (*de lege lata*) and what it ought to be (*de lege ferenda*). According to this distinction current law is separated from politics in general. Made concrete by legal scholars, *de lege ferenda* often comes to mean suggestions or recommendations directed to the legislator but also to courts of justice (Ross 1971, 421 and 472). Swedish legal theses often contain a short concluding section with discussions about whether current law, in the specific area with which the thesis deals, is satisfactory or whether other regulations or interpretations of the law are to be preferred. In legal scholarship there is no disunity concerning the substance of these conceptions. Under certain conditions it is desirable to argue, for instance, for the amendment of an act. Such statements are not considered controversial for legal scholars (Lauridsen 1974, 70), but they are regarded as being beyond the purely descriptive view of *de lege lata*.

In this context, when considering what the law ought to be, an additional distinction is made between controversial party politics and politics supported by consensus. The latter is seen as the type of politics that legal scholars can appropriately deal with (Ross 1971, 417 and Blandhol 1999, 139).

To sum up, all the above examples express a conception of a separating line between law and politics. Actions and decisions in legislation, adjudication and legal scholarship are made as if it is possible to separate law and politics. The separating

9 One illustrative legal case is NJA 1997 p. 538.

concept influences what is regarded as being of legal and non-legal relevance. Moreover, the boundary is moveable. It changes, meaning that an issue considered as political can shift and become judicial, and vice versa. As I have indicated, the conception of a dividing line between law and politics is of great importance as it decides whether an issue is to be regarded as of legal or non-legal relevance.

Points of Contact

Swedish Debates on the Relation Between Law and Politics

Debates about the tension, the relationships and boundaries between law and politics occur in the Nordic countries, as in other democracies. The nature of this relationship attracts both national and international interest.[10] This is not surprising because drawing a line around another discipline partly decides the nature and limits of one's own. When this relationship is specifically dealt with by legal scholars, however, it is often done through the more critical currents in legal scholarship. The separating concept is challenged, for instance, by feminist legal scholars. The object of study in mainstream Swedish legal scholarship is, however, dogmatic and mainly directed to issues of current law. At a cursory glance law and politics seem quite different, and yet the relationship between law and politics is continuously discussed amongst legal practitioners, legal scholars, politicians and political scientists.

One distinguishing feature of the Swedish debate is the presumption that the outcome can be described as a zero-sum game. The authority to decide and to legislate comes to the forefront and the implication is that as the influence of law and legal practitioners grows, so politics and politicians lose, proportionally. Often these discussions relapse into specific understandings of democracy. From one position, legislation is primarily seen as a political means of bringing about social and economic transformation in order to achieve justice and equality. Courts and authorities, such as regional social insurance offices or any public authority, are charged with implementing political decisions but are not to work as an independent judicial power. Since law and legal authority are seen as congruent, the political majority is free to make any decision it wants. The representative of the people, that is the parliament, cannot resign its constitutionally-conferred power. Thus, power cannot be delegated to multiple authorities, such as a specific court considering constitutional issues. There is a fear that a consequence of more independent courts, which pay less heed to the intentions of the political majority as expressed in written documents explaining and motivating the legislation, would be increased judicial power and reduced parliamentary power. The intentions of the parliament or the government would not reach into the courts which in this view is inconsistent with democracy (Nordquist 2001, 66 and Petersson 2005, 113).

The opponents of this view emphasize that comprehensive legislation creates risks regarding individual freedom. The law may not regulate the life of the nation's

10 The theme for the 21st Congress of the International Association for Philosophy of Law and Social Philosophy (IVR) was 'Law and Politics – In Search of Balance'.

subjects in detail; instead it must protect the individual against the majority or state authority. The normative foundation for this latter attitude to legislation has varied, sometimes, for example, being promoted in terms of historical norms embedded in cultural heritage. (Peczenik 1998–99, 468). Sometimes it is justified in terms of religious norms or norms that lie deep in people's hearts (Strahl 2003, 7, 92 and 137). This position advocates less parliamentary influence and greater judicial power. It argues that the importance of human rights should be highlighted through the strengthening of constitutionally protected civil liberties. Courts should be more independent vis-à-vis the majority in the parliament, not just an authority merely carrying out the decisions of politicians. In my view the debates described above amongst legal practitioners, politicians and representatives of legal scholarship and political science, on the relation between law and politics, do not lead anywhere. Increased parliamentary power is advocated from one position while increased judicial power is recommended from the other. The adherents of law and politics simply look to the interests of their own subject or discipline by drawing lines of exclusion around it, thus failing to question the essence of law and perhaps also politics. Such debates can be described as a form of trench warfare.

Different Views of the Legislator

Several circumstances are likely to play a part in drawing a boundary between law and politics. One factor concerns different ways of viewing the legislator. The concrete meaning of 'legislator' is usually interpreted as the parliamentary majority (Nergelius 1997, 433).[11] Parliamentary decision-making in the form of legislation is emphasized in both legal scholarship and political science but from different angles. The main interest for Swedish legal scholars dealing with current law, concerns decision-making in the form of the legislator. In contrast to legal scholarship, political science has traditionally more interested in the politicians and the political parties beyond the legislator.

Initially the political parties were at the forefront of research in political science. Although that interest still remains, research in the discipline has become wider (Ruin 1990, 1). Thus, from a legal point of view decision-makers are regarded as the legislator. Nonetheless, from a political point of view, the same decision-makers are designated as politicians or political parties.

When legal scholars and legal practitioners are analysing current law it is essential to understand the intentions of the legislator. In the Swedish legal tradition it is therefore often necessary to consult preparatory works (Peczenik 1999, 12). However, this does not reach to the interests beyond the legislator, i.e. political parties, occupational and other lobby groups and so forth. The legislator is also an essential research object for an expert in political science. The legislator, from this view, is seen as the majority in the legislative body where the political parties are actors. The politicians that form the majority in the parliament play a crucial part in legislation (Bäck and Möller 2003, 23).

11 The legislator can also for instance be the European Council and the European Parliament, see article 251 in the treaty establishing the European Community.

Politicians reach collective and binding decisions in the form of legislation. The preparatory works preceding legislation and presented in written documentation, usually represent the opinions of more than one political party. However, in Sweden the preparatory works often represents the opinion of one party because of the dominance of the Social Democratic Party in the post-war period. The parliamentary situation has, until just recently, been very similar to the predominant party system (Sartori 1976, 192) As majority governments or clear parliamentary majorities have proved impossible, the legislation passed is the result of power games, compromises, evaluations and various other kinds of considerations. Legislation can, therefore, be understood as a determination of values (Lewin 2002, 36; Isberg 1999, 18 and Nergelius 1997, 433).

Regarding parliamentary decision-making as described above, that is in the form of the legislator or the politicians, the political parties and other interest beyond the legislator, implies that the exercise of law, is permeated with, and rests on, objectivity. In contrast, politics is seen as subjective with valuations and ideologies being of great importance. This distinguishing feature can make it seem as if law and politics are as different as chalk and cheese. At the same time there is no doubt that law and politics are connected even if it is not clear precisely in what the connection consists (Eckhoff 1989, 29). It seems to me that the concept of a dividing line between law and politics, where law is regarded as objective while politics is seen as subjective, creates a means by which some issues are kept outside the legal sphere.

A Mixture of Law and Politics in Actions

Even when legislation from different legal areas is taken into consideration nothing really supports a separating concept. There is rather, on the contrary, a connection between law and politics. The difficulties of separating law and politics are in my view a consequence of the nature of law, as comprising both ethics and politics. Law is sometimes described as a 'bridge' between them (Eckhoff 1989, 10). From this position it is impossible to make a theoretically-based division between law and politics. A presumption of the separating concept is that law and politics are opposites, and that it is important to maintain a clear-cut division where law is objective and politics is subjective. If law and politics are not seen as contradictory, the limit cannot be maintained either theoretically or practically. The separating concept is simply a fiction used to dissociate law from politics.

Various legal areas exhibit a mixture of law and politics, for instance labour law, administrative law, tax law and EC law (von Eyben 1991, 3). The same can be said about social law and sex-equality regulations. It is probably possible to add any branch of law to some extent, though in traditional Swedish legal scholarship some areas are regarded as more political than others. Yet as the examples above illustrate, adjudication presents action or argumentation given both in legislation and adjudication as if a distinct line divides law from politics.

When legislation is put into practice, legal practitioners not only have to interpret the law but also evaluate both general and unspecified principles such as discretionary rules, general clauses, standards, policies, legal principles, rules of thumb and guiding norms (Strömholm 1996, 234). A common account of Swedish legal practice centres on the characteristics of pragmatism, caution and loyalty towards the state authority (Peczenik 1999, 11). The Swedish legal method points out relevant legal sources such as preparatory works including directives, official reports, proposed bills circulated for consideration, government bills, committee reports and parliamentary messages to the government, and also sources such as precedents, and doctrine. As mentioned above, preparatory works which precede legislation are widely used. In an international context, preparatory work holds an exceptionally important position, which may perhaps change over time as a consequence of EC membership (Frändberg 2001, 9).[12] For the time being, however, it remains of great importance in interpreting and analysing the law. For this reason commentaries on preparatory works are often used by legal scholars (Hellner 1994, 83).

Occasionally the loyalty towards the legislator is questioned. Even the Supreme Court has been criticized for lacking independence in this regard (Nergelius 1997, 433 and Hellner 1991–92, 262). The far-reaching loyalty accorded to the legislator in courts is sometimes seen as one of the most important unwritten principles of 'objectivity' behind Swedish legal usage (Peczenik 1998–99, 466). However, even if the procedure is criticized it is seldom designated as a political principle.

Yet in many cases the legal sources contain no unambiguous answer to how a legal matter is to be solved. Both legal practitioners and legal scholars need to become more aware of the insufficiency of legal sources, and that one's own standpoints are not objective. A greater awareness contributes to raising awareness of the preferences and social comprehensions underlying various standpoints. This will open up possibilities for criticizing and discussing such preferences and comprehensions (Eckhoff 1989, 47).

Sometimes law is understood as a subsection of politics where law is equivalent to the activity in court, characterized as the power to authoritatively and definitively record a verdict in a specific case. Through their verdicts courts consciously influence the allocation of values in society (Holmström 1998, 33 and 41). It is hardly controversial to say that courts, especially the Supreme Court, allocate values in society. To what extent it is done consciously, however, is open to debate. This reinforces the point made earlier that connections between law and politics are more likely to exist than limits and boundaries between them. As outlined at the outset, if one looks only at definitions, law and politics initially seem quite different. Yet, when confronting a broad definition of politics with an understanding of law from the dogmatic position, both are seen to be described as determining values in society. The examples referred to concerning legislation, adjudication and the scholarly view also indicate connections. When confronting law with a narrow definition of politics, focusing on the political institutions, and especially parliamentary decision-making, law and politics also come together, and overlap with each other. The substance or the content of the concepts, whether defined broadly or narrowly, cannot be used as grounds for separation.

In a scholarly view of law there are also efforts to set limits. Legal scholarship is generally separated from, for instance, feminist legal theory, which is described

12 See also Bernitz 1991, p. 35 concerning the importance traditionally given to preparatory work in Sweden which is not matched in the rest of Europe.

as a theory outside the law itself (Sandgren 2004–05, 299). The distinction gives expression to a conflict between a narrower view of law and legal scholarship, and a more extensive one. It also expresses an order of precedence where some legal analyses are seen as more central, or even more judicial than others. The ranking order is however questioned by legal scholars, contributing to an expanded understanding of law (Gustafsson 2006, 19).

A Mixture of Law and Politics in Decisions

When decisions made in a judicial or political sphere are systematized it becomes even clearer that it is not their substance which makes them either judicial or political. Decisions, as opposed to certain actions, judgements, activities or bodies, made in judicial or political spheres, can be classified as political or non-political. Three kinds of decisions can be distinguished: those with political effects; those based on political considerations regarding potential effects; and finally those involving controversial political struggles. Political effects are seen as social effects, such as distribution of income, state of health and state of production. These aspects are usually considered by politicians before they make decisions. Sometimes the outcome of judgements coincides with political effects, even though the courts do not consciously act with that in mind. A decision made with regard to its social effects is classified, in this analysis, as a decision based on political considerations. Even effects on certain occupational groups or on the power relations between political parties and groupings are considered in this way. One conclusion drawn is that decisions or judgements connected with politically controversial issues become political when used for political purposes (Eckhoff 1989, 30).[13]

It is plausible to characterize decisions as either judicial or political, and to mark a certain usage as judicial or political. I find it likely that the attributes judicial and political are also strongly connected to different views of parliamentary decision-making and the form of decision-making. Consequently, the formal decisions taken by courts are to be seen as judicial while their substance may be of a political nature. And the opposite is also possible, i.e. decisions made by a political institution can be described as political irrespective of their content. If this reasoning is accepted, substance or content cannot be used to separate law and politics. The separation is made on the basis of the idea that a statement about law constitutes an objective statement, separated from politics.

Stressing the form of decision-making, in contrast to its substance, resembles the international trend towards judicialization, which means that an increasing number of issues, that were earlier decided by political bodies such as the government or the parliament, are now decided by legal institutions (Vallinder and Tate 1995, 2; Holmström 1995, 345). This is not followed, however, by a parallel change in the substance of the decisions. It is simply that the forum where decisions concerning legal matters are made has changed. Decisions that were earlier considered to be political, and thus made by politicians, are no longer reserved to politicians alone

13 The second type of decisions mentioned is very much like what is designated, in another analysis, as rules for goals or means, see Hydén 2002.

(Nergelius 1999, 55). Judicialization manifests a clash with the framework of contemporary national constitutions, which accord with Montesquieu's division of state authority on institutional and functional grounds. The split is based on a distinction between the legislative, executive and adjudicative functions of the state (Holmström 1998, 23; Montesquieu 1998, 10). Confronting the separation of law and politics with the three-way division above is not without objections. Usually legislation and the exercise of executive power are related to political institutions, while adjudication is not. In reality, however, even institutions other than courts, and consequently people other than judges, deal with law. An assertion concerning a corresponding area in politics where courts are political bodies or make political decisions is more controversial. It might be seen as an attack on the actions of the courts and even on the honour of the judges (Holmström 1998, 41). In this context, politics is considered to be emotive in a negative sense and closely linked to partiality and non-objectivity. Assertions that claim 'law is politics or claims that courts are political bodies, are often understood as accusations of abandoning the ideals of law' (Eckhoff 1989, 30, my translation).

A Mixture of Law and Politics in the Academic Distinction

Apart from the aim of dividing law and politics in legislation and adjudication there is a further area of controversy over limits, namely the academic distinction between what the law actually prescribes, and what it ought to prescribe. The academic distinction includes not only a distinction between law and politics, but also between politics that are a suitable subject for legal scholarship, and party politics. Thus, not all statements about what the law ought to be are seen as suitable material for legal scholarship.

As indicated above, the politics suitable for inclusion in legal analysis are of a special kind that do not cause any controversy or dispute amongst political parties (Eckhoff 1989, 47) Only when the parliamentary political parties have reached consensus concerning an issue does it become a suitable subject for legal scholars. The distinction between what law prescribes and the normative considerations of what it ought to describe, which are neither controversial nor of interest for party politics, can also be questioned.

This implies that the legal profession can ignore party politics and give their normative considerations an air of objectivity. The distinction differentiates between various sets of values (Eckhoff 1989, 47). The basis for this is unclear but nevertheless influential.

Conclusions and Reconceptualizations

The relationship between law and politics is complex. From a scholarly view connections between law and politics are sometimes admitted. At the same time decisions based on a presumed separation between them, find expression within legislation, adjudication and the scholarly view. A separating concept operates by excluding some issues and circumstances as being of a political nature, and therefore of no legal relevance. This seems to be almost natural and argument rarely occurs. Accepting an apparent boundary is almost a prerequisite for engaging in any type of legal work: issues with the attribute 'political' are practically excluded from the legal scene or, it is argued, they should be. Having said that, several analyses by Scandinavian legal scholars and political scientists reject the possibility of an exclusionary boundary between law and politics which has a theoretical foundation (Bolding 1968; Eckhoff 1989; Holmström 1998; Persson 2004, and Petersson 2005). Neither politics in its broad or narrow sense, makes a clear-cut division between law and politics when confronting these definitions with an understanding of law from the dogmatic position.

One conclusion drawn is that trying to make a clear division between law and politics involves setting boundaries in vain. Every court, and particularly the Supreme Court, consciously and authoritatively allocate values in society, directly by bringing about social effects or indirectly as part of the consequences of the power of the social actors. An additional conclusion, based on acceptance of the traditional views of politics, is that the majority of activities in court must be seen as political (Holmström 1998, 35).

Law and politics can be described as the outcomes from separate fora for decision-making but also as different spheres for decision-makers. The former seem to be a determining factor when ascribing attributes such as judicial and political, or objective and subjective. Different spheres, understood as different objects, cannot however serve as grounds for the separation. Even if politics is dressed in legal attire it hardly becomes less political.

The idea of law as something distinct from politics could perhaps, from an interdisciplinary view, be understood as if the representatives of both legal scholarship and political science were trying to protect their respective territories and to maintain the power that comes with room to manoeuvre. But what is to be said from a legal point of view?

Settlements diverging from the purposes or the declarations made by the legislator are considered non-political. Even a reluctant attitude towards the legislator, at least regarding sexual violence and abuse, is also seen as non-political. These different attitudes mean that the results of the division between law and politics differ depending on which legal area is concerned. It would be equally reasonable to regard a reluctant attitude as political. The closeness between law and politics is perhaps clearest regarding sexual violence and abuse.

One way of understanding the attempts to construct and maintain a clear-cut limit is to acknowledge the influence of Scandinavian realism. This derived its inspiration from a new school of philosophy taught at Uppsala University at the beginning of the twentieth century.[14] I think it likely that it influenced the claim that there is, or at least should be, a division between law and politics (see Svensson this volume). A central part of this approach was the theory of value-nihilism, where estimations of values such as good or bad, right or wrong, were seen as emotional and expressing

14 Axel Hägerström (1868–1939) was the founder of the school. Followers were the Swedes, Vilhelm Lundstedt (1882–1955) and Karl Olivecrona (1897–1980) and also the Dane, Alf Ross (1899–1979).

only feelings of like or dislike. Values could never be proven to be true or false and they said nothing about reality (Källström 1986, 19).

Furthermore this perspective considered statements about the existence of binding rules to be mere hocus-pocus because they did not correspond to anything in reality. Historically people believed in mysticism, to which words like right and duty belonged. When law developed, certain features of mysticism died but people still used the words and with the same psychological effect and limitation as before. Individual rights and duties according to law were brought into effect by means of normative statements concerning what should be the rights and duties of individuals. An understanding of law as a series of imperatives, as conveyed in the teaching, in fact did presuppose a moral duty. Seen in this light legal scholarship worked with normative comprehensions and was seen as unscientific (Källström 1986, 40). Another argument was that the distinction which was claimed to exist between the judicial and the normative within law was simply illusory (Hägerström 1917, 128). The conclusion was that the existing unscientific legal scholarship had to acquire a more scientific character by discarding its values and its subjectivity. The priority was to gain objectivity. In courts this was expressed through the notion that courts owe a high level of loyalty to the legislator. The judges had to avoid normative matters of judgement otherwise they risked being seen as subjective. This value-nihilism took possession of both the courts and legal scholarship (Källström 1986, 19 and 42).

Aspirations for a screen to ward off subjectivity from law and legal scholarship can also be seen in recent legal scholarship. The foundation for the distinction differs from that claimed by the school of philosophy at Uppsala but the striving to separate law and legal scholarship from subjectivity is much the same (Sandström 2002, 282). Swedish legal methodology, with its special legal sources, also plays a part in the striving for separation between law and politics.

Legal scholarship is sometimes described as a manifold activity, full of nuances (Wahlgren 2002, 293) but this does not find expression in a proportional number of methods advocated in the dogmatic position. Dealing merely with the evaluation of legal sources leads to the legal professions being impossibly isolated (Bolding 1968, 97). The legal methodology employed may become self-fulfilling, reproducing and even exclusive (Gunnarsson 2003, 23).

The play on the separation between law and politics seems especially to affect gender-related areas. In this light the lively theorizing amongst feminist legal scholars is not surprising as it presupposes a reflexive and critical approach to law. The separating concept seems to work as an obstacle against some, often gender-related, issues being considered as legal, placing them outside the legal system as having no legal relevance.[15] The sluggishness in remodelling law reflects the traditional way of viewing law as conservative *per se* (Eckhoff 1989, 47). It hinders matters perceived as 'political' being adequately dealt with by law. Matters considered to be of lower priority – outside the law and legal scholarship – are less likely to be incorporated into the body of legislation and, of course, adjudication.

15 See Burman and Svensson this volume apropos the terms inside and outside.

The separating concept presents law as an objective set of rules applied by unprejudiced adjudication. Politics, on the contrary, is seen as an act of volition. It intimates an understanding of law as objective and independent, but could it not be the opposite? For instance, in the custody dispute referred to above, the Supreme Court did not reject the application for legal aid by referring to any legal principles such as the child's best interest or equality before the law. Is the court's argumentation to be understood as judicial? Under present conditions, with great loyalty towards the legislator, it is. But would it have been *less* judicial to ignore the government's reason for restriction and argue instead from the basis of these other important principles? A sceptical attitude towards preparatory work is however often regarded as being subjective or political. Maybe the standpoint of the court above depends on presumptions concerning the essence of law, rather than law itself. Both matters concerning aliens and, for instance, environmental issues, embrace policies, discretionary considerations and so forth. Yet it seems that matters concerning aliens have been considered as having a more political nature than, for instance, environmental issues, which are settled by courts. This indicates the presumption of a clear-cut division between law and politics. The separating concept not only makes distinctions between law and politics, but also between party politics and other politics. It is very doubtful whether this latter distinction benefits legal scholarship at all: maybe it is time to leave it behind.

Nevertheless it makes it possible for legal scholars to leave aside party politics and to give their valuations the impression of objectivity and impartiality. The drawing up of boundaries indicates possibilities of really demarcating law from politics, where law is considered to be a closed system, with its own limits.

A view of law as uniform, in the sense of using a common methodology and legal sources, is probably predominant among the legal professions (Sandgren1999–2000, 872). There are claims that law is an open system since certain rules of law, and indeed the whole system, depend on interpretation (Aarnio 1988, 16). Assuming law to be an open system leads to the acceptance of influences from outside.

Furthermore feedback between legal regulation and these outside influences is essential if the legitimacy of law is to be maintained (Gunnarsson 1995, 26). A law which gratuitously makes differences among values runs the risk of being out of touch with reality and consequently has less legitimacy.

It may perhaps be a shocking thought that law must integrate with social science, politics and public debate on the problems of a modern society (Bolding 1968, 1 and 89). It is time to fully acknowledge a mutual relationship between law and politics, supplemented with an understanding of law as an open and inadequate system, as opposed to a closed and coherent one.

The separating concept, which divides objectivity from subjectivity, is a construction rather than an emanation from the nature or substance of law itself. Possibly there is only a desire for a clear-cut division between law and politics. Perhaps it is not surprising that the political scientists seem to consider the relation with less prejudice than legal scholars. The point of departure for many legal scholars seems to be the separating concept (Persson 2004, 299). Theoretically grounds for such a separation do not exist, yet the separating concept is influential. The concealing of evaluating strains in both law and legal scholarship is facilitated and maintained by the play on a boundary between them and politics. This constructed boundary works ideologically and hides a great deal of evaluating in both law and legal scholarship.

References

Government Bills

Prop. 1983/84:105, *om ändring i brottsbalken m.m. (sexualbrotten)* [Governments proposal, Changes in the Penal Code (sexual offence)].

Prop. 2004/05:170, *Ny instans- och processordning i utlännings- och medborgarskapsärenden.* [Governments proposal, A new order for court hierarchy and procedures in matters concerning aliens and citizenship].

Government Committees and Other Official Documents

Utdrag ur protokoll vid sammanträde 2005-05-09, *Ny instans- och processordning i utlänningsärenden m.m.* [A new order for court hierarchy and procedures in matters concerning aliens and citizenship. Extract from the report of the proceedings in session].

SOU 1999:58, *Löser juridiken demokratins problem?* Demokratiutredningens skrift nr. 23 [Report from the Commission on Democracy].

Bet. JuU 1983/84:25 *om sexualbrotten* [Bet. JuU 1983/84:25 on sexual offences].

NJA 1997 s. 538 [Supreme Court Decision NJA 1997 s. 538].

NJA 2000 s. 390 [Supreme Court Decision NJA 2000 s. 390].

Literature

Aarnio, Aulis (1988), 'Om rättssystemets slutna natur', in Tuori, Kaarlo (ed.) (1988, *Rättsdogmatikens alternativ* (Tampere: Juridicia). (ed.) 9–16.

Algotsson, Karl-Göran (1987), *Medborgarrätten och regeringsformen. Debatten om grundläggande fri- och rättigheter i regeringsformen under 1970-talet* (Stockholm: Norstedts).

Algotsson, Karl-Göran (1993), *Lagrådet, rättstaten och demokratin under 1900-talet* (Stockholm: Norstedts Juridik).

Andersson, Ulrika (2004), *Hans (ord) eller hennes? En könsteoretisk analys av straffrättsligt skydd mot sexuella övergrepp* (Lund: Bokbox Förlag).

Bäck, Mats and Möller, Tommy (2003), *Partier och organisationer* (Stockholm: Norstedts Juridik AB).

Bernitz, Ulf (1991), Utblick på EG-rätten. In '*Författningsdomstol och lagprövning i nordisk och europeisk belysning*', 32–38.

Blandhol, Sverre (1999), *Juridisk ideologi. Alf Ross' kritikk av naturretten* (Copenhagen: Jurist- og økonomförbundets Förlag).

Bolding, Per Olof (1968), *Juridik och samhällsdebatt* (Stockholm: Almqvist & Wiksell).

Easton, David (1965), *A framework for Political Analysis* (Englewood Cliffs, N.J.: Prentice Hall).

Eckhoff, Torstein (1989), *Juss, moral og politikk* (Oslo: Universitetsforlaget).

von Eyben, Bo (1991), 'Om politik og retspolitik', in *Suum quique, Retsvidenskabelige afhandlinger* (Copenhagen: Jurist- och Økonomförbundets Förlag), 3–13.

Frändberg, Åke (2001), 'Rättsordningen och rättstillämpningen', in Strömholm, Stig (ed) (2001), *Svensk rätt – en översikt* (Uppsala: Iustus Förlag AB). 7–26.

Gunnarsson, Åsa (1995), *Skatterättvisa* (Uppsala: Iustus Förlag).

Gunnarsson, Åsa (2003), *Fördelningen av familjens skatter och sociala förmåner* (Uppsala: Iustus Förlag).

Gustafsson, Håkan (2006), 'Cyklopens öga. En betraktelse av rättsvetenskapens könsblindhet', in *Retfærd* 2/113, 3–26.

Hägerström, Axel (1917), *Till frågan om den objektiva rättens begrepp, Bd 1 Viljeteorin* (Uppsala: Skrifter utgivna av K. Humanistiska vetenskapssamfundet i Uppsala).

Hague, Rod, Harrop, Martin and Breslin, Shaun (1998), *Comparative government and politics. An introduction*, 4 ed, (Basingstoke: Macmillan).

Hellner, Jan (1991-92), 'Medverkan till skada vid strikt ansvar', in JT 1991/92, 252–274.

Hellner, Jan (1994), *Rättsteori. En introduction* (Stockholm: Juristförlaget).

Henricson, Rolf, Hydén, Håkan, Lindgren, Lena and Widerberg, Karin (1976), *Likhet inför lagen* (Lund: Juridiska Föreningen).

Holmström, Barry (1995), 'Sweden', in Vallinder, Torbjörn and Tate, C. Neal (eds) (1995), *The Global Expansion of Judicial Power* (New York: New York University Press), 346–367.

Holmström, Barry (1998), *Domstolar och demokrati. Den tredje statsmaktens politiska roll i England, Frankrike och Tyskland* (Uppsala: Acta Universitatis Upsaliensis).

Hydén, Håkan (1999), *Rättssociologi som emancipatorisk vetenskap* (Lund: Sociologiska Institutionen, Lunds Universitet).

Hydén, Håkan (2002), *Normvetenskap* (Lund: Sociologiska Institutionen, Lunds Universitet).

Isberg, Magnus (1999), *Riksdagsledamoten i sin partigrupp. 52 riksdagsveteraners erfarenheter av partigruppernas arbetssätt och inflytande* (Hedemora: Gidlunds Förlag).

Källström, Staffan (1986), *Den gode nihilisten. Axel Hägerström och striderna kring uppsalafilosofin* (Stockholm: Rabén & Sjögren).

Lauridsen, Preben Stuer (1974), *Studier i retspolitisk argumentation* (Copenhagen: Juristforbundets Förlag).

Lewin, Leif (2002), *Ideologi och strategi. Svensk politik under 130 år* (Stockholm: Norstedts Juridik AB).

Lind, Johan (1996–97), 'Högsta Domstolen och frågan om doktrin och motiv som rättskälla' in JT 1996/97, 352–370.

Montesquieu, baron de, Charles de Secondat (1998), *Om lagarnas anda* [translation of 1757 edition] (Stockholm: Ratio).

Nergelius, Joakim (1997), 'Domstolarna, grundlagen och rättighetsskyddet – några reflektioner kring de senaste årens debatt och praxis' in SvJT 1997, 426–457.

Nergelius, Joakim (1999), 'Maktdelning och politikens judikalisering', in SOU 1999:58, 55–84.

Nordquist, Jonas (2001), *Domstolar i det svenska politiska systemet. Om demokrati, juridik och politik under 1900-talet* (Stockholm: Stockholms Universitet, Statsvetenskapliga Institutionen).

Peczenik, Aleksander (1995), *Vad är rätt? Om demokrati, rättssäkerhet, etik och juridisk argumentation* (Stockholm: Fritzes).

Peczenik, Aleksander (1998–99), 'Värdenihilismen och den konstruktiva rätten', in JT 1998–99, 462–491.

Peczenik, Aleksander (1999), 'Lagstiftningen, domstolarna, rättsmedvetandet och rättsvetenskapen', in SOU 1999:58, 7–54.

Persson, Åsa (2004), *De politiska partiernas rättspolitik* (Uppsala: Iustus Förlag).

Petersson, Olof (2005), *Rättsstaten – frihet, rättssäkerhet och maktdelning i dagens politik* (Stockholm: Norstedts Juridik).

Rättsfonden (1991), *Författningsdomstol och lagprövning i nordisk och europeisk belysning* (Stockholm: Rättsfonden).

Ross, Alf (1971), *Om ret og retfærdighed. En indførelse i den analytiske retfilosofi* (Copenhagen: Nyt Nordisk Förlag Arnold Busck).

Ruin, Olof (1990), *Statsvetenskap. Rapport nr 1990:3* (Stockholm: Statsvetenskapliga institutionen, Stockholms Universitet).

Sandgren, Claes (1999-2000), 'Vad gör juristen? Och hur? – del II', in JT 1999–2000, 867–893.

Sandgren, Claes (2004-2005), 'Om teoribildning och rättsvetenskap', in JT 2004-05, 297–333.

Sandström, Marie (2002), 'Rätt eller vetenskap? Till frågan om rättsvetenskapens nytta', in SvJT 2002, 282–292.

Sartori, Giovanni (1976), *Parties and Party systems* (New York: Cambridge University Press).

Strahl, Ivar (2003), *Makt och rätt. Rättsidéns gång genom historien – från Babylon till FN* [revised by Stig Strömholm] (Uppsala: Iustus Förlag).

Strömholm, Stig (1996), *Rätt, rättskällor och rättstillämpning. En lärobok i allmän rättslära* (Stockholm: Norstedts Juridik).

Strömholm, Stig (ed.) (2001), *Svensk rätt – en översikt* (Uppsala: Iustus Förlag AB).

Tuori, Kaarlo (ed.) (1988), *Rättsdogmatikens alternativ* (Tampere: Juridica).

Wahlgren, Peter (2002), 'Syfte och nytta med rättsvetenskapliga arbeten', in SvJT 2002, 293–303.

Vallinder, Torbjörn and Tate, C. Neal (1995), 'The Global Expansion of Judicial Power. The Judicialization of Politics' in Vallinder, Torbjörn and Tate, C. Neal (eds) (1995), *The Global Expansion of Judicial Power* (New York: New York University press), 1-10.

Vallinder, Torbjörn and Tate, C. Neal, 'The Global Expansion of Judicial Power. The Judicialization of Politics' in Vallinder and Tate (eds), 1–10.

Vängby, Staffan (1996), 'Aktuella spörsmål. Till frågan om 2 kap. 18 § andra stycket regeringsformen', in SvJT 1996, 892–898.

Wennstam, Katarina (2002), *Flickan och skulden. En bok om samhällets syn på våldtäkt* (Stockholm: Bonnier).

Chapter 4

Legal Texts as Discourses[1]

Johanna Niemi-Kiesiläinen, Päivi Honkatukia and Minna Ruuskanen

Exploiting the limits of law often means that the focus of the inquiry is on the relationship between the legal system and the other normative systems of a society. The question whether the legal system can or should be delimited and defined as opposed to other social systems and social practices can be approached from different angles. In legal theory, a relationship between legal arguments and other value arguments is often acknowledged, either openly or discreetly, in the formulation of legal principles or teleological arguments (see for example Aarnio 1997, 185). In this chapter we explore the interaction between legal and other social discourses, including the discourses of other scientific disciplines. Our starting point is that the limits of the legal system are constructed and that other social discourses participate in the construction of the concepts and limits of law. Likewise legal discourse is an important social discourse that participates in the construction of social phenomena.

We have found the discourse analytical methods developed in sociology and cultural sciences fruitful for the analysis of legal discourses, and we discuss the application of these methods to legal texts. As we will explain later, discourse analysis refers to symbolic and language based methods of constructing reality. By using examples from our own work we wish to show that this approach is fruitful for an understanding of the relationship between what is normative and what is factual and for grasping the relationship between social and legal theory.

Our interest in discourse analytic readings of legal texts arises out of our research on legal issues related to violence against women. It is common knowledge in the social sciences that violence against women is a widespread and persistent problem

1 The authors participated in Research Project VISE: Violence in the Shadow of Equality: Hidden Gender in the Legal Discourse, funded by the Finland's Academy in 2001-2004. We thank other participants of the project, especially Sari Näre, PhD, Heini Kainulainen LL and Helena Karma LLM and Dr of Law Kaijus Ervasti for vivid discussions on social construction of reality. We wish to thank participants of the doctoral seminars in Helsinki and Umeå (2002-2005), of the panel on Sociology of Law at the Law and Society Conference in Vancouver, June 2002, and of Socio-legal Research Methods Workshop, Onati, April 2003 and of the 5th European feminist research conference in Lund, August 2003 for constructive critique and comments. We also thank an anonymous referee whose vehement critique has considerably improved this chapter.

An earlier version of this chapter has been published in Finnish in Niemi-Kiesiläinen, Honkatukia, Karma and Ruuskanen 2006.

and that it is often either neglected or ignored by the criminal justice system.[2] For example, the police often do not recognize violence against women committed by their partners if the violence followed a quarrel or if the woman was hysterical or drunk at the time. In addition, the fact that violence or the threat of violence is repeated or habitual is often considered to be irrelevant in a case of battery. Women's claims of self-defence are often ignored, and rape cases involving acquaintances are often down-graded (Honkatukia 2001; Ruuskanen 2001, 319).

When we started our respective studies on the approaches of the Finnish legal system towards violence against women, our initial problem was that the problems which we studied eluded us. The legal language of court cases, police protocols, *travaux preparatoires*, etc., was sex and gender[3] neutral. The legal discourse did not recognize issues related to violence against women. We were even told by some colleagues and judges that there were no legal problems associated with violence against women because the law is the same for everyone. If, for example, the cases are not reported to the police, the problem lies within the community, not in the criminal justice system itself. The legal discourse even resisted taking specific legal measures to combat such violence.[4]

We became intrigued by this apparent neutrality of language and started to ask whether there were hidden assumptions about sex and gender behind the seemingly neutral language of the law. In addition, we started to ask how the assumptions about sex and gender were reflected in discourses on other legally relevant concepts, such as violence, sexuality in rape law, and the distinction between private and public domains (Ruuskanen 2001; Honkatukia 2001; Niemi-Kiesiläinen 2004, 167). In short, we became interested in how concepts are constructed in legal texts.

As a sociologist and two lawyers with an interest in sociology of law, we started to look at how we could read the legal texts as social discourses. We started to look at how language is used by, and in relation to, law and its institutions using discourse analysis as a method. We soon discovered, however, that this kind of reading was not at all common within sociology of law, and theorized even less. As we will argue

2 There is an abundance of evidence of inefficient response to violence against women by the police. An important classic in this, as in so many other issues concerning domestic violence against women, is Dobash and Dobash 1992. Even though notable improvement has taken place due to the conscious policy reforms, problems still exists. See, for example; Boychuck and Ferraro 1992; Edwards 1996; Hoyle 1998; Lundberg 2001. For example, in Sweden about one third of complaints to the police did not lead to prosecution; see SOU 1995:60 B. The situation had not considerably changed by 2004; see SOU 2004:121, 87.

3 In this chapter we use the phrase 'sex and gender' and avoid the debate on whether this distinction is theoretically founded. While all the studies we use as examples are based on the theoretical belief that sex and gender are, at least partly, socially constructed, some of the studies are more interested in the construction of social meanings connected to sex (for example studies on rape law), while some of the studies are more interested in social and gendered roles in the society.

4 See, for example, the discussion about the reform to amend the Swedish Criminal Code with a special section on breach of women's peace, Nordborg and Niemi-Kiesiläinen 2001; Svensson 2001.

in this chapter, one reason for this situation is that this kind of discourse analysis approaches texts in a fundamentally different way from legal scholarship.

Feminist legal studies, on the contrary, has taken up the challenge of the 'linguistic turn' (see Svensson this volume) in social sciences. Several reasons have contributed to this development in feminist legal studies. First, as Nicola Lacey argues, the constructionist understanding of sex and gender is a common characteristic of various branches of feminist theory, including feminist legal theory (Lacey 1998, 3). Irrespective of whether or not biological sex is a category that predates language, for the most part the meanings attributed to sex and gender are constructed discursively (Naffine and Owens 1997). Second, it can hardly be denied that the duality of sexes is an organizing factor in our society and social relations, including law (Lacey 1998; Svensson 2001). Third, despite their importance, sex and gender are not explicitly recognized in many social contexts, including the contemporary Nordic legal system (Nousiainen and Niemi-Kiesiläinen 2001). Fourth, contemporary feminist theory is essentially interdisciplinary. Feminist legal studies is undertaken in interaction with feminist studies in other disciplines and, especially, in women's studies and feminist theory. Feminist theories offer a theoretical context which helps to identify discourses of sex and gender in law and to reveal assumptions hidden within the law.

In this chapter we reflect on discourse analysis both as a theory and as a method of reading legal texts. Our point is largely pedagogic in that we wish to point out the differences between the doctrinal legal scholarship and the discourse analytic reading of legal texts as well as between dominant forms of the sociology of law and the discourse analysis. In doing so, we often paint a simplified picture of the models of thinking and reasoning that we contrast with each other. We believe, however, that this use of 'ideal types' is justified to highlight the differences in the reasoning.

First, we briefly discuss the dominant conceptualizations of the sociology of law and contrast them with social constructionism and discourse analysis. In the second part of the chapter we explore social constructionism as the theoretical background of discourse analysis and discuss its theoretical assumptions by contrasting them with the approach in (normative) legal scholarship. In the third part of the chapter we discuss discourse analysis in more concrete terms. As we are interested in the relationship between the legal discourse and other social discourses, our interest is focused on critical discourse analysis.

The Identity of the Sociology of Law

A few years ago, Nordic legal sociologists became engaged in a lively debate on the disciplinary identity of the sociology of law in *Retfærd: The Nordic Journal of Law and Justice*. The discussion was initiated by Reza Banakar, who argued that the sociology of law lacked a fundamental paradigm capable of uniting the various socio-legal approaches (Banakar 1998). Although this thesis was largely undisputed by those who responded to Banakar's article, no agreement was reached on whether this shortcoming was beneficial or to the detriment of the sociology of law. Nor was an agreement reached on whether it was feasible to construct such a fundamental paradigm (Hydén 1999; Dahlberg-Larsen 2000).

Banakar used the metaphor 'stepchild' to describe the position of the sociology of law between sociology and legal scholarship. As many scholars have observed, the two disciplines have quite different expectations of the sociology of law (Banakar 1998, 7; see also Cotterrell 1998 and Nelken 1998). These conflicting expectations may have contributed to the situation in which there has been relatively little theorizing about discourses in the sociology of law.

For lawyers, the sociology of law is often an auxiliary discipline that is oriented to produce empirical data to the legal decision-making and law drafting. Those who draft laws are especially keen on empirical information about the frequency of certain behaviour. The interest of the courts in sociological knowledge is somewhat different and perhaps less common. The courts are more interested in behavioural sciences, such as psychiatry and psychology, in the form of expert evidence. The pattern of social knowledge is the same, however. The questions that arise might take the form of, for example, how typical certain behaviour is for a rape victim or perpetrator, for a victim of domestic violence, etc. The problem is that the courts always decide individual cases, whereas the knowledge produced by social sciences almost always concerns populations. Thus, there seems to be a constant dilemma between sociological data and decision making by the courts.

Social theorists, to the contrary, have been interested in posing grand questions and, as Banakar put it, to answer them by grand theories (Banakar 1998, 9). Functionalism has been especially influential in the sociology of law. Indeed, it seems more than appropriate to ask questions concerning the functions of law and of legal practices in socio-legal studies.[5] In addition, sociological inquiry during the 20th century has studied 'social structures', i.e. political, economic and other social institutions, from the point of view of the existence of a society as an integrated whole. In Talcott Parsons' (1902–79) structural and functionalist theory, the underlying structures are assumed to exist deeper than the surface of social life which we can observe and which they affect. In sociology of law, Niklas Luhmann's theory of autopoetic law has been a well known and much cited example of system theory (Luhmann 2004).

These lawyers' and sociologists' approaches to the sociology of law seem difficult to reconcile. Furthermore, neither the lawyer's nor the social theorist's approach as outlined above focus on the sociological aspects of legal thinking.[6] In recent years, interesting qualitative socio-legal studies have emerged, including work using different forms of discourse analysis. For example, ethnomethodological and anthropological studies of legal and other normative systems have analyzed the construction of norms and interaction between different norm systems (see for example Banakar and Travers 2005).

The epistemological relationship and interaction between what is normative and what is factual should be a target for socio-legal inquiry. If we take seriously the

5 A vivid observation on the influence of functionalism on sociology of law was presented by Mathiesen in the debate Banakar initiated in Retfærd:Nordic Journal of Law and Justice. Mathiesen 1998, 68.

6 We do not want to underestimate the need for empirical sociological inquiries into legal and quasi-legal practices, nor the importance of structural analyses of the legal system and its functions. Both are needed.

critique of the autonomy of the legal system and the exploration of its limits, we need to explore the ways in which the normative is influenced by the factual. To explore that relationship, analysis of discourses and especially of inter-textual discourses, is essential. As Nelken argues 'the attempt to deploy social insights so as to help law's reflexivity requires us to pay *more* rather than less attention to their disciplinary and discursive connections' (Nelken 1998, 410).

In the following discussion of discourse analysis as a socio-legal method, we make an attempt to contrast it with the legal way of thinking in order to illustrate how discourse analysis could contribute to legal scholarship.

Discourse Analysis and the Lawyer

Both legal scholarship and discourse analysis concern reading and interpreting texts, are preoccupied with the meaning of texts, and both seem to assume that texts have a life of their own that is independent of their authors. For a lawyer, however, there is a crucial difference between applying methods of legal interpretation and using methods of discourse analysis in the study of legal texts.

Lawyers are trained to apply a set of norms (law) to existing facts. For a lawyer, the facts exist independently of any legal text or discourse, and the law is applied to the facts. These facts are organized in a certain way, independently of the normative world, for example in predetermined categories of two sexes. Discourse analysis, on the other hand, is based on social constructionist theory, which sees discourse, including legal discourse, as constructing the social world. For a constructionist, legal discourse is involved in constructing what is factual and what is conceptual. In discourse analysis, concepts such as sex and gender or debtor and creditor are not categories existing independently of law but concepts that are constructed socially in the legal discourse.

While this fundamental difference in thinking may work as a barrier against using discourse analysis as method, we will in the following discuss the background theory of discourse analysis, social constructionism.

Social Constructionism as a Challenge to Legal Scholarship

Social constructionism has taken distance from grand sociological theories. The roots of social constructionism can be traced back to the phenomenological sociology founded by Edmund Husserl (1859–1938) and further developed by Alfred Schutz (1899–1959). The American sociologist Harold Garfinkel (1917–) turned its more or less abstract ideas into the practice of conducting empirical research on everyday interactions between people, calling this approach 'ethnomethodology'. Further, in their classical book *The Social Construction of Reality* (Berger and Luckmann 1966) Peter L. Berger and Thomas Luckmann brought Max Weber's and Herbert Mead's basic assumptions on the importance of meaning of social actions together with the phenomenological tradition to form their own theory. Berger and Luckmann emphasized the meaning of everyday knowledge and interaction between people.

Social constructionism and discourse analysis were influenced by the 'linguistic turn' in the social sciences and helped to draw the attention of social scientists to the significance of the linguistic and symbolic processes for social life (Howarth 2000, 1, 16). Above all, Foucault's theoretical work and work on 'grand' historical processes, work which showed how social phenomena (such as sexuality or punishment) are construed in professional discourses, has strongly influenced later discourse analysis (Foucault 1977, 1978). Further, discourse analysis derives from postmodernism, which criticizes the Enlightenment's undertaking to search for truth with the aid of objective and rational methods. Instead, it emphasizes the co-existence of a multiplicity and variety of meanings (Burr 1999, 12–17) and their conditions for existence (Foucault 1989). Nowadays, the term discourse analysis comprises a cluster of methodologies in different disciplines, based on somewhat different epistemological premises (Howarth 2000).

Legal scholarship also theorizes about legal discourses, that is, legal argumentation. In European legal theory, a school that can be called theory of legal argumentation or legal justification[7] has been very influential during the past twenty years. This theory, represented by such prominent scholars as Robert Alexy, Neil MacCormick, Aulis Aarnio, Alexander Peczenick and Jerzy Wróblewski, is a normative theory about argumentation in the interpretation of law and the justification of legal decisions. A central tenet of such normative theories is the doctrine of legal sources, that is, which arguments are valid arguments in the interpretation of law. For example, Wróblewski and MacCormick state the purpose of such a normative theory in the following way: 'The process of stating reasons for a decision or an opinion on the law ought to be treated as one aimed at showing how and why the decision is a justified decision in its legal context.' Furthermore, in legal theory the interest is not on how a certain decision is constructed in practice. According to the same authors, '[t]heir adequacy or lack of it as statements of justificatory reasons are wholly independent of their accuracy or lack of it as accounts of the way in which the Court came to regard the decision as the one to be given in the case' (Wróblewski and MacCormick 2003).

The normative theory on legal argumentation has been strongly influenced by hermeneutics and Jürgen Habermas' theory of communicative action (Habermas 1992). The latter theory is also connected to the normative nature of legal argumentation theory as it explores the conditions of valid communication (Tuori 2002; Habermas 1981).

The hermeneutic legal theory has made an attempt to analyse the relationship between the application of a norm and the selection of relevant facts in a case. The crucial concept for hermeneutics is pre-understanding. The judge, from whose point of view the theory is usually constructed, has a pre-understanding of both the legal system and the factual world. Through reflection the judge then proceeds along a hermeneutic circle, selecting the relevant norms to be applied as well as the relevant facts (see for example Aarnio 1997, 103). According to the hermeneutic theory, the interpretation of facts by courts is guided by legal concepts that are applied to the case in question. While discourse analysis is closely related to hermeneutics, we find the hermeneutic approach insufficient, because it assumes that it is possible to

7 Even the term 'discursive theory' has been used. See Aarnio 1997.

arrive at a correct interpretation of the law and the application of law to given facts. The hermeneutic legal theory is still the perspective of legal institutions, particularly the courts, and an 'inside'-perspective of law. We wanted to explore the processes in which the facts and concepts are constructed and, thus, become relevant to legal interpretation, in a wider social context.

Legal argumentation theory has been influenced by John Austin's theory of speech acts. His theory is concerned with performative speech acts, that is, constitutive expressions that may have legal character (for example, promises) and the capacity to change relationships, status, or factual circumstances (Austin 1984). Austin's theory analyses speech acts that bring about changes in (legal or other) positions and statuses, whereas our interest here focuses on the underlying assumptions of legal discourses and non-determinate construction of social reality, concepts and relations through legal language. Our interest in legal discourses as social processes that construct the social world is more closely related to John Searle's analysis of how institutional facts are constructed through social and linguistic processes (Searle 1995).

While these theories are related to social constructionism and the 'linguistic' turn, we will here follow theories and methodological approaches that have more in common with the study of everyday discourses, especially those methodological approaches which are inspired by French philosophy and pay attention to the construction of identities, social change and power relations (Burr 1999, 47).

Therefore, we have been especially interested in the idea that people construct their own and each other's identities through their encounters with other people. We have felt that understanding of legal practices should not be sought (solely) in social structures but in the interactive processes that routinely take place between people in courtrooms, police stations and various legal texts. We think that the construction of meanings in legal texts can be studied in the same way as Berger and Luckmann studied the interaction between ordinary people and focused on what is regarded as [self evident] knowledge and how that kind of knowledge is constructed. In particular they considered the use of language as crucial in how we construct meanings and knowledge (Berger and Luckmann 1966).

Furthermore, it is important to study how interaction constructs social institutions and structures. From the 1970s onwards, the constructionist orientation has been concerned with social problems, for example, by studying how claims to bring about social change are made. Strict constructionists are interested solely in the processes of defining whereas contextual and critical constructionists pay attention to societal and political situations, cultural features and historical processes (Burr 1999, 7; Jokinen and Juhila 1999, 51). The aim of bridging cultural phenomena and societal structures has also been visible in the work of later sociologists, including Giddens, Bourdieu and Habermas (Heiskala 2000, 102–103).

The Relationship Between Reality and Language

The relationship between language and reality constitutes our primary concern here, which is why we shall discuss the principles of social constructionism further by focusing more closely on the role of language in social research.

In this part of the chapter we will contrast the two basic understandings of the relationship between reality and language, which we call the positivist and constructionist approaches.[8] We will highlight the differences between them to make our point. In doing so, we downplay the fact that the borderline between quantitative empirical research and qualitative methods in social sciences is not at all clear cut. To the contrary, even though some methodological disputes still exist, the methodological positions of 'empiricists' and 'constructionists' seem to approach each other. In particular, many researchers who use quantitative empirical data are conscious that the way data is gathered has an impact on the content of it and few constructionists deny the importance of quantitative analyses. Nevertheless, we believe that the following exposition of the different understandings of the relationship between reality and language is justified by pedagogic reasons and still reflects to some extent different research traditions.

The positivist approach has been the foundation of social science from its beginning (Burr 1999, 6) and it is still often used in quantitative empirical research, such as surveys. According to positivist epistemology, knowledge is a reflection of reality and language is a means to study the facts that exist in reality (Alasuutari 1993, 9; Silverman 1993, 90–91). Language is used in order to describe reality in the search for the truth (Burr 1999, 6). A researcher poses questions concerning a reality that exists independently of the researcher and the respondents answer these questions. The researcher follows certain procedures to ensure access to the facts. For example, sample size, the selection process of potential interviewees, respondents or source document, the use of standardized questions and statistical tests are important criteria for the validity of the results. The research questions can be of following types: how many, what proportion, which subgroups, what causes what etc. On the basis of such research the social scientist is qualified to make generalizations and suggest explanations.

The picture of sociology that many lawyers interested in the sociology of law have is informed by these kinds of procedures for good quantitative research and the structural theories of society we described in the preceding part of this chapter. We often encounter doctoral students in law who want to probe deeper into legal decisions or other legal practices. These students often think that the only purpose of socio-legal inquiry is to make generalizations. They become anxious when they realize that they cannot achieve this because of their small sample of cases, interviews, contracts or other legal documents. As a result, they experience what we could call 'validity angst'.

8 Also realism and anti-realism or positivism and post-positivism have been used. See Eskola and Suoranta 1998; Taylor 2001, 11. We have chosen positivism/constructionism to emphasize the epistemological notions of the terms.

The second approach, which can be called constructionist, sees reality and language as intertwined. Language is not just a reflection of reality. The constructionist approach assumes that reality cannot be approached independently of language. This does not, however, mean that reality does not exist without language, but that human activity and language are very deeply intertwined (Eskola and Suoranta 1998, 221). A person always interprets and constructs his/her actions via language and needs language and conceptual thinking to describe actions and observations. Thus, it is emphasized that there are different realities and potential meanings of things. Also, situationality, which indicates that the language or the text is produced in a certain situation, is regarded as important (Alasuutari 1993, 21).

A constructionist researcher sees, for example, interviewees as experiencing subjects who actively construct their social worlds and give meanings to the facts and experiences that they report. Data are never raw or pure data but situated and contextual, and this is reflected in the analysis (Silverman 1993, 90–95, 199, 208). Facts are always socially constructed, no matter who presents them (Juhila and Suoninen 1999, 234).

Discourse analysis is based on the constructionist approach. Using discourse analysis and other qualitative methods the researcher can make observations about what discourses exist and how they are used. These are often the questions a socio-legal scholar wants to ask of his or her data. To answer these types of questions one does not necessarily need statistically large samples. When answering such questions as 'what kinds of discourses exist?' the concept of saturation is used. When the data do not contain new discourses, its saturation point is achieved and there is no need to collect more data. A fairly small sample may be sufficient. For the purposes of conducting an analysis of how discourses are used, even one text, such as a Supreme Court decision may be enough, even though we are generally cautious about relying on such limited data.[9] Our student is relieved of her 'validity angst' once she realizes that by using discourse analysis and other qualitative methods she can analyse the existence of discourses and the meanings they construct. She cannot make general statements regarding the frequency of various practices but that is often not necessary for a legal scholar with a socio-legal interest.

In the following we discuss four fundamental assumptions of social constructionism and how they can be interpreted and used when doing legal research. For this purpose we take Vivien Burr's list of four key assumptions of social constructionism as our point of departure (Burr 1999, 3–8).

A Critical Standpoint Towards Taken-for-Granted Knowledge

In the civil law cultures of the Nordic countries, law is regarded as a normative science, within which taken-for-granted knowledge and a hierarchy of knowledge play central roles. This is most obvious in the doctrine of 'sources of law' or of 'sources of legal information'. What law prescribes can hardly be questioned. In written law countries, the rulings of the Supreme Court are a most valuable source

9 Taylor 2001, 25, on the selection of highly specific documents for the analysis because of their powerful origin.

when deciding on how to interpret the law.[10] Also, the writings of certain authors are often more authoritative than those of others and are often referred to as a source of authoritative information or reference is made to the prevalent opinion in the relevant field of law. A philosopher or a mathematician would call this an *ad hominem* argument and in legal theory the statements of the legal scholars are valued according to the reasoning they contain. Nevertheless, in the legal community this kind of argumentation is used to confirm the normative content of the law.

A critical standpoint towards taken-for-granted knowledge means, according to Vivien Burr, that social constructionism questions the validity of statements that we usually take as authoritative (Burr 1999). Discourse analysis focuses on how meaning is constructed through various forms of linguistic exchanges and expressions. The meanings constructed in a discourse are not necessarily, nor usually, the same as the meanings that the participants intended to confer on their contributions. In the discourse analysis of legal texts we may have a special interest in the discourses of the Supreme Court, but unlike doctrinal studies, this interest is primarily not concerned with the legal implications of what the Supreme Court intends to express in its decisions, but in how the discourse of the Court constructs basic categories of social life, such as sex or gender, violence or sexuality. These constructions do not necessarily correspond to the way the member of the Court would express their opinions when asked.

Even though the meanings constructed in the texts are not necessarily the same as those the participants intend to express, the position or role of the participant may be important in the analysis. These positions are also constructed in the discourses as are other identities.

Historical and Cultural Specificity of Ideas

Our ideas and concepts are historically specific. In addition, all ways of understanding are historically and culturally relative. Foucault's broad historical analyses of the historical construction of punishment and sexuality are perhaps the most famous examples of this kind of analysis (1977, 1978).

What does the historical and cultural specificity of meanings mean in legal research? Legal concepts have also their historical and cultural background. They have been developed under certain circumstances within a certain kind of society. For example, one can analyse self-defence, a concept in criminal law, from a historical and cultural viewpoint. One can ask whom this type of justification was designed to protect and, more importantly, whether this intention is valid and whether it still influences our thinking. It can be said, for example, that the rules of self-defence were designed to meet the needs of someone who was defending himself and his family and his property against an illegal intruder or against an attack by a stranger. When attacked, the use of the same kind of weapon as the attacker was accepted. He

10 We do not have a possibility to discuss different doctrines of legal sources here. It has to be noted, however, that the position of case law is quite different in Common law countries and the countries which rely more on statutory law. Differences exist also inside those groups. For a comparison see MacCormick and Summers 1997.

was not allowed to use force if the attacker had already turned his back etc. Do we perhaps still regard these 'fair fight' rules as the key elements of an argument based on self-defence? And if so, do we realize that we are indeed talking about the rules of 'fair fight' when we talk about the use of 'equal force'? (Ruuskanen 2001).

In discourse analysis, we try to make visible the historical and cultural connections and underpinnings of concepts.[11] In the further legal analysis, we may discuss the consequences of working with concepts from another time and from another culture than the one that we live in.

Knowledge is Created and Mediated in Social Processes

According to the third principle of social constructionism, knowledge is created in interaction between people, particularly through language. The focus is on the processes and dynamics of social interaction. What is regarded as truth is a result of on-going social processes and interactions. Therefore, discourse analysis asks *how* questions instead of *why* questions. For example, confusion surrounds the concept and definition of sexual harassment. A positivistic researcher would solve the problem by accepting a certain definition and trying to find out how common it is and why it happens. Likewise a lawyer would ask what is the legal definition and apply it the facts. From a discourse analytic perspective, by contrast, the confusion over the definition is a research topic; the question is how or through which kind of processes is sexual harassment defined and what consequences might different definitions have (Thomas and Kitzinger 1997).

What might this mean in the context of legal knowledge? It might mean, for example, that legal truth is created in interaction between lawyers and/or legal scholars and judges. Situating the participants of the discourse is important, since some positions are more powerful in the discourse than others.

The argument that the language used by courts is not objective raises questions. One could argue, for example, that the court only uses the language that the parties themselves have used. But while the court has to translate, so to speak, the language used by the parties into legal jargon, it also interprets what the parties have said. And even if the court uses the language used by the parties, in most cases it has to make a choice between at least two different discourses, since the language used by the parties, or by the witnesses, often reflects different conceptions of the same phenomenon.

Constructionist reading cannot take the legal system as an autonomous system. On the contrary, the constructionist is interested in and explores the relationship between legal discourse and other normative systems of a society. It is acknowledged that laws reflect their historical and cultural background. In the legal field we have at least two types of social interaction: everyday interaction and legal interaction. The interpretations produced in these two forms of interaction may reinforce but also

---

11 A fascinating example of historical specificity of legal ideas is presented by Robberstad 1999, where she explores the transformation of the criminal procedure from a 'fair fight' between the victim (including her kin) and the offender to a trial between the prosecutor and the suspect.

challenge each other. The concepts used in everyday interaction (or exchanges) may be applied in the legal discourse and have an effect on legal reasoning. For example, everyday concepts of violence against women may influence the legal analysis of the cases. Legal language also constructs reality and everyday understanding of what is violence against women.

Knowledge and Social Action go Hand in Hand

The fourth main principle of social constructionism states that knowledge and social action go hand in hand. Legal knowledge is created in interaction between individuals. It is constructed in courts, law offices and universities by people for other people and for a purpose.

This concerns also the relationship between the legal scholar and the object of research, as a researcher not only describes social reality but also creates it. At this point one must emphasize that the way in which we understand a certain phenomenon affects the way in which we deal with it. For example, in some societies drunkenness is no longer regarded as a crime but instead as a form of sickness, a change which scientific discourse has influenced and which has brought changes to how the problem is dealt with (Burr 1999, 5).

Consequently, it is important that as researchers we acknowledge our own position. As researchers, we not only explain and describe, but also partake in the process in which knowledge is created. The scientific knowledge contains in itself powerful discourses that construct social relationships, but it is all too easy to forget it from the inside perspective of the research.

Reading Legal Texts

Rather than a method, discourse analysis is a methodological framework that allows many ways of conducting a study. In this section, we examine some concrete questions in our critical discourse analytical approach. Discourse analysis is interested in the different meanings that people give to social events and interaction and asks what consequences these meanings might have. We define a discourse as a coherent expression or a meaning structure that constructs reality in a certain way. It does not simply represent the world but signifies, constitutes and constructs social identities, (power) relations between people and systems of knowledge (Fairclough 1996). The researcher's job is to analyse how this is done. Identification of discourses, thus, includes interpretations of data by the researcher.

A common problem for those who have attempted to provide discourse analytic readings of legal texts is that the technical nature of many legal texts masks their embeddedness in discourse. Partly, the problem is that it is difficult to change the role and read the texts as constructing instead of defining.[12] For most lawyers, it is

12 This is a problem that almost all lawyers interested in discourse analysis recognize, stating that it is very difficult to 'find discourses' in legal texts. Social scientist, who are more familiar with the method, do not think legal texts are somehow specific in this respect and many of them have met us with critical comments on this issue.

very difficult to distance oneself from the 'lawyer's way of reading' the texts. How, then, can we develop our methods and strategies to recognize discourses?

Legal texts are almost always written in an objective and neutral style from a position of a legal authority or expert that masks their discursive and constructive nature. One way of reading the text is to look at what it excludes and silences, thus, constructing the normality. For example, a decision of the European Court of Human Rights (ECHR) may include a technical and complicated discussion of the admissibility of the case, while the substantive reasoning for the decision is short.[13] We have read the decision *Christine Goodwin* v. *Great Britain* of the said court concerning the rights of a transsexual person (11.7.2002) and analysed how sex and gender are constructed in the decision. We find a medical discourse on sex that alternates with a discourse based on sex and gender as a choice of a person. The text does not include references to heterosexuality but, in our analysis, it constructs the sexes as binary and heterosexual.

There are two basic starting points for recognizing discourses. According to one view, represented by ethnomethodology, phenomenology and analytic discourse analysis, the researcher should approach the texts without preconceived ideas of relevant discourses. The researcher should be as open-minded as possible and let the text speak for itself. The scarcity of (substantive) discourses in legal texts easily leaves a researcher empty-handed, especially if the researcher is not well trained in discourse analysis. A theoretical argument against this view is that as no researcher can relieve him/herself from all preconceptions, it is better to be conscious of one's theoretical assumptions and anticipated discourses. Even so, a researcher should be open-minded towards other discourses. Our experience is that one usually finds also some unanticipated discourses.

In our research project we have been influenced by critical discourse analysis (see for example Fairclough 1996; Van Dijk 2001). Studies utilizing critical discourse analysis have often been interdisciplinary and have concentrated on social problems. They have analysed the abuse of social power, how dominance and inequality are reproduced and resisted, and they have also taken an explicit position to 'understand, expose and resist social inequality' (Van Dijk 2001, 352–353). Critical discourse analysis focuses on the use of discourses as a means of exercising power. Power can be interpreted as inequalities concerning access to such desirable resources as money, leisure time etc. as well as the capacity to have some influence on one's own and other people's lives (Foucault 1978; Fairclough 1996, 12; Burr 1999, 62). Power makes itself visible as a strategy used by different people in the discourses that they use. Thus, some 'truths' or states of affairs are legitimated and others marginalized. We want to ask what discourses are used to silence others and what states of affairs are made possible by using certain discourses and what kinds of oppressive relationships are created and reproduced (Eskola and Suoranta 1998, 199).

We usually find a complex of discourses in the text that we have chosen to study. It is possible to analyse what kinds of roles (subject positions) are given to different actors and the relationships between different actors in the discourses. For

13 In all fairness, it must be noted that the ECHR is known for its good and full argumentation.

example, we have discovered two discourses of violence against women in the legal documents we have studied, two explanations for its causes and consequences. The first discourse, 'violence as power and control', talks clearly about the perpetrator and the victim and sees men's use of violence as an expression of an unequal power relation between the parties. The second discourse, 'interaction or family discourse', describes violence as mutual and seeks to explain it in terms of the relationship between the parties. Anyone taking part in the legal process can take part in either or both of these discourses, including the parties themselves and their lawyers. This kind of analysis sheds light on the contradictory nature of accounts: one and the same person can use different discourses. Discourses are cultural resources that are mobilized in different situations.

Here discourse analysis stands in contrast to the legal reading of a source, especially as practised in the Continental civil law traditions, where lawyers seek a systematically coherent interpretation of the law (Aarnio 1997; Nousiainen and Niemi-Kiesiläinen 2001). While discourse analysis reveals contradictory discourses, it does not directly contribute to doctrinal studies of law, which are based on the traditional forms of legal interpretation. Rather, it can challenge generally accepted interpretations of law by analysing and revealing their underlying concepts and taken-for-granted assumptions.

Power relations can be studied by asking which discourses become dominant and which are silenced and how this happens or what strategies are used in different discourses. A dominant discourse within the criminal justice system is a powerful tool in silencing other discourses. It appears as uncontested truth (for a critical account see Smart 1991). Sometimes the technical legal discourses, which we referred to above, operate by excluding some and including some other identities or relations and, thus, are quite powerful.

The power strategies include, for example, appeals to nature (sexuality is typically constructed as 'natural' in one way or another) or categorizing people by giving them inflexible identities. For example, in her study of young girls and their relationship towards delinquent behaviour Honkatukia conducted group interviews with adolescent girls (Honkatukia 1999). She analysed a particular feature of the interviews: how the interviewees repeatedly referred to other girls whom they disliked or despised. These girls were given inflexible identities, such as 'sluts', violent girls or girls who drink too much. They were seen solely as representatives of those negative femininities from which the girls wished to disassociate themselves. Other strategies in attempting to gain a hegemonic position for a certain discourse are, for example, references to general or expert knowledge or to cultural or religious conventions.

Power is also analysed when a researcher asks what consequences the usage of certain discourse may have (Jokinen, Juhila and Suoninen 1993). Discourse analysis is interested in different explanations that are used in social interaction, and it asks what consequences these explanations may have (Juhila and Suoninen 1999, 247–248). For example, the way in which violence against women is explained has legal consequences. The court does not have to take a specific stance on the underlying causes when handling a case. However, using discourse analysis one can find that the court often does in fact take a stand, and that this stand has social and legal consequences.

If the court, when describing violence against a woman in a relationship, states that 'the parties frequently argued and the arguing led to violence' or 'A and B quarrelled a lot which has led to threats against life and physical abuse' the formulations have social and legal consequences in and beyond the ruling of the case. In these two formulations, the court describes violence as mutual and draws a parallel between arguing, which refers to a verbal confrontation, and physical violence. In a way, the system is in accordance with the understanding that draws parallels between verbal confrontation and physical confrontation and therefore shows a tendency to blame the victim. One possible legal consequence might be that if the criminal justice system sees violence in a relationship as mutual and as part of the relationship, it is difficult for a woman to put forward a claim of self-defence. After all, how can one justifiably defend oneself against a relationship? (Ruuskanen 2001, 2005).

Legal discourses do not appear out of the blue, but are part of social discourses and influenced by them. Legal scholars may be informed of the everyday discourses and may reflect on their relationship to legal discourse. As an example of 'intertextuality' (Fairclough 1996), it has been shown that the discourses of 'violence as power and control' and of 'interaction and family' identified earlier have their firm roots in the process by which violence against women has been defined as a social problem in the Finnish society at large (see for example Nyqvist 2001).

Another approach is to turn to the theoretical social sciences. Our work has been influenced by feminist theories and the construction of gender and gendered subjectivities. Our reading of the Goodwin decision was informed by theories of heteronormativity, developed especially in queer studies. Sometimes comparative materials help to identify relevant discourses. Reading and comparing texts from different legal cultures or historical periods may make the researcher more sensitive to the meanings that are given in the discourses of one's own culture. In a historical and comparative study of Finnish and Swedish rape law, the historical constructions of subjectivity and sexuality were used to help to recognize and highlight the cultural constructions in the comparative legal texts. The discourses in the *travaux preparatoires* reveal that the Finnish rape law of 1998 is based on liberal assumptions of sex and sexuality. A Swedish reform proposal, to the contrary, constitutes an attempt to incorporate a feminist view into the law (Niemi-Kiesiläinen 2004).

Conclusion

Feminist theory has been the most important theoretical influence on our analyses of legal discourse. We believe, however, that feminist theory has relevance beyond our individual development as researchers. As we explained in the beginning of this chapter, feminist legal scholarship shares the view that sex and gender are constructed categories but, nevertheless, quite fundamental to legal interpretation. Therefore, feminist legal theory offers the most fundamental challenge to contemporary legal theory. It challenges the objectivity of legal language, the autonomous character of the legal system and it encourages exploring the relationship between legal discourse and other social discourses.

The benefits of discourse analysis are by no means limited to feminist analysis. On the contrary, discourse analysis can be utilized to examine any legal discourse in which identities, categories, boundaries and concepts are defined. Discourse analysis does not challenge legal dogmatic science in the search for a correct interpretation of law. While discourse analysis is concerned with how cultural and social values are reflected in the concepts and interpretations of the law, such analysis may indirectly have consequences for the interpretations of law. Moreover, legal discourses have a privilege among the social discourses as they have the power of the state behind them. This status gives legal discourses an exceptional power to shape social relations and should therefore be of special interest to social and socio-legal scholars.

References

Government Committees and Other Official Documents

SOU 1995:60, *Kvinnofrid.* [Woman's Peace].
SOU 2004:121, *Slag i luften.* [Strike in the air].

Literature

Aarnio, Aulis (1997), *Reason and Authority. A Treatise on the Dynamic Paradigm of Legal Dogmatic* (Aldershot: Dartmouth).

Alasuutari, Pertti (1993), *Laadullinen tutkimus* (Tampere: Vastapaino).

Austin, John L. (1984), *How to do things with words: The William James Lectures delivered at Harvard University in 1955* (Oxford: Oxford University Press).

Banakar, Reza (1998), 'The Identity Crisis of a 'Stepchild', 81 *Retfærd: Nordic Journal of Law and Justice* 1998, 3–22.

Banakar, Reza and Travers, Max (eds) (2005), *Socio-legal Theory and Method* (Hart: Publishing: Oxford).

Berger, Peter L. and Luckmann, Thomas (1966), *The Social Construction of Reality. A Treatise in Sociology of Knowledge* (New York: Doubleday and Co.).

Boychuck, Tascha and Ferraro, Kathleen (1992), 'The Court's Response to Interpersonal Violence. A Comparison of Intimate and Nonintimate Violence', in Buzawa, E. and Buzawa, C. (eds), *Domestic Violence. The Changing Criminal Justice Response* (Westport: Auburn House).

Burr, Vivien (1999), *An Introduction to Social Constructionism* (London & New York, Routledge).

Cotterrell, Roger (1998), 'Why must Legal Ideas Be Interpreted Sociolgically', *Journal of Law and Society* 1998, 171–192.

Dahlberg-Larsen, Jørgen (2000), 'Sociology of Law from a Legal Point of View', 89 *Retfærd:Nordic Journal of Law and Justice* 2000, 26–39.

Dobash, R. Emerson and Dobash, Russel (1992), *Women, Violence and Social Change* (New York: Routledge).

Edwards, Susan (1996) *Sex and Gender in the Legal Process* (London: Blackstone Press).

Eskola, Jari and Suoranta, Juha (1998), *Johdatus laadulliseen tutkimukseen* (Tampere: Vastapaino).

Fairclough, Norman (1996), *Discourse and Social Change* (Cambridge: Polity Press).

Foucault, Michel (1977), *Discipline and Punish: The Birth of the Prison* (New York: Pantheon).

Foucault, Michel (1978), *The History of Sexuality I: An Introduction* (New York: Pantheon).

Foucault, Michel (1989), *The Archaeology of Knowledge* (London: Routledge).

Habermas, Jürgen (1981), *Theorie des kommunikativen Handelns* (Suhrkamp: Frankfurt a.M.).

Habermas, Jürgen (1992), *Faktizität und Geltung* (Suhrkamp: Frankfurt a.M.).

Heiskala, Risto (2000), *Toiminta, tapa ja rakenne: kohti konstruktionistista synteesiä yhteiskuntateoriassa* (Helsinki: Gaudeamus).

Honkatukia, Päivi (1999), 'Gender, Social Identity and Delinquent Behaviour', 86 *Retfærd: Nordic Journal of Law and Justice* 1999, 41–52.

Honkatukia, Päivi (2001), 'Ilmoitti tulleensa raiskatuksi. Tutkimus poliisin tietoon vuonna 1998 tulleista raiskausrikoksista' (Helsinki: Tilastokeskus).

Howarth, David (2000), *Discourse* (Buckingham: Open University Press).

Hoyle, Carolyn (1998), *Negotiating Domestic Violence: Police, Criminal Justice and Victims* (Oxford: Clarendon Press).

Hydén, Håkan (1999), 'Even a Stepchild Eventually Grows Up' 85 *Retfærd: Nordic Journal of Law and Justice* 1999, 71–80.

Jokinen, Arja and Juhila, Kirsi (1999), 'Diskurssianalyysin suhde sukulaistraditioihin', in Jokinen, A. Juhila, K. and Suoninen, E. (eds), *Diskurssianalyysi liikkeessä* (Tampere: Vastapaino), 37–53.

Jokinen, Arja, Juhila, Kirsi and Suoninen, Eero (1993), *Diskurssianalyysin aakkoset* (Tampere: Vastapaino).

Juhila, Kirsi and Suoninen, Eero (1999), 'Kymmenen kysymystä diskurssianalyysistä', in Jokinen, A. Juhila, K. and Suoninen E. (eds), *Diskurssianalyysi liikkeessä* (Tampere: Vastapaino), 233–252.

Lacey, Nicola (1998), *The unspeakable subject: Essays in feminist legal theory* (Oxford: Hart).

Luhmann, Niklas (2004), *Law as a social system* (Oxford: Socio-legal studies).

Lundberg, Magnus (2001), *Vilja med förhinder. Polisers samtal om kvinnomisshandel* (Stockholm: Brutus Östlings Bokförlag Symposion).

MacCormick, Neil and Summers, Robert (eds) (1997), *Interpreting Precedents. A Comparative Study* (Ashgate: Aldershot).

Mathiesen, Thomas (1998), 'Is it all that bad to be a stepchild? Comments on the state of sociology of law', 83 *Retfærd: Nordic Journal of Law and Justice* 1998, 67–76.

Naffine, Ngaire and Owens, Rosemary J. (1997), *Sexing the subject of law* (North Ryde: Sweet & Maxwell).

Nelken, David (1998), 'Blinding Insights? The Limits of a Reflexive Sociology of Law', 25 *Journal of Law and Society* 1998, 407–426.

Niemi-Kiesiläinen, Johanna (2003), 'Collective or Individual? Constructions of Debtors and Creditors in Consumer Bankruptcy', in Niemi-Kiesiläinen, J., Ramsay, I. and Whitford, W. (eds), *Consumer Bankruptcy in Global Perspective* (Oxford: Hart), 41–60.

Niemi-Kiesiläinen, Johanna (2004), 'The Reform of the Sex Crime Law and the Gender-Neutral Subject', in Pylkkänen, Anu, Svensson, Eva-Maria and Niemi-Kiesiläinen, Johanna (eds) *Nordic Equality at a Crossroads. Feminist Legal Studies Coping with Difference* (Aldershot: Ashgate), 167–194.

Niemi-Kiesiläinen, Johanna, Honkatukia, Päivi, Karma and Ruuskanen, Minna (eds) (2006), *Oikeuden tekstit diskursseina* (Helsinki: Finnish Lawyers' Association).

Nordborg, Gudrun and Niemi-Kiesiläinen, Johanna (2001), 'Women's Peace: A Criminal Law Reform in Sweden', in Nousiainen, Kevät, Gunnarsson, Åsa, Lundström, Karin and Niemi-Kiesiläinen, Johanna (eds), *Responsible Selves: Women in the Nordic Legal Culture* (Aldershot: Ashgate), 353–373.

Nousiainen, Kevät and Niemi-Kiesiläinen, Johanna (2001), 'Introductory Remarks on Nordic Law and Gender Identities', in Nousiainen, Kevät, Gunnarsson, Åsa, Lundström, Karin and Niemi-Kiesiläinen, Johanna (eds), *Responsible Selves: Women in the Nordic Legal Culture* (Aldershot: Ashgate), 1–22.

Nyqvist, Leo (2001), *Väkivaltainen parisuhde, asiakkuus ja muutos* (Helsinki: Ensi- ja turvakotien liitto).

Parsons, Talcott (1951), *The Social System* (Glencoe, IL: Free Press of Glencoe).

Robberstad, Anne (1999), *Mellom tvekamp og inkvisisjon. Straffeprosessens grunnstruktur belyst ved fornærmedes stilling* (Oslo: Universitetsforlaget).

Ruuskanen, Minna (2001), 'The Good Battered Woman', in Nousiainen, Kevät, Gunnarsson, Åsa, Lundström, Karin and Niemi-Kiesiläinen, Johanna (eds), *Responsible Selves: Women in the Nordic Legal Culture* (Aldershot: Ashgate), 311–329.

Ruuskanen, Minna (2005), *Hätävarjelu ja parisuhdeväkivalta. Rikosoikeudellinen ja diskurssianalyyttinen tutkimus* (Helsinki: Finnish Lawyers' Association).

Searle, John R. (1995), *The Construction of Social Reality* (London: Penguin Books).

Silverman, David (1993), *Interpreting Qualitative Data. Methods for Analyzing Talk, Text and Interaction* (London: Sage Publications).

Smart, Carol (1991), *Feminism and the Power of Law* (London: Routledge).

Smart, Carol (1995), *Law, Crime and Sexuality: Essays in Feminism* (London: Sage).

Svensson, Eva-Maria (2001), 'Sex Equality: Changes in Politics, Jurisprudence and Feminist Legal Studies', in Nousiainen, Kevät, Gunnarsson, Åsa, Lundström, Karin and Niemi-Kiesiläinen, Johanna (eds), *Responsible Selves: Women in the Nordic Legal Culture* (Aldershot: Ashgate), 71–104.

Taylor, Stephanie (2001), 'Locating and Conducting Discourse Analytic Research', in Wetherell, M., Taylor, S. and Yetes, S. (eds) *Discourse as Data. A Guide for Analysis* (London: Sage), 5–48.

Thomas, Alison and Kitzinger, Celia (1997), *Sexual harassment: Contemporary feminist perspectives* (Buckingham: Open University Press).

Tuori, Kaarlo (2002), *Critical Legal Positivism* (Aldershot: Ashgate).

Van Dijk, Teun A. (2001), 'Critical Discourse Analysis' in Schiffin, D. Tannen, D. and Hamilton, H. (eds) *The Handbook of Discourse Analysis* (Malden, Massachussets and Oxford: Blackwell Publishers), 363–415.

Wróblewski, Jerzy and MacCormick, Neil (2003), 'On Justification and Interpretation', in Atria, F. and MacCormick, N. (eds) *Law and Legal Interpretation* (Aldershot: Ashgate), 421–434.

Chapter 5

Beyond Constructed Boundaries in Criminal Law Discourse

Monica Burman

Contemporary feminist legal studies in Sweden are often based on a social constructionist theory and methodology of law.[1] Studies of criminal law and men's violence against women, however, are an important exception. The shortcomings of criminal law in addressing men's violence against women have been on the feminist legal studies agenda for quite some time. But not until recently has social constructionist thinking begun to have a serious impact on feminist legal scholarship in the field of rape and men's violence against women. One important factor behind the increasing interest in confronting criminal law with social constructionist theories and methods is the general conclusion that a dogmatic approach to criminal law seems, from a feminist perspective, to be a dead end. This, among many other things, has led to suggestions that discourse analysis should be used as a way to further explore and analyse men's violence against women in criminal legal discourse.[2]

In this chapter my intention is to reflect on how social constructionism and discourse analysis relate to the dominant theory and methodology of criminal law and legal scholarship in Sweden. I want to raise and discuss the following questions: What are the differences between traditional, dogmatic criminal legal scholarship and discourse analysis? Why do Swedish feminist legal studies of criminal law seem to be shifting from dogmatics to approaches inspired by social constructionism? And finally, how can discourse analysis be described in terms of carrying out criminal legal scholarship?

The Dogmatic Conception of Criminal Law and Criminal Legal Scholarship

In contemporary Swedish criminal legal scholarship, law is most often conceptualized as a formal, closed and coherent system of rules and principles. In this system concepts and legal dogmas are created for the purpose of supporting a harmonious unity (Nousiainen 1999, 9–10). Legal argumentation is formal and closed; legal arguments must be grounded in legal sources, defined and accepted within the system. The systemic character of criminal law, the creation of dogmas and the closed

1 For example Svensson 1997; Lundström 1999; and Kouvo 2004.

2 The first doctoral thesis in criminal law using discourse analysis was presented in 2004 by Ulrika Andersson. See Andersson 2004.

argumentation are seen as important elements in upholding legality in criminal law, as guarantees against unpredictability and unequal treatment.

The ideological background of contemporary criminal legal scholarship in Sweden is Scandinavian neoclassicism and the 'defensive' model of criminal law policy. Neoclassical ideology started as a critical response to treatment ideology, which dominated criminal policy in Sweden until the 1970s (Tham 1995). The core element of treatment ideology was that in its choice of sanction the court in particular should keep in mind that the purpose of the sanction was to foster the sentenced offender's rehabilitation into society. Neoclassicism, however, does not support the 'law-and-order' movement in terms of increased criminalization and harsher punishments as instruments for controlling criminality in society. Indeed, scepticism about the efficacy of deprivation of liberty as a penalty is an important characteristic.

In order to maintain a critical position regarding the treatment ideology and to simultaneously be able to ward off demands for harsher punishments, neoclassicism emphasizes a moral principle of fairness and traditional principles of justice. Legality, proportionality and predictability are upheld, and the criminal justice system is characterized as rational, humane, just and effective (Anttila and Törnudd 1992, 13).

One central element in neoclassicism is that proportionality between the blameworthiness of the crime and the punishment should guide sentencing rather than considerations of what sanction is regarded as being best suited to rehabilitating the criminal. The criminal act as such, not the perpetrator (his attitudes, former criminality and so on), shall be decisive in determining the sanction (Leijonhufvud 1996, 102). Neoclassical ideology has had consequences beyond the question of sanctions and punishment. One example is contemporary theories about *mens rea*.[3] The criminal act and not the perpetrator are considered to be the appropriate basis for judging whether or not the requirement of intention is fulfilled.[4]

Criminal law has traditionally had a relatively low-key role in the Nordic welfare states (Niemi-Kiesiläinen 2001, 297). One important factor behind this is how the purpose, justification and limits of criminal law have been conceptualized in the defensive model of criminal law policy. *Criminal law* policy is constructed as a much narrower concept than *criminal* policy. Criminal policy encompasses all discussions and decisions that concern criminality in any sector of society. Almost all policies, for example educational, traffic and social policies, are regarded as having a criminal policy aspect (Jareborg 1995, 19–20).

Criminal law policy is restricted to issues related to the criminal legal system and its three levels, which are criminalization, sentence and execution of the sentence. Various forms of justification are seen as appropriate to different levels of the system. While criminalization is justified by a need for general prevention, sentencing is justified by retribution (just desert). Finally, the justification for execution is that a person has been sentenced to undergo punishment. The protection of individual, collective and state interests from being violated is considered to be the purpose of

3 The mental element of liability (*det subjektiva rekvisitet*).

4 See for example Jareborg 1992; Träskman 2002.

the criminal legal system as a whole. It is, however, generally believed that the main point in having a criminal justice system is its legality, that is, for the protection of the offending individual from any abuse of power by the state or other individuals. Consequently the object of criminal law policy is how criminal and procedural law should be constructed while respecting demands for efficiency, justice and human rights (Jareborg 2001, 20).

The defensive model of criminal law policy builds on neoclassical values and stresses that values such as legality, proportionality and fairness cannot be subordinated to the need to prevent crime through criminalization. In line with Hart's mixed theory of punishment (Hart 1968), general prevention is considered to be the general justifying aim for criminalization at the same time as arguments related to prevention are considered irrelevant when it comes to distribution of punishment. Instead retribution and legality (just desert) are upheld as main principles in deciding when and how to criminalize and punish. It is not regarded as an important task for criminal law to contribute to solving social problems and criminalization is regarded as the *ultima ratio*, as a last resort, to be used only when every other measure for addressing social problems has failed. On the contrary, it is considered an important task for criminal law to create *hindrances* to criminalization.

Abolitionist thinking also has an influence on the defensive model. This reveals itself in a lack of faith in punishment, especially imprisonment. But at the same time a criminal legal dogmatic scholar 'must' believe that a system of criminalization and punishment makes sense. Therefore 'the utmost a dogmatist may do is to argue that criminal law should be strictly limited and its use minimalized' (Nousiainen 1999, 15).[5] So, the need for criminalization is not denied. Instead legal dogmatic scholars have set up models and principles for providing answers to the question of *what* should be criminalized and – if the behaviour in question should be criminalized – *how* this should be done.[6]

The dogmatic conception of criminal law and its ideological background influences what criminal legal scholarship is understood to be. Dogmatic criminal legal scholarship is considered the most important kind of criminal legal scholarship (Jareborg 2001, 19; Lahti 1992, 6). Its main subject, according to Nils Jareborg, one of the most influential criminal legal scholars in the Nordic countries, is to construct the criminal legal system and to serve as a pathway between law and the practical application of law. Dogmatic scholarship in this view strives to find better concepts and systematics and to capture the correct interpretation of law in the same way as a judge would do (Jareborg 2001, 19).

Dogmatic criminal legal scholarship is comprehended as an internal systematic perspective within boundaries that are set up by the legislator and the courts. There is certainly considered to be room for proposals *lex ferenda*, but the normal purpose of such suggestions should be to support the criminal legal system and its foundations. For example, it is regarded as necessary to take coherence in the legal system into consideration (Asp 2002, 312). It is also regarded as possible for a criminal dogmatic scholar to search and argue for an ideal criminal justice system or an ideal solution

5 For an example, see Jareborg 1995, 33.

6 See for example Jareborg 2001, 45–65.

to criminal legal problems, but the boundaries surrounding the criminal legal system are considered necessary to take into consideration.[7]

Descriptions of the field tend to picture dogmatic criminal legal scholarship as a rather narrow and non-theoretical activity. Other fields of criminal legal scholarship, for example criminal legal history and philosophy, are considered mainly as auxiliaries to dogmatics (Jareborg 2001, 19). Apart from traditional criminology, results or theories from research fields other than law are seldom considered relevant to criminal legal scholarship.

As is pointed out by Eva-Maria Svensson in this volume, dogmatic legal scholarship can be characterized as not making any explicit distinction between the object, the Law, and the academic model of it. A conception of law as an existing object and an epistemology that perceives the bases of knowledge in the essence of the object, easily leads to an understanding of law as fact, not as norms or values created by humans (Svensson 2001, 81). Svensson argues that the construction of law as an existing object makes a distinction between object and subject possible and that this exercise can be comprehended as part of the attempt to accord law the characteristics of autonomy, scholarly status and objectivity (Svensson 1997, 259–265).

Another characteristic of dogmatic legal scholarship is a general desire to strictly separate law from ethics and politics. Law is often regarded as objective while politics is considered subjective (Persson in this volume; Persson 2004; Svensson 2001, 81). The concept of criminal law policy can be analysed as a way of detaching the 'legal' part of criminal policy from the overall 'political' criminal policy. Quite a number of efforts have also been made to define clear boundaries between the criminal legal system on the one hand and the social and political context on the other. Several attempts have been made for example to formulate a legal principle that, regardless of values or political considerations, can provide normative answers to the question of what kind of interests should or should not be protected by criminalization (Lernestedt 2003).

Madeleine Leijonhufvud's opinion is that dogmatic criminal legal scholars sometimes disguise the fact that neoclassicism and the defensive model of criminal law policy are based on values. Instead, they are presented as objective and scholarly products emanating from criminal legal and criminological scholarship (Leijonhufvud 1996). In my opinion the conception of a boundary line between criminal law and criminal law policy on the one hand and the general criminal policy on the other, also makes it possible to designate as 'political' any aspects defined as coming from outside the dogmatic sphere of criminal law. Such aspects might therefore be regarded as, if not irrelevant, then at least as less important than the 'legal' and legality aspects.

Constructing the criminal legal system in accordance with the defensive model and neoclassical ideals, however, can be a problematic project for dogmatic criminal legal scholarship. The social, moral and political context of criminal law continuously exerts pressure on the criminal legal field to implement values and to find solutions that are considered better, more reasonable and fairer.

7 See for example Jareborg 2004, 4.

The dogmatic conception of criminal law and legal scholarship is also challenged from a variety of critical positions. Critical criminal legal scholarship presents a critique of the liberal system of criminal law because it fails to raise social justice issues associated with socio-economic status, race or ethnicity, and gender (Norrie 2001). The classical concepts of modern criminal law have also been criticized as not being in line with scientific and technological advances, political changes and social upheavals during the 20th century.[8] And feminist legal studies have focused on the inability of criminal law to address and deal with rape and men's violence against women.[9]

Problematic Boundaries

Feminist legal studies in the Nordic countries started to (and partly still do) criticize criminal law by putting women as a category into law and focusing on how female experiences fit poorly into law. The next step has been to criticize the material content of law and to suggest legislative changes in order to make law better suited to women. This approach is valuable as a tool for making visible the significance of gender and gender-related effects of law in a strong formal gender-neutral regime.[10] However, basic theoretical assumptions about criminal law and the legal subject or methodological assumptions in mainstream legal research or in the practical application of law have not really been challenged. The Women's Peace Reform and the introduction of a new crime 'Gross violation of a women's integrity' in 1998 can be characterized as following this tradition.[11]

After some time however feminist legal scholars started to recognize that the dogmatic conception of criminal law involves obstacles and dilemmas for feminist demands that there should be a criminal law that is more responsive to men's violence against women. These obstacles and dilemmas are of various kinds, but they all contribute to the construction and upholding of boundaries that are difficult to transgress.

In Sweden it is quite generally accepted, at least most people pay lip service to it, that men's violence against women in intimate relationships is a significant social problem. At the same time there is a tendency in mainstream criminal law

---

8 Ezzat A. Fattah has presented a profound critique of the classical and fundamental concepts of modern criminal law based on the argument that criminal law has not kept pace with developments during the 20th century. Fattah believes that abstract and metaphysical notions in criminal law, such as, 'moral guilt', and the notion of retributive justice should be replaced by a secular notion of 'harm' and distributive justice. See Fattah 1992.

9 See for example Pohjonen 1995; Edwards 1996; Nordborg and Niemi-Kiesiläinen 2001; Larsson 2002; Sutorius and Kaldal 2003; Andersson 2004.

10 This first feminist legal studies approach shows some similarities to liberal feminism as described in Naffine and Owens 1997, 4.

11 The purpose of the new crime 'Gross violation of a women's integrity' was to create a crime that recognizes the process-like nature of men's violence against female partners or ex-partners and the multiple effects of various acts and to give repeated violence in intimate relationships a more adequate penal value.

and legal scholarship to articulate 'women interests' as political or as 'special' interests, incompatible with the 'general' (male) interests of criminal law. Gender-related violence and violence related to other types of power or discrimination are considered to be 'different' or 'strange' and therefore not appropriate for inclusion in the criminal legal system. The difficulties of dealing with such violence within the criminal legal system are not, however, connected with the system itself. Instead of reflecting, for example, on how legal concepts and dogmas or the legal subject of criminalization or protection are constructed in criminal law, the difficulties are attributed to the 'problematic nature' of men's violence against women. Examples of the problematic features that are pointed out are that the violence occurs in private with no witnesses outside the family and that the psychological effects of such violence do not fit into the criminal legal concept of injury.

One fundamental problem is that the norms are considered to be sex/gender-neutral. Argumentations based on the relevance of sex/gender can therefore be rejected as irrelevant (Svensson 2001, 82). The criminal legal system consequently lacks any internal imperatives to consider gender-related issues. Gender-based or crime-victim-related arguments do not fit into the system and the concept of criminal law as an almost totally internal and closed system makes it very difficult to legitimize such arguments (Berglund 1995, 1997).

But implementing gender-related aspects into criminal law is also problematic. Feminists in Sweden quite often point out that the law is a tool by means of which aims related to gender equality decided by parliament could be achieved (Svensson 2001, 96). But the neoclassical and defensive criminal legal approach has forced feminist demands into a rather uncomfortable choice between prevention and legality (Nousiainen 1999, 16). Feminist demands for reform risk being associated with 'forbidden' arguments based on general prevention and therefore labelled 'offensive'[12] by mainstream criminal legal scholars in Sweden.

The offensive model of criminal law policy is constructed as the opposite to the defensive model and therefore as a threat to basic assumptions about the purpose, justification and limits of criminal law. It is characterized as specifying prevention and not legality as the fundamental basis for the whole criminal legal system and as regarding 'the criminal justice system as an at least potential repertoire of methods for solution of social or societal problems' (Jareborg 1995, 24–25). While the defensive model is described in terms of principles and safeguards, the offensive model is considered best described in terms of its methods and consequences (Jareborg 1995, 24–26). This description tends to 'de-legalize' feminist political demands as well as the critique that feminist legal studies level against criminal law. Accordingly the space for a discussion about *possibilities* within criminal law or *use* of criminal law is very limited. Furthermore legality is often used as a basis for counteracting gender- or crime-victim-related arguments.[13] The principle of *ultima ratio* and legality-based arguments often leads to the conclusion that means other than criminal law have to be implemented.

12 Nils Jareborg uses the word 'offensive' as an opposite of 'defensive'.

13 Andersson argues that the contradictions often made between crime-victim aspects and legality is unnecessary. See Andersson 2003.

How gender-related arguments can be met with resistance is clearly illustrated in the way the legal community responded to a proposal for a new crime entitled 'A Serious Breach of a Woman's Peace'. The proposal was presented in 1995 by the Commission on Violence against Women as a part of The Women's Peace Reform (SOU 1995:60; Prop. 1997/98:55). The proposed crime focused on repeated violence aimed at a lasting violation of the woman's integrity and damage to her self-respect. The proposed law text mentioned acts that had already been criminalized but also included other acts of a physical or psychological character that were not offences according to the current criminal code, but which nevertheless effectively contributed to the mental processes of abuse, violence and mental terror (Nordborg and Niemi-Kiesiläinen 2001, 360–361). The legal community expressed a systematic reluctance to accept the proposal and both the need for and the construction of the crime were questioned (Bjelle 2000).[14]

One important aspect behind questioning the need for criminal legal reforms is the traditional Nordic conception of men's violence against women as primarily a social policy question (Niemi-Kiesiläinen 2001; Elman 1996). A conclusion that frequently follows is that measures other than criminal law have to be implemented in order to prevent and combat such violence. Alternative measures proposed often consist of therapy or treatment for the perpetrator, the victim or both or of social efforts to support the female victim's opportunities to separate from the abusive man and recover from the consequences of violence.

Another common way of arguing is to refer to the need to deal with the 'real' cause behind men's violence against women. When The Office of the Prosecutor General gave its view on the proposed crime 'A Serious Breach of a Woman's Peace', men's violence against women was considered to be a social and human problem rather than a problem that should be solved through criminal law. Thus the Office believed that other ways had to be sought and pointed to alcohol and drugs policies as important areas in this context. In addition, the Office found that improved knowledge was more important than new legislation. More knowledge was considered sufficient to solve existing problems with criminal investigation and evidence (Ds 1996:28, 10). If such a policy is repeatedly recommended in connection with men's violence against women, while other forms of violence are still considered to be best treated by criminal law, an understanding of the former as 'a misfortune rather than a wrong' is perpetuated (Nousiainen 1999, 17).[15]

The critique of the construction of the proposed crime 'A Serious Breach of a Woman's Peace' was based on the principle of legality and the argument that the prerequisites for criminal liability were not formulated precisely enough. The proposed crime was also considered incompatible with the prevailing doctrine of self-defence. A new crime entitled 'Gross violation of a woman's integrity' was finally enacted, but only after fundamental changes to the construction of the crime in accordance with the opinions of the legal community. It was reduced to more severe

14 The legal critique and the processes and outcome of the Women's Peace Reform are described and analysed in Nordborg and Niemi-Kiesiläinen 2001.

15 In a Finnish context there seems to be an especially strong conception of domestic violence as a family problem and not as a crime. See Ruuskanen 2001; Elman 1996.

sanctions for acts that are already criminalized. This result, as has been pointed out by Gudrun Nordborg and Johanna Niemi-Kiesiläinen, is also problematic in the Scandinavian context of liberal criminal policy, especially since severe sanctions have hardly ever been a goal of the feminist movement (Nordborg and Niemi-Kiesiläinen 2001, 370).

Despite the legal critique having a strong influence on the outcome, the legal community has continued to criticize the crime 'Gross violation of a woman's integrity'. A criminal legal scholar has characterized the new crime as a problematic construction. It is regarded as a strange element in Swedish criminal law, especially from the perspective of dogmas and ideas about how a crime might be constructed (Wennberg 2000). In the first Supreme Court Case (NJA 1999 s 102) regarding the new law the opinions among the judges differed in a remarkable way. The judges found several criminal legal problems connected with the crime, which they wanted to deal with in various ways. They also interpreted the prerequisites for criminal liability differently. The majority focused on the formulation of the law text and made a very strict interpretation of the legality principle, with the consequence that the new crime could not comprise the kind of cases that had been the object. This case led to a semantic change in the law in order to make it applicable in the manner intended.[16]

The new crime 'gross violation of a woman's integrity' is in my opinion a good example of how feminist demands for a more effective criminal law to protect women's rights and interests have been forced to adapt to criminal legal dogmatics and/or the defensive model of criminal law policy. Because dogmatic criminal legal scholarship is bound to its object there is little possibility of arguing for something considered to fall outside the boundaries of criminal law (Svensson in this volume). Feminist demands also tend to be constructed as offensive and are therefore rejected or considered to be in need of adjustment.

While recognizing these problematic boundaries, most contemporary feminist criminal legal scholars in the Nordic countries have abandoned belief in the possibilities offered by dogmatics. Today the need for a more profound critique of the basic assumptions and concepts of modern criminal law is on the agenda. Inspired by the international development in feminist legal studies, Nordic feminist legal scholars have started to explore criminal law using a social constructionist approach. There is also a growing interest in using discourse analysis in feminist criminal legal scholarship.[17]

---

16 Law SFS 1999:845 and Prop. 1998/99:145.

17 See for example Andersson 2004; Niemi-Kiesiläinen 2004a. A research project in Finland during 2001–2004, 'Violence in the Shadow of Equality: Hidden Gender in Legal Discourse', dealt with how implicit perceptions about violence against women are reflected and reproduced in legal discourses, and discourse analysis was a central method. The project included seven people, both lawyers and social scientists. See http://www.jus.umu.se/personal/johanna_vise.htm. One example of ongoing research is my own PhD project on 'Men's Violence Against Women in Criminal Legal Discourse'.

Approaching Criminal Law using Social Constructionism and Discourse Analysis

A central tenet of a feminist social constructionist theory of law is to regard law as a discourse, as a practice which produces certain kinds of statements. With a social constructionist view, our understanding of the world (or parts of it) is created through discourses and law produces an understanding that has consequences, for example for the way we view the nature of men's violence against women.

In discourse analysis the main focus is on the different meanings that are given to social events and interaction and what consequences these meanings might have (Niemi-Kiesiläinen *et al.* in this volume). But discourse analysis is not one single method, instead it is a framework of related methods concerning how to read texts and analyse their meanings (Niemi-Kiesiläinen 2004b, 655). Furthermore it is not simply a method for data analysis. Theory and method are intertwined, to form a theoretical and methodological whole, building on a social constructionist basis (Philips and Winther Jørgensen 2002, 4). Apart from social constructionism, two further important starting points characterize discourse analysis. Language is considered to be the mechanism through which the social world is constituted and the subject is seen as being created in discourses, not as a pre-given category (Philips and Winther Jørgensen 2002, 8–16).

The notion of knowledge is connected to the social and linguistic turn. Instead of upholding a notion of a true foundation for knowledge, knowledge is understood as something contextual and constructed (Svensson in this volume). Law is believed to play a crucial role in the construction of facts, concepts and subjects, in that law not only regulates something that exists prior to law, but is in itself also a part of the social construction of that same reality (Niemi-Kiesiläinen *et al.* in this volume). In criminal law this can mean, for example, seeing the subject of criminal protection as constructed in legal discourse instead of being a pre-determined category (Andersson 2004). In contrast to dogmatics, where the interest lies in finding the correct interpretation of the law and the application of law to given facts, the interest in discourse analysis lies in exploring the processes in which facts and concepts are constructed and become relevant for legal interpretation (Niemi-Kiesiläinen *et al.* in this volume).

Performing discourse analysis often means revealing the discourses operating in a text. In this context a discourse is regarded as a certain way of speaking of and understanding a phenomenon.[18] Constructions of central notions can be revealed by identifying the discourses in legal texts. In her study of legal reasoning in cases

18 The notion of 'discourse' can be defined in many different ways. In feminist legal scholarship the word is generally used in one of two possible meanings. 'Law as discourse' indicates a social constructionist understanding of law functioning as a discourse, closely related to Michel Foucault's notion of 'discourse'. See for example Svensson and Pylkkänen 2004, 31. The other way of using the word is associated more specifically with discourse analysis, in other words, how a phenomenon is spoken about in a legal context. This is often expressed in terms of 'legal discourses' or 'discourses in law'. For example Niemi-Kiesliäinen et al in this volume defines a discourse as 'a coherent expression or a meaning structure that constructs reality in a certain way'.

concerning sexual offences from Swedish courts of appeal, Ulrika Andersson has found (among others) discourses on the victim's expression of will. The legal reasoning naturally included such discourses, which produced a victim with an open and accessible body and an accessible, passive sexuality, a subject which is clearly feminine (Andersson 2004, 276–277).

In performing discourse analysis the focus lies on *what* is spoken and *how* it is spoken about (Andersson 2003, 2). Legal texts can be deconstructed by looking behind the surface of the texts to reveal discourses that contribute to the construction of, for example, gender, body and sexuality. This can be done through careful reading with the purpose of identifying recurrent patterns that form discourses. What is not spoken about is also relevant (Andersson 2004, 41). Discourse analytical readings of legal texts do not directly contribute to legal interpretation, but they can provide grounds for reconsidering accepted interpretations by being critical towards them and revealing how cultural and social values are reflected in legal concepts and interpretations of law (Niemi-Kiesiläinen *et al.* in this volume).

Power is a central issue for feminist legal studies. Gender relations are often defined as power relations. The understanding that Swedish feminist legal studies have of power and gender relations is influenced by the *Genus System Theory*, developed by Yvonne Hirdman. Contemporary sex-equality politics in Sweden is also based on this theory.[19] The theory understands *genus* as a socially constructed relationship between men and women. This relationship is characterized by two principles. First, the two sexes are detached and man is formed, manifestly divided from woman.. Second the male is the standard for a human being. The *genus* system consists of normative and stable patterns and is active in reproducing gendered patterns of power and inequality, but is still subject to change. *Genus* is used as an analytical and abstract concept to describe how the relationship between the meanings of man and woman is expressed at the symbolic, structural and individual levels.[20]

Discourse analysis provides tools for dealing with power, power relations and the relation between power and knowledge. Common ideas that occur in feminist legal studies are, for example, that the very structure and method of modern law is hierarchically gendered and that law in its claim to enunciate the truth disqualifies other knowledges and experiences (Lacey 1998, 2; Smart 1989, 11). These ideas can be further elaborated by using discourse analysis.

Feminist legal studies in Sweden and Finland seem to be especially inspired by critical discourse analysis. Critical discourse analysis deals with the relationship between discourse and power and focuses on the use of discourses as means of exercising power (Van Dijk 2001, 363). By asking which discourses become dominant and which are silenced power relations and the consequences of dominant discourses within the criminal justice system can be studied (Niemi-Kiesiläinen *et al.* in this volume; Andersson 2004, 42).

---

19 The *Genus System Theory* was presented by Yvonne Hirdman in an official report in 1990, SOU 1990:44, and is further elaborated in Hirdman 2003.

20 The genus system theory is described and problematized in a legal context in Svensson 2001.

Another way of dealing with power is to focus on discourses struggling to provide meaning. In this tradition, relations are seen in terms of antagonism, but the main interest does not lie in the operation of dominant discourses. Instead power struggles between discourses and instability are the main focus.[21]

Inside or Outside the Paradigm?

Social constructionist and discourse theories and methods have inspired feminist legal thinking in many ways. These approaches are attractive because of their 'unpacking of what has been normalized or of the taken-for-granted truths of modernity' (Kouvo 2004, 71). Social constructionism is important for feminist deconstructions of law's claim to be enunciating truths and discourse analysis is one method among others which provide the tools for exploring gendered constructions and power relations in law and legal concepts. More or less hidden assumptions in legal argumentation about gender, power and gender relations can also be revealed.

As argued by Niemi-Kiesiläinen *et al.* in this volume, the key-assumptions of social constructionism, feminist legal theory and discourse analysis have the potential to present critical perspectives on law and dogmatic legal scholarship, perhaps even to offer the most fundamental challenge to contemporary legal theory. They seem to gratify feminist legal theory aspirations to reveal the ways in which law reflects, reproduces, expresses, constructs and reinforces power relations along sexually-patterned lines and to contribute to the feminist questioning of the law's claim to autonomy and the feminist representation of law as a practice which is continuous, with deeper social, political and economic forces which constantly seep through its supposed boundaries (Lacey 1998, 7).

Contemporary ways of defining criminal legal scholarship presuppose and construct limits to criminal law and criminal legal scholarship. A social constructionist and discourse analytical approach challenges these limits. So these approaches seem promising in that they offer a way of transcending the constraints of dogmatics. But how can social constructionism and discourse analysis be understood in relation to dogmatic criminal legal scholarship? Dogmatic criminal legal scholarship could be characterized as an 'inside view' of law. An inside view includes 'a faith in the capacity of the conceptual framework to generate determinate answers to substantive questions of law; and a belief in the timeless validity of the "general principles of criminal law"' (Lacey *et al.* 2003, 39).

At first sight, social constructionism and discourse analysis seem to be an 'outside view' of criminal law. Theories concerning outside views of law have developed (especially) in the discipline of the Sociology of Law. This view is defined as looking at the legal system from the outside, focusing on the functions of law in a broader social context and a conception of law as a social function interacting with surrounding normative systems (Gustafsson 2002, 61). However, the concept 'outside view' is problematic, because it reproduces conceptions of boundaries in

21 This tradition is often associated with Ernesto Laclau and Chantal Mouffe. See for example Philips, and Winther Jørgensen 2002, 24–59; Bergström and Boréus 2000, 228–233.

criminal law and legal scholarship instead of promoting pluralism. If feminist legal studies in criminal law defines itself as an 'outside view' of law, the whole field of research risks being labelled 'non-legal' or being considered outside the boundaries of criminal legal scholarship. Furthermore, discourse analysis might be considered a strange methodology in criminal legal scholarship.

One way to avoid being trapped between the dogmatic ideal and the exclusion mechanisms inherent in the concept 'outside view of law' might be to comprehend the difference between inside and outside views of law as an epistemological difference instead of an ontological one. With an epistemological approach it is possible to see the two views as a whole, not as two separate or hierarchical aspects of conducting legal research. Instead of choosing theory or method from a hierarchical point of view, it would be a choice between different 'explanatory scopes' (Gustafsson 2002, 71–89).[22]

Defining discourse analysis as an 'inside methodology' is another alternative. Feminist legal studies have revealed the contextualized nature of criminal law, both in respect of criminal law as a practice and its theoretical foundations (Lacey 2002). It would be possible to argue that criminal law *is* contextualized and that dogmatic criminal legal scholarship *is* a contextualizing method, but frequently used in an unreflected manner. Discourse analysis would then simply be a method for exploring these aspects of criminal law and criminal legal scholarship.

Even though I find the last approach interesting, I believe it is better to define the feminist legal studies position as neither 'inside' nor 'outside'. Discourse analysis and social constructionism are, as I have described them, critical positions – they are at once inside and outside. Another consideration is that as long as the dogmatic conception remains the dominant paradigm, criminal law's 'special' characteristics must be acknowledged and reflected on. But with a social constructionist approach this will be done from a critical position and without accepting dogmatic presuppositions as unconstructed truths. A theoretical starting point with criminal law as discourse and performing discourse analysis is perhaps best described as a striving to reach beyond constructed boundaries.

References

Governmental Bills

Prop. 1997/98:55, *Kvinnofrid.* [Governments proposal, Woman's Peace].

Prop. 1998/99:145, *Ändring av fridskränkningsbrotten.* [Governments proposal, Amendment of the Peace Crime].

Government Committees and Other Official Documents

SOU 1990:44, *Demokrati och Makt i Sverige* [Democracy and Power in Sweden].

22 Hydén has developed a theory of norms which he believes will make it possible to combine an inside and outside view of law. See Hydén 2002, 274.

SOU 1995:60, *Kvinnofrid* [Woman's Peace].
Ds 1996:28, *Remissammanställning. Kvinnofrid.*

Literature

Andersson, Ulrika (2003), 'Offrets rättsskydd eller förövarens rättssäkerhet – en nödvändig motsättning?', in Mohr, Tilmann and Nemitz, Jan Christoph (eds), *Strafrecht aus nordischer Perspektive. Festschrift für Karin Cornils zum 25-jahrigen Jubiläum als Referentin am Max-Planck-Institut* (Aachen: Shaker Verlag), 1–4.

Andersson, Ulrika (2004), *Hans (ord) eller hennes? En könsteoretisk analys av straffrättsligt skydd mot sexuella övergrepp* (Lund: Bokbox Förlag).

Anttila, Inkeri and Törnudd, Patrik. (1992), 'The Dynamics of The Finnish Criminal Code Reform' in Lahti, Raimo and Nuotio, Kimmo (eds), *Criminal Law Theory in Transition. Finnish and Comparative Perspectives* (Helsinki: Finnish Lawyers' Publ.), 11–26.

Asp, Petter (2002), 'Rättsvetenskap och lagstiftningsarbet', 87 *Svensk Juristtidning* 2002, 311–318.

Berglund, Kerstin (1995), 'Rättens användbarhet vid brott mot kvinnor', in Herrlin, Monica (ed.), *Kvinnor och miljöer. Rapport från det 9nde nordiska kvinnojuristmötet 19–21 maj 1995* (Helsingfors: Helsingfors Universitet), 213–228.

Berglund, Kerstin (1997), 'Den kvinnliga rätten vid sitt första skifte', in *de lege. Juridiska fakulteten i Uppsala. Årsbok årgång 7, 1997* (Uppsala: Iustus), 157–183.

Bergström, Göran and Boréus, Kristina (2000), *Textens mening och makt. Metodbok i samhällsvetenskaplig textanalys* (Lund: Studentlitteratur).

Bjelle, Britta (2000), 'Arbete och strategier för kvinnofrid', in Nordborg, Gudrun, Ågren, Karin and Nilsson, Eva (eds), *Strategier och kontrakt för ekonomi och kärlek. Rapport från 10:e Nordiska KvinnoJuristmötet* (Uppsala: Iustus), 91–98.

Edwards, Susan S.M. (1996), *Sex and gender in the legal process* (London: Blackstone Press Limited).

Elman, Amy (1996), *Sexual Subordination and State Intervention. Comparing Sweden and the United States* (Providence: Berghahn Books).

Fattah, Ezzat A. (1992), 'Beyond Metaphysics: The need for a new Paradigm. On actual and potential contributions of criminology and the social sciences to the reform of the criminal law', in Lahti, Raimo and Nuotio, Kimmo (eds), *Criminal Law Theory in Transition. Finnish and Comparative Perspectives* (Helsinki: Finnish Lawyers' Publ.), 64–101.

Gustafsson, Håkan (2002), *Rättens polyvalens. En rättsvetenskaplig studie av sociala rättigheter och rättssäkerhet* (Lund: Sociologiska Institutionen, Lunds Universitet).

Hart, H.L.A. (1968), *Punishment and Responsibility. Essays in the Philosophy of Law* (Oxford: Clarendon Press).

Hirdman, Yvonne (2003), *Genus: om det stabilas föränderliga former* (Malmö: Liber).

Hydén, Håkan (2002), *Normvetenskap* (Lund: Sociologiska Institutionen, Lunds Universitet).

Jareborg, Nils (1992), *Straffrättsideologiska fragment* (Skrifter från Juridiska fakulteten i Uppsala, nr. 92. Uppsala: Iustus).

Jareborg, Nils (1995), 'What Kind of Criminal Law Do We Want? On defensive and offensive criminal law policy', in Snare, Annika, (ed.), *Beware of Punishment. On the Utility and Futility of Criminal Law.* (Oslo: Pax), 17–36.

Jareborg, Nils (2001), *Allmän kriminalrätt,* (Uppsala: Iustus).

Jareborg, Nils (2004), 'Rättsdogmatik som vetenskap', 89 *Svensk Juristtidning,* 1–10.

Kouvo, Sari (2004), *Making Just Rights? Mainstreaming Women's Human Rights and a Gender Perspective* (Uppsala: Iustus).

Lacey, Nicola, Wells, Celia and Quick, Oliver (2003), *Reconstructing Criminal Law. Text and Materials* (London: LexisNexis UK, Third Edition).

Lacey, Nicola (1998), *Unspeakable subjects. Feminist essays in legal and social theory* (Oxford: Hart Publishing).

Lacey, Nicola (2002), 'Violence, Ethics and Law: Feminist Reflections on a Familiar Dilemma', in James, Susan and Palmer, Stephanie (eds), *Visible Women. Essays on Feminist Legal Theory and Political Philosophy* (Oxford: Hart Publishing), 117–135.

Lahti, Raimo (1992), 'Criminal Sciences and the Finnish Criminal Code Reform', in Lahti, Raimo and Nuotio, Kimmo (eds), *Criminal Law Theory in Transition. Finnish and Comparative Perspectives* (Helsinki: Finnish Lawyers' Publ.), 4–9.

Larsson, Monica (2002), 'Kvinnors rätt till nödvärn', 87 *Svensk Juristtidning,* 668–685.

Leijonhufvud, Madeleine (1996), 'Rättsvetenskap och kriminalpolitik', in Rosén, Jan (ed.), *Lex Ferenda* (Stockholm: Skrifter utgivna av Juridiska fakulteten vid Stockholms Universitet, nr. 50. Juristförlaget), 95–105.

Lernestedt, Claes (2003), *Kriminalisering. Problem och principer* (Uppsala: Iustus).

Lundström, Karin (1999), *Jämlikhet mellan kvinnor och män i EG-rätten: en feministisk analys* (Uppsala: Iustus).

Naffine, Ngaire and Owens, Rosemary J. (1997) 'Sexing law', in Naffine, Ngaire and Owens, Rosemary J. (eds), *Sexing the subject of law* (Sydney: The Law Book Co. Ltd), 3–21.

Niemi-Kiesiläinen, Johanna (2001), 'Criminal Law or Social Policy', in Nousiainen, Kevät, Gunnarsson, Åsa, Lundström, Karin and Niemi-Kiesiläinen, Johanna (eds.), *Responsible Selves. Women in the Nordic legal culture* (Aldershot: Ashgate), 289–309.

Niemi-Kiesiläinen, Johanna (2004a), 'The Reform of Sex Crime Law and the Gender-Neutral Subject', in Svensson, Eva-Maria, Pylkkänen, Anu and Niemi-Kiesiläinen, Johanna (eds), *Nordic Equality at a Crossroads. Feminist Legal Studies Coping with Difference* (Aldershot: Ashgate), 167–194.

Niemi-Kiesilänen, Johanna (2004b), Anm. av Ulrika Andersson, Hans (ord) eller hennes?, (2004) 89 *Svensk Juristtidning,* 653–659.

Nordborg, Gudrun and Niemi-Kiesiläinen, Johanna (2001), 'Women's Peace: A Criminal Law Reform in Sweden', in Nousiainen, Kevät, Gunnarsson, Åsa,

Lundström, Karin and Niemi-Kiesiläinen, Johanna (eds), *Responsible Selves. Women in the Nordic legal culture*. (Aldershot: Ashgate), 353–373.

Norrie, Alan (2001), *Crime, Reason and History. A Critical Introduction to Criminal Law* (London: Butterworths).

Nousiainen, Kevät (1999), 'Equalizing Images? Gendered Imagenary in Criminal Law' (1999) 24 *Antropologi i Finland. Journal of the Finnish Anthropological Society*, 7–24.

Persson, Åsa (2004), *De politiska partiernas rättspolitik* (Uppsala: Iustus).

Philips, Louise and Winther Jørgensen, Marianne. (2002), *Discourse as Theory and Method* (London: Sage Publications).

Pohjonen, Soile (1995), 'Kvinnor, våld och straffrätt', in Gudrun Nordborg (ed.), *13 kvinnoperspektiv på rätten*, (Uppsala: Iustus), 197-223.

Ruuskanen, Minna (2001), 'The Good Battered Woman', in Nousiainen, Kevät, Gunnarsson, Åsa, Lundström, Karin and Niemi-Kiesiläinen, Johanna (eds), *Responsible Selves. Women in the Nordic legal culture.* (Aldershot: Ashgate), 311–329.

Smart, Carol (1989), *Feminism and The Power of Law* (London and New York: Routledge).

Sutorius, Helena and Kaldal, Anna (2003), *Bevisprövning vid sexualbrott* (Stockholm: Norstedts Juridik AB).

Svensson, Eva-Maria and Pylkkänen, Anu (2004), 'Contemporary Challenges in Nordic Feminist Legal Studies', in Svensson, Eva-Maria, Pylkkänen, Anu and Niemi-Kiesiläinen, Johanna (eds), *Nordic Equality at a Crossroads. Feminist Legal Studies Coping with Difference* (Aldershot: Ashgate), 17–46.

Svensson, Eva-Maria (1997), *Genus och rätt, en problematisering av föreställningen om rätten* (Uppsala: Iustus).

Svensson, Eva-Maria (2001), 'Sex Equality: Changes in Politics, Jurisprudence and Feminist Legal Studies', in Nousiainen, Kevät, Gunnarsson, Åsa, Lundström, Karin and Niemi-Kiesiläinen, Johanna (eds), *Responsible Selves. Women in the Nordic legal culture* (Aldershot: Ashgate), 71–104.

Tham, Henrik (1995), 'From Treatment to Just Deserts in a Changing Welfare State', in Annika Snare (ed.), *Beware of Punishment. On the Utility and Futility of Criminal Law* (Oslo: Pax), 89–122.

Träskman, Per-Ole (2002-2003), 'Uppsåtets tredje form – sannolikhet, eller…?' 14 *Juridisk tidskrift*, 2002-03, 616–626.

Van Dijk, Teun A. (2001) 'Critical Discourse Analysis', in Schiffrin, Deborah, Tannen, Deborah and Hamilton, Heidi E. (eds), *The Handbook of Discourse Analysis* (Malden and Oxford: Blackwell Publishers), 363–415.

Wennberg, Suzanne (2000), 'Grov kvinnofridskränkning – en problematisk brottskonstruktion' 85 *Svensk Juristtidning,* 792–804.

Chapter 6

Children Crossing Borders – On Child Perspectives in the Swedish Aliens Act and the Limits of Law

Eva Nilsson

> On the one hand there is the letter of the law exalted in these documents, which describes a specific range of rights and precepts. On the other hand there is the spirit of the law, the symbology of freedom, which is in some ways utterly meaningless or empty – although at the same time the very emptiness provides a vessel to be filled with possibility, with a plurality of autonomous yearnings. (Williams 1993, 16)

Introduction

In the middle of the 1990s, there was an intense debate in Sweden questioning whether Sweden was fulfilling its obligations under the United Nations Convention on the Rights of the Child[1] (CRC). The Aliens Act (SFS 1989:529) and its application were subjected to particularly severe criticism. In a number of cases, which attracted much attention, adverse remarks were made about the practice applied, as it was considered to conflict with children's rights. Representatives of occupational groups with experience in aliens' matters such as lawyers, medical experts, psychologists and others, objected to the application of the law. Particularly important from a legal standpoint were statements that expert opinions about children had not been given adequate consideration and that children's own grounds for being granted residence permits had not been heeded (SOU 1996:115, 24).

On account of the criticism, a parliamentary committee (the Committee on the Convention of the Rights of the Child and Swedish Legislation, henceforth the Child's Committee) was set up in February 1996, to make a broad survey of the standing of Swedish legislation and practice in relation to the provisions contained in the CRC. The Committee was instructed to give priority to the situation of children in matters involving the Aliens Act (Dir. 1996:15, 76). The object when dealing with the various dilemmas and conflicts that had emerged, was to seek to find ways and means that would allow Sweden to live up to the spirit and intentions of the Convention in the best way (SOU 1996:115, 24).

1 Convention on the Rights of the Child, 29 November 1989, UN Doc. A/Res/44/25.

The Child's Committee found in its review that the Swedish aliens' legislation was mainly consistent with the Convention. Due to the criticism of the application of the law, however, the Committee delivered a number of proposals and views concerning the application and also certain changes to the law (SOU 1996:115, 12–13). In the bill, the Government declared that it was of the opinion that in various respects it was possible to move beyond current applications, and 'several concrete improvements of the child's position within aliens law [my translation]' were therefore proposed: changes that, in the Government's view, were in the spirit of the CRC (Prop. 1996/97:25, 248). These proposals resulted in some amendments of principal importance in the Aliens Act *inter alia*, a rule concerning the child's best interests in the introductory provisions of the Act and a rule about hearing children in the course of proceedings.[2] The amendments came into force in January 1997.[3]

The Aliens Act has been criticized as being difficult to apply, not least after the revision mentioned above.[4] A number of legal clashes may occur and different interests conflict in its application. As regards the rule about the child's best interests, the Swedish Council on Legislation also remarked, in its expert opinion on the government bill, that the proposed formulation of the rule would provide little guidance to the authorities in the difficult task of balancing interests, which quite frequently occurs in these matters. The Council concluded that it was not possible, at that moment, to give a definite answer about whether the rule would have a real tangible impact on the application of the law (Prop. 1996/97:25, 363). It may therefore, not come as a surprise that applications have continued to be the subject of harsh criticism, especially in matters concerning children.[5] Studies made so far, suggest that these rules have had limited, if any, impact on practical applications.[6]

---

2 1 Chapter 1 Section 2 § Aliens Act and 11 Chapter 1 a Section Aliens Act, respectively.

3 SFS 1996:1379; Prop. 1996/97:25; 1996/97:SfU5; rskr. 1996/97:80. The changes were made in connection with other major alterations in the Aliens Act, for instance changes in the rules granting subsidiary protection, the introduction of a possibility for the Government to pass regulations on a time-limited residence permit for groups in mass flux situations and limitations of immigration on grounds of family ties. For an overview of the changes, see 1996/97:SfU5, 1–2.

4 It was also remarked in the government bill that the proposed changes were relatively comprehensive and that this entails in part a lack of lucidity, which brings to the fore an overhaul of the whole Aliens Act. See Prop. 1996/97:25, 31.

5 The criticism has principally concerned the asylum process. See for instance Barnombudsmannen 2000; Halvorsen 2004; Juhlén 2003.

6 In the above-mentioned study by Karin Juhlén, 32 per cent of the children who were seeking asylum together with their family, and claiming their own reasons for asylum or humanitarian reasons, had their claims thoroughly assessed, in the decision. See Juhlén 2003, 5. In an earlier study made by Johanna Schiratzki it was concluded that the best interests of the child was primarily considered when determining whether a residence permit should be granted on humanitarian grounds. See Schiratzki 2000, 90. See also memorandum by Dagerås, UD 98/601/MP, 14; Juhlén 2003, 44; Barnombudsmannen 2000, 11. Children were considered, however, in such way, even before the amendments. See SOU 1996:115, 66–67, where the Child's Committee refers to a survey of practice made by Barbro Thorblad, on behalf of the Committee on Refugee Politics. The Child's Committee concluded in its own

The apparent gap between the legislator's intentions and the application of the law raises questions about the limitations of law and how the spirit and intentions in the CRC have been implemented in the Aliens Act, and, in view of this, the limits of law. In this chapter, I aim to discuss two questions regarding this comprehensive issue, that is what are the legal premises for the rules in question and what are their implications for a legal study about children in matters concerning residence permits. However, as my perception of law and legal knowledge is significant for the analysis, I will start with a theoretical background and the assumptions on which that analysis is based. Furthermore, the strategies that shape the legislation, procedurally as well as materially, are important premises for effective implementation and therefore central to the questions asked, and consequently to the methods used, in the study. A description of these premises will therefore be given in the following part. Finally, I will discuss the implications these premises might have for a legal study and why studies in this field of law are relevant. I will also, as a part of this concluding discussion, argue for different feminist approaches to the subject, for I believe that they can supply new and valuable knowledge.

The chapter is based on findings from an ongoing doctoral study concerning the status of children in the determination of residence permit. After the chapter was finished in October 2004, there have been comprehensive changes concerning the legislation described. Most important is that a new Aliens Act (SFS 2005:716) has come into force. The new law involves a changeover from a handling by administrative authorities and the Government to a system where appeals are tried in administrative courts. It has however been questioned whether the new law implies any vital changes concerning the material regulations. Where necessary, elements of the new legislation are addressed

Feminist Approaches to Children's Rights and Child Law

Feminist perspectives on gender relations have in many ways illuminated power relations other than those concerning gender. There are indeed clear parallels between women and children. A case in point is that historically women and children have been considered to be in need of particular protection, which has motivated a specific regime of rights – but also exclusion from rights. For this reason, theories that have been developed by feminist legal scholars also form a part of the discourse on children's rights and child law.[7] Many of these scholars emphatically disclaim

---

survey of practice, which was made shortly after the alterations came into force, that it was difficult to form an opinion as to whether the legislators' intentions about the child's best interests had had any impact on the application. See SOU 1997:116, 164.

In 2003, a committee was set up to overhaul the material rules in the Aliens Act. See Dir. 2003:28. An integral part of their assignment was to direct particular attention to how the rule about the child's best interests is applied in matters where children are concerned. The Committee in its report, SOU 2004:74, has *inter alia* proposed a new rule about the granting of residence permits on humanitarian grounds to children.

7 For example, see Minow 1986, 9. Drawing parallels between women and children may, however, also be considered problematic. See for instance Bhabha 2002.

their ability to provide one answer to what the law is or what it should be and criticize any such analysis (See Ratner and Slaughter 1999, 413).[8] Instead they challenge the very categories of 'law' and 'non-law', and seek to expose and question the limited bases for law's claim to objectivity and impartiality (Charlesworth 1999, 379; see also the discussion on page 392). Hence, the concept of law and the production of legal (and other) knowledge in itself, is an important part of what is analysed, that is what knowledge is privileged and what knowledge is silenced and devalued. (See Gerhard 2001, 156ff.; Svensson 2001, 23; Charlesworth 1999, 380, 386; see also Bridgeman and Monk 2000, 2).

Many of these scholars also take a critical stand towards the concept of the subject and the holder of rights and the private/public divide, which historically have implied the exclusion and subordination of women; this is a basic philosophical critique of the subjectivity of western philosophy, the enlightenment concept of reason and rationality and modern social contract theories (see Gerhard 2001, 151ff., 158ff.).[9] This critique has been equally affirmed in children's rights theory.[10] In brief the argument is that the legal theories that have formed western thinking about rights, for instance 'the will theory', have implied that rights are seen as the exercise of free will and the ability to enforce the performance of an obligation. The 'interest theory', however, has made it possible to define children as rights' holders – *just* because of the child's presumed lack of experience and particular need for protection. The individual's capacity or competence is therefore central to our understanding of rights, regardless of whether we emphasize self-determination and free will or interest and protection (see for instance Hunt Federle 1994, 343, with further references). Thus, the analogy between women and children is flawed, because children, as Katherine Hunt Federle points out, have not been able to redefine themselves as competent beings (Hunt Federle 1994, 344, 354).[11] Instead, as argued

---

8 Svensson argues that legal dogmatics 'presuppose a fiction that it is possible to freeze the constantly changing law in specific moments or situations [my translation]'. See Svensson, 1997, 32. The idea that there is 'no one answer' is, however, shared by most legal scholars and by academics in general. According to Ratner and Slaughter, because of this '[t]he debate should instead be recast in terms of *relative* indeterminacy: between methods insisting that because there is no *one* answer, any answer is possible, and those that contend that even in the absence of a single answer, some answers are manifestly *better* [my italic] than others and that the lawyer's job is to narrow that range.' See Ratner and Slaughter 1999, 420. This is however a theoretical standpoint that is just as political as any other standpoint. See for instance discussion by Davies 2002, 11. See also note 12, below.

9 For a reply to the feminist critique from the standpoint of the Kantian thesis, see Tesón, 1998, 157–178.

10 See for instance Minow 1986, 17–18, where Martha Minow argues that rights rhetoric makes an account of rights for children problematic by unnecessarily excluding interpersonal relationships and emphasizing individual autonomy. According to Hunt Federle, the emphasis on relationships may, however, be problematic in connection with children's rights. See Hunt Federle 1994, 354ff.

11 Still, it can be argued that women too 'are on the margins of the international legal system [...] viewed in a very limited way, chiefly as victims, particularly as mothers, or potential mothers, and accordingly in need of protection.' See Charlesworth and Chinkin

by Jo Bridgeman and Daniel Monk, 'children are perceived in terms of lack and, consequently, as vulnerable and in need of protection' (Bridgeman and Monk, 2000, 5). This perception of children, that they have needs that must be protected by adults is, as described by Anna Hollander, anchored in the CRC and also predominates in the Nordic children's rights movement (Hollander 1998, 194).

The category of child has been, and continues to be, seen as natural. Our perception of children as vulnerable and in need of protection is, however, according to Bridgeman and Monk, one of the implications of the dominance of the discourse of developmental psychology and its construction of childhood as a process, which ends when a child becomes an adult. But attitudes towards children, expectations of them and understandings of their capacities are not unitary, fixed or static, which implies that the meanings given to childhood are historically and culturally specific, that is socially constructed. Furthermore, Bridgeman and Monk argue, legal discourse is 'heavily implicated in the production of the category childhood.' (See Bridgeman and Monk 2000, 3–5, with further references).

As it appears, this is a contextualized approach to law and legal knowledge which builds on social constructionist thinking.[12] As described by others in this volume, a social constructionist theory of law focuses on how law relates to the social, in that it not only regulates something that exists prior to law, but also is in itself part of the social construction of the same reality. The interest in law as discourse, how it contributes to the construction of both social and legal concepts and how law is contextualized, Monica Burman notes, poses the need for methodological tools other than those the traditional legal dogmatic[13] approach can provide. She advocates the use of discourse analysis. In discourse analysis the theory and method are intertwined, as a theoretical and methodological totality building on social constructionism (see Burman, this volume).[14] However, among feminist legal scholars, there are no homogeneous theoretical formations. As pointed out by Hilary Charlesworth, no single theoretical approach or method seems adequate when confronted with a

2000, 48, with further references; see also the discussion on p. 335; Charlesworth 1999, 381; Kouvo 2004, 35.

12 According to Svensson, contemporary academic thinking in general has abandoned the search for the foundation of knowledge. Instead, knowledge is seen as something contextual and constructed, where different variants of constructionism are common. See also Niemi-Kieseläinen, Honkatukia and Ruuskanen, this volume. Nevertheless, Svensson argues, jurists often act as if legal knowledge has a true foundation. See Svensson, this volume.

13 About the academic dogmatic position in Swedish legal scholarship, see Svensson this volume.

14 For an introduction to social constructionism, see for instance Burr 2003. For a critical analysis of how to use the conception 'social constructionism', see Hacking 1999, 9–10. Hacking is of the opinion that the concept has often been misused. He takes female refugees as an example and asks why anyone would use the title 'The Social Construction of Women Refugees', when it is obvious that women are refugees as a consequence of a sequence of social events. What is socially constructed is, according to Hacking, not in the first instance the individual people, the women refugees, but the classification 'woman refugee'. This kind of person, as a specific *kind* of person, the *idea* of the woman refugee, is socially constructed.

concrete issue. Instead, a range of theories and methods may be necessary to excavate the issues (Charlesworth 1999, 381; see also Svensson, this volume).[15] The use of a range of techniques may lead to charges of methodological and theoretical impurity, but according to Charlesworth, such impurity is inevitable in the analysis of complex situations (Charlesworth 1999, 381). For all that, Eva-Maria Svensson argues, the use of a variety of methods makes it possible to highlight a problem in many ways, which should produce a more complete description and a more nuanced answer than if only one method is used (Svensson 1997, 30). The approach in feminist legal studies is, however, rather to ask questions and start a conversation than to yield a 'single triumphant truth' (see for instance Ratner and Slaughter 1999, 415, 417, 421; see also Svensson 1997, 23). The output of this process is not knowledge in terms of statements, but may very well be 'consciousness raising' or 'exposing notions' (Wennström 2003, 342, in reference to MacKinnon 1989; Svensson 1997; see also Burr 2003, 55).

In brief, this feminist critique and approach to law, contains the theoretical frame for my analysis. The assumptions that it is based on were, however, not a part of my understanding when I began the study. Rather, they have developed during the research process, in reciprocal activity with the material. That is, I initially had a traditional approach to the study but found early on that, because of the character of the legislation, a traditional legal study would not suffice and that other methodological tools would be necessary to probe the subject. Furthermore, even if I had an idea at the beginning of the study that there would be parallels in feminist legal theory and theories about children's rights and child law, it was not until I had started to study the application of the law, that I found that feminist legal theory would work as an analytical tool which would explain my findings, both regarding the application *and* the legislation. For this reason, my theoretical assumptions and the results are interconnected. This may be inconsistent with general scientific ideals, as the object should be separated from its subject (see Svensson, this volume), but social constructionist theory of law denies that such a separation is possible. According to Vivien Burr, the task of researchers is, therefore, rather to acknowledge and work with their own intrinsic involvement in the research process and the part that this plays in the results that are produced (Burr 2003, 152).[16] Thus, what follows below is my understanding of the law and the legal premises. It is neither objective nor complete. From a social constructionist perspective, it never could be.

---

15 For an example within child law, see Bridgeman and Monk 2000, which contains a variety of feminist and critical theoretical perspectives, such as discourse analysis, autopoiesis and poststructral and comparative approaches together with empirical research.

16 'Reflexivity' is a term that is widely used in social constructionist writing. It refers, among others, to the fact that social constructionism itself is not exempt from the critical stance it brings to bear on other theories. See Burr 2003, 157. See also Charlesworth 2000, 22.

The Law and the Legal Premises

The legal premises for the rules are, as argued above, important for the aims and methods used in my study. I will therefore continue with a description of these premises: the general provisions of the proceedings, the technical formulation (legal construction) of the Aliens Act and the rules in question, as well as the material content (constructions in law) of these rules.

General Provisions of the Proceedings

In March 2006, a new Aliens Act came into force in Sweden, which introduced new rules relating to the circumstances in which judicial review would be available as well as a new process for dealing with such reviews. As already mentioned the new order involves a changeover from a handling by administrative authorities and the Government to a system where appeals are tried in administrative courts. The possibility that the Government has had to direct the application of the law by issuing regulations however remains.

The Aliens Act does not make clear the child's legal status in the process. It is nevertheless, clear that the child is a party and has a right to plead but no right to take proceedings (see also Migrationsverket 2001, 7).[17] The child is normally represented in the matter by a parent or another legal guardian. Sometimes a joint public counsel is appointed for the child and the parent.[18] If the child is unaccompanied, a custodian is appointed for the child.[19] When a public counsel is appointed for an unaccompanied

17 In practical applications it has, however, been accepted that unaccompanied children may submit their own application. See also the internal handbook of the Migration Board, for the handling of asylum matters, Section 37.1, about children without legal guardians in Sweden.

18 In the internal handbook of the Migration Board, for the handling of asylum matters, in Section 37.2, about children in families, it is stated that, as a rule, there is no need for a public counsel for the child, as the counsel that may have been appointed for the family will also protect the child's interest.

19 4 Chapter 3 Section 2 § Act on Certain International Judicial Circumstances Concerning Marriage and Guardianship (Lag om vissa internationella rättsförhållanden rörande äktenskap och förmynderskap [IÄL], SFS 1904:26 s. 1) compared to 11 Chapter 1 Section 11 § Parental Code (Föräldrabalken [FB], SFS 1949:381). See also description of current order in prop. 1996/97:25, 233. It has emerged that there is a need to strengthen the protection for unaccompanied children. The major problem is considered to be that the present custodians for unaccompanied children can only take the place of the child's guardian, that is their authority mainly concerns economic affairs. The possibilities the custodian has to decide in matters concerning the personal relations of the child are thus strictly limited. In the interim report, SOU 2003:51, it was suggested that a possibility for a chief guardian to appoint a custodian, who can take the place of the caretaker as well as of the guardian, is created within the scope of a specific legislation aiming at unaccompanied children. It was also suggested that a child who has reached the age of 15 should be allowed to file an application for a residence permit. In order to ensure that a child who has not yet reached the age of 15 is also given the right to have an application for a residence permit examined, the inquiry proposed that a new section should be entered in 11 Chapter 1 c Section Aliens Act, which prescribes

child, the counsel is the child's representative in the matter to which the appointment refers, without being specially appointed.[20]

While a child has no right to take proceedings, the child has a right to be heard. As mentioned initially, the rule concerning the child's best interests and the rule about hearing children in the course of proceedings are fundamental to my study. The rules are based on articles 3 and 12 respectively, in the CRC;[21] but these articles should not be seen in isolation, as 'the Convention is indivisible and its articles interdependent'.[22] The articles in the Convention should also be considered in connection with other international obligations.

As the CRC is neither incorporated nor self-executing in Swedish law, the Swedish legislation, preparatory work and practice are the primary basis for the interpretation of the rules.[23] It is, however, considered as a general principle that Swedish legislation should be interpreted in conformity with international obligations. When there is a conflict between a rule in the Convention and an explicit regulation in law, the regulation shall nevertheless take precedence (Prop. 1996/97:25, 245; see also Strömberg and Melander 2003, 26).

The government bill concerning the rules in question states that the formulation of the Act concerning children emanates in the first place from the basic respect for

---

that a custodian, or a public counsel, has an obligation to apply for a residence permit on account of the unaccompanied child, if the child has a need for such a permit.

20 11 Chapter 1 b Section Aliens Act.

21 Provisions for protection of children have been expressed in most instruments dealing with human rights. At a European level, there are for instance references to the principles about the best interests of the child and respect for the views of the child in the Charter of Fundamental Rights of the European Union, OJ C 364 18.12.2000, 11-22.

22 Implementation Handbook for the Convention on the Rights of the Child, UNICEF (1998), XVII. The Committee on the Rights of the Child has highlighted articles 3 (1) (best interests of the child) and 12 (respect for the views of the child) alongside articles 2 (non-discrimination) and 6 (child's right to life and maximum survival and development) as general principles of relevance for the implementation of the whole Convention. The articles must also, of course, be viewed with regard to the general provision on parental guidance laid down in article 5 (general provisions of the CRC are laid down in articles 1–5 and 41).

23 No specific legislative measures were taken when ratifying the CRC, since Swedish law was considered to be in accordance with the Convention. See Prop. 1989/90:107, 28. It has, however, been commonly accepted that treaties must be incorporated into Swedish law in one way or another, in order to be applied by Swedish courts and authorities. In Sweden, incorporation and transformation have been applied in practice, to incorporate treaties. Presumption of norm harmony, either by the Parliament or by interpretation in conformity by courts, has also been applied to avoid conflicts between national law and treaties. The Constitutional Committee of the Swedish Parliament has pronounced that incorporation and transformation are acceptable from a constitutional point of view. See 1995/96:SoU4; 1995/96: KU2y. Whereas whether presumption of norm harmony can be seen as an independent method for incorporation has been called into question. See Strömberg and Melander 2003, 23ff. The distinction between monism/dualism has, however, been questioned by Swedish legal scholars. Also, as regards general international law, Swedish legislation and practice, to a lesser extent, bear the stamp of dualism. See Bring and Mahmoudi 2001, 43ff. See also SOU 1996:115, 22–23.

human rights (Prop. 1996/97:25, 244). As regards consideration of the CRC, it was pointed out that children's specific vulnerability and needs in many ways motivate special treatment in relation to adults. It was also noted that there are good reasons for giving particular consideration to children in the asylum process, as they have not themselves chosen to leave their country and cannot survey the consequences in the same way as an adult (Prop. 1996/97:25, 246). Furthermore, the Government referred to a statement by the Child's Committee that the basic outlook in the CRC, non-discrimination, the child's best interests, the right to be heard and the right to life and development, determines a conduct towards children at the international level and that 'this attitude, this child perspective, shall permeate all decisions that concern children [my translation].' (Prop. 1996/97:25, 245).

Legal Construction and Constructions in Law

The Swedish Aliens Act is of a pronounced framework legislation character, which allows an extensive scope for assessing the circumstances in each case.[24] The first section of the Act contains a declarative regulation, with the introductory provisions of the law. The rule concerning the best interests of the child is placed in this section. The second paragraph in the section prescribes that '[t]he Act shall be applied in such a way that the liberty of aliens is not restricted more than necessary in each individual case. In cases where a child is involved, special attention shall be given to what is required, bearing in mind the child's health and development and the best interests of the child otherwise.' The positioning of the rule in the introductory provisions signifies that it will function as a general rule for interpreting the law (Wikrén and Sandesjö 2002, 40). The Government was also of the opinion that *all* kinds of matters should be covered by the regulation. Without generally bowing to the public interest in regulating immigration, such a rule would have a strong and meaningful significance. It would, it was declared, have a real significance, '[b]oth when assessing whether humanitarian grounds for granting a residence permit are present as well as in the whole asylum process [my translation].' (Prop. 1996/97:25, 248).

Deciding about residence permits comprises both assessing the best interests of the child and balancing interests. Regarding the assessment of the child's best interests, it was noted in the government bill that what is best for a child in a given situation is not usually unequivocal. However, the ethnocentric view, which is sometimes expressed in the political migration debate, that it is almost always considered best for children to stay in Sweden, irrespective of linguistic, cultural and national background and belonging, was repudiated (Prop. 1996/97:25, 249).

When determining the best interests of the child, one important question is how these interests are to be determined *vis-à-vis* the child's parents. This issue, of the extent to which the authorities should intervene in the private sphere and how conflicting interests within the family should be resolved in the decision about a residence permit, has not been thoroughly pursued in the preparatory work. This issue

24 See Lagrådet 2002; See also discussion in Prop. 1988/89:86, 51, in reference to SOU 1983:29, 71. Generally on framework legislation, see Chapter 1, this volume.

was, however, discussed briefly by the Child's Committee, its principal standpoint being that the parents have the main responsibility and that it is primarily they who can best decide what is best for the child. At the same time it was pointed out that this does not relieve the authorities of their responsibility to consider the child's best interests in various decisions and that society has a responsibility to implement the rights stated in the CRC. It was then declared that '[i]f the parents act in a way that would be contrary to the child's best interests (despite that not being their intention) then the authority has an obligation to attend to the best interests of the child [my translation]' (SOU 1996:115, 53).

The Government did not specifically address this problem, but did touch upon it, in connection with a discussion about children in families that are in hiding. In that case it was clearly stated that it is self-evident that the parents have the main responsibility for their children, but that this does not release the authorities from their responsibility. Furthermore, the Government pointed out that parents assume a heavy responsibility by hiding their children from the authorities rather than leaving the country. There is in these situations, it was remarked, a major risk that the child will be harmed. The Government found, however, that information to the parents and others involved would probably not achieve a great deal. Instead efforts with regard to these exposed children must be directed, as far as possible, towards preventing such situations arising where absence without leaving is a way of gaining a residence permit (Prop. 1996/97:25, 252).

Also of importance regarding the best interests of the child in relation to the parents is a statement, in the description of current order in the government bill, that in matters where children are concerned by reason of family ties, it is evident that great consideration must be taken to the children's situation and whether they would be subjected to a separation from either of the parents (Prop. 1996/97:25, 107, in reference to Prop. 1994/95:179, 20). It was, however, also remarked that at the ratification of the CRC it was considered that the Convention does not involve any prohibition of a separation of parents and children when some of them are hiding or kept hidden, nor in other cases, but it was also noted that as a guiding principle measures that lead to a separation should be avoided (Prop 1996/97:25, 23, in reference to 1989/90:SoU28, 20). In connection with this it should also be noted that article 8 (the right to respect for private and family life) of the European Convention for the Protection of Human Rights and Fundamental Freedoms,[25] was specifically mentioned in the outline of international obligations in the government bill.[26]

25 European Convention for the Protection of Human Rights and Fundamental Freedoms, 4 November 1950, ETS No. 5. The Convention is contained in Swedish law, by incorporation (SFS 1994:1219).

26 See description of current order in Prop. 1996/97:25, 225 (see also references in the section about grounds for migration policy, page 48). Provisions for the protection of the unit of a family have been expressed in the CRC and in most instruments dealing with human rights, beginning with the Universal Declaration of Human Rights (1948), GA Resolution 217 A (III). The 1951 Refugee Convention (Convention relating to the Status of Refugees, 28 July 1951, 189 UNTS 137) and the 1967 Protocol (Protocol relating to the Status of Refugees, 31 January 1967, 606 UNTS 267) does not, however, refer to the principle. The only reference occurs in the final act of the conference that adopted the Convention. See Final Act of the

Concerning applications by parents for family reunification in Sweden, if there is no 'need of protection',[27] the starting point regarding unaccompanied children is that all actions possible are to be taken, so that the children shall be able to reunify with their parents in their home country as soon as possible. Nevertheless, if after a careful investigation, it is shown that the child has been abandoned in the real sense, a permanent residence permit is to be granted (Prop. 1996/97:25, 250–251).[28] Of interest in connection with this issue is also a discussion in the government bill about the need for a representative for unaccompanied children, where the situation concerning the granting of a residence permit was compared with that in cases where the *Care of Young Persons Act* (SFS 1990:52) is applied. It was then concluded that in these cases, a conflict of interest can be presumed between the custodian and the child and that the situation differs from that in an application for a residence permit. The Government, however, was of the opinion that a similar order should be introduced in the aliens province for other reasons and it referred to the fact that sometimes it may take some time before a custodian is appointed and to the 'regular' character and aim of such an appointment. It was also emphasized that the task of an appointed custodian is to look after the child's best interests as a whole,[29] while the task of the public counsel is merely to represent the child in the proceedings concerning the residence permit. Furthermore, it was pointed out that in many situations it is not the best solution for the child to reside in Sweden instead of being with her or his family in the country of origin and that in these cases it is the important task of the custodian to protect the child's overall interest (Prop. 1996/97:25, 258).

Regarding the balancing of interests, it was pointed out that the basic balancing between different interests takes place in the legislative procedures. It was, however, at the same time remarked that interests must be balanced in each case for each child who is affected by the decision and that it is necessary to be able to consider the specific circumstances that may occur in the individual case. Furthermore, it was concluded that the child's best interests could be provided for by, for example, the possibility of granting a residence permit on humanitarian grounds, where the reasons may be somewhat less serious and weighty when children are concerned (Prop. 1996/97:25, 284; see also 248-249 and description of current order 228).

As mentioned earlier, the Government was of the opinion that the rule would have a real significance, not only when assessing humanitarian grounds, but in the whole asylum process. It was, however, not expounded in the government bill

---

United Nations Conference of Plenipotentiaries on the Status of Refugees and Stateless Persons, 1951, UN doc. A/CONF.2/108/Rev.1, 26 Nov. 1952, Recommendation B.

27 The term 'aliens in need of protection' [skyddsbehövande] comprises refugees as defined in the 1951 Refugee Convention and the 1967 Protocol relating to the Status of Refugees, as well as 'aliens in need of protection otherwise', that is reasons due to a need for international protection. Humanitarian reasons are, however, not included in the definition and also fall outside the scope of the asylum process in Sweden.

28 See also description of current order, Prop. 1996/97:25, 229, where the Government pointed out that in many cases parents have been granted residence permits for family reunification in Sweden.

29 Compare with note 19, above.

exactly how the rule could have a strong and meaningful significance in the asylum determination process. It was observed, nevertheless, that the principle of the best interests of the child indicates that a permit to stay in Sweden may be granted in a considerable number of cases. It was pointed out, however, that it cannot be said that it would generally harm the psychosocial development of a child to accompany her or his parents to another country, particularly if it is the child's home country. According to the Government, this is also true for children who have been in Sweden throughout the considerable, but limited, time that a final decision about granting a residence permit may take under normal circumstances. It was also remarked that it is inevitable that the deciding authorities will have to strike a balance between the best interests of the child and other interests, even in those cases where a return may entail serious strains on the child. The necessity of upholding the requirements for settlement in Sweden constitutes such an interest. It should be decisive as, 'to what degree the child's psychosocial development can be presumed to be permanently harmed by moving back to the home country, to be distinguished from the, in most cases, temporary strains that a migration to other environments often involves for a child [my translation]' (Prop. 1996/97:25, 249–250).

The rule about hearing children in the course of proceedings prescribes that '[w]hen assessing permit cases under this Act, the viewpoints of any children affected by a decision in the matter shall be ascertained, unless this is unsuitable, and consideration shall be given to what a child has said if this is justified bearing in mind the child's age and level of maturity.' The rule thus contains both a procedural and a material part. In the commentary to the statute in the government bill, it was stated that, as a rule, the child should be heard in connection with an inquiry when applying for a residence permit. It was also noted that the rule is formulated in such a way that it is more far-reaching than article 12 in the CRC, which is limited to the child's opinion. It was, however, at the same time pointed out that the child should not be heard when it is unsuitable, which, for instance, may be the case if the child is young or if the child's mental health precludes the child being heard (Prop. 1996/97:25, 297–298).

It is not, the Government pointed out, sufficient to allow a parent to express the child's view when there may be conflicting interests or if there are reasons to believe that the parent will not be able to deliver the child's opinion. It was, however, at the same time remarked that it could not always, at least not without hesitation, be said to be in the best interests of the child to be heard. The child would in such a case be placed in an exposed situation, with pressure from her or his parents and the child herself/himself to support unambiguously the parents' story. In a case where their story is false this would be too hard for the child. It should, the Government declared, be up to the Migration Board to determine from the individual child's age and maturity if and how the child should be allowed to express her or his views. Furthermore, the Government shared the opinion of the Child's Committee that the right to be heard should be directed to elucidating the child's situation. It was, however, noted that it is inevitable that the child's statements may have an influence on the asylum inquiry for the whole family. The inquiry, it was pointed out, should not only ensure that the reasons for asylum are elucidated, but also elicit any circumstances that may reveal the existence of other reasons for granting a residence permit. It was thus concluded that there is also a basis for assessing what is in the best interests of the child (Prop. 1996/97:25, 262–263).

... a Vessel to be Filled ... with Plurality and Autonomy – or Family Unity?

As described above the Swedish Aliens Act is of a pronounced framework legislation character. Furthermore, the principle concerning the child's best interests has been incorporated into the Swedish Aliens Act as an introductory provision. Hence, it is constructed as a procedural rule which is intended to have significance for the material determination of the grounds for the granting of a residence permit. According to Stig Strömholm, such introductory provisions constitute a kind of *leges imperfectae*. There are, in his opinion, reasons to question how the legislator can conduct itself in a way that must be considered fundamentally unfamiliar for its assignment and, furthermore, what functions policy statements such as this might have in the practical application of the law. Strömholm nevertheless finds it likely that these rules could have some real impact, as data for interpretation, 'states of direction', in the application of concrete rules in the legislation at issue. The guiding power of framework legislation, in his opinion, is the same as in the case of introductory provisions (see Strömholm 1996, 263ff.).

The rule concerning the child's best interests constitutes a rule of adjustment, which means that it is constructed in order to make it possible to balance different interests in *each* decision. The preparatory work, however, lacks more specific guidance about how the best interests of the child are to be assessed or balanced against other interests (see the criticism by the Council on Legislation, commented on above). The reference in the government bill to the degree the child's psychosocial development can be presumed to sustain permanent harm, however, limits the range for the balancing of interests. The balancing of interests thus builds on considerations of a goal-rational character, as it forces the decision maker to assess the risks which might follow from a refusal of entry or an expulsion. These are considerations that are largely based on knowledge from other disciplines, such as expert opinions about mental health and suicide risk etc.

Likewise, the procedural rule about hearing children also constitutes a rule of adjustment, since there is to be an assessment of whether it is inappropriate to elucidate what the child has to say and because the child's age and maturity has to be factored into the consideration. The rule thus contains a balance between the interest of hearing the child and the child's need for protection. In this case too the balancing of interests builds on considerations of a goal-rational character, as it forces the decision maker to assess the risks which might follow from the child being heard. Furthermore, there is an assessment of maturity. This is an assessment that is normally made by other professions, but in these matters is made by the deciding authority itself.

The wording in the rule about the child's best interests as well as the rule about hearing children in the course of proceedings suggests that they are duty-imposing norms (see Eckhoff and Sundby 1991, 67), directed to the authorities applying the law – but without sanctions. As described, it is clear nonetheless that both rules are constructed as rules of adjustment, involving considerations of a goal-rational character. According to Håkan Hydén, rules of adjustment are connected with a balancing of interests model, where the aim is to achieve a compromise between conflicting interests. The legal assessment in this model is made in the light of each specific case, a form of *ex existere* judgement (Hydén 2002, 139). Adjustment rules, according to Torstein Eckhoff and Nils Kristian Sundby, are norms that are open in that they give free rein to discretion so that the legal decision becomes dependant on adjustments between various factors, such as considerations, arguments and interests. There are often correcting-lines tied to these rules, that define which factors are relevant (or irrelevant) and sometimes also how these factors are to be taken into consideration (Eckhoff and Sundby 1991, 108ff.). The reference in the government bill to the degree the child's psychosocial development can be presumed to sustain permanent harm constitutes such a correcting-line.

According to Hydén, goal-means rules state certain goals that the decision maker must endeavour to attain and the means that are available for this purpose. In the goal-rational model of argumentation decisions are taken on the basis of a prediction of the consequences of the decision. The decision is distinguished by considerations *ex ante*, which means that the decision maker must make predictions about the future that are tied to the decision. This concerns a position taken towards causal relations, which presupposes knowledge about how reality is constituted. Hence, rules constructed in this way build on standpoints that presuppose other than legal knowledge. The significance of professional knowledge and expert participation is increased in this model (Hydén 2002, 137–140).

In summary, the normative content of the rules is not clear, as the preparatory work provides little guidance about how the rules are to be interpreted or applied in the individual case (compare also with Schiratzki 2000, 83). This is due to the legal construction, which *aims* to make it possible to take individual considerations in each case. In addition, case law has primarily considered children in connection with humanitarian grounds. The precedent value of these cases is, in most cases, limited because of their individual character.[30] Moreover, the doctrine in this legal field is very limited (see for instance Norström 2004, 31–32, 181, 257, 281, with further references).

Notwithstanding this normative uncertainty, it is obvious that children are perceived by the legislator as being dependant and vulnerable, in need of protection, primarily from their parents, but also from conflicts with their parents.[31] In my opinion, it is also clear that it is mainly the child seeking asylum that is seen as an individual, concerning need for protection, due to a risk of persecution or for humanitarian reasons – *but also,* and not least, protection from her or his parents' harmful measures to gain a residence permit in cases where the application was determined as being unfounded to begin with. Thus, the legislator does recognize

---

30 About the individual character in these cases, see description of current order in Prop. 1996/97:25, 229.

31 The notion that children are to be protected from conflicts with their parents is an expression of what can be defined as 'the principle of shared interests'. According to Minow, this principle suggests that 'individual rights are not just unnecessary, but may actually damage the relationships between parent and child'. See Minow 1986, 13.

some need for intervention between children and parents. Apart from this, children are viewed as appendages of their parents, objects that can easily be moved from one place to another, as long as they are not separated from a parent. In other respects, children's rights are reduced to *just* family unity. The principle of family unity or, at least, the active, competent and independent subject defined in it,[32] however, seems also to set the standard in the asylum process, even though children appear to be in focus in this process, for the legislator seems to have forgotten the meaning of childhood when determining asylum. This can be gleaned from our understanding of children as well as our understanding of persecution and the grounds for it. (For a more thorough discussion about children in the asylum process, see Nilsson 2005.)

The Borderland of Law – Limitations and Possibilities

As mentioned initially, this concluding part of the chapter aims to discuss the implications the legal premises that have been described might have for a legal study and why it is important to conduct studies in this field of law.[33] Furthermore, I will argue in favour of various feminist approaches to the subject.

32 In the earlier-mentioned recommendation B on family unity (see note 26, above), the states were recommended to take the necessary measures for the protection of the refugee's family, especially with a view to ensuring that the unity of the refugee's family is maintained 'particularly in cases where *the head of the family* [my italics] has fulfilled the necessary conditions for admission to a particular country.' See Final Act of the United Nations Conference of Plenipotentiaries on the Status of Refugees and Stateless Persons, 1951, UN doc. A/CONF.2/108/Rev1., 26 Nov. 1952, Recommendation B. The significance of the principle of family unity when determining refugee status for a minor is, according to the UNHCR Handbook, that if a minor is accompanied by one (or both) of his parents, or another family member on whom he is dependent, who requests refugee status, the minors' own refugee status will be determined according to the principle of family unity. See UNHCR Handbook on Procedures and Criteria for Determining Refugee Status under the 1951 Convention and the 1967 Protocol relating to the Status of Refugees, HCR/IP/4/Eng/REV.1, paragraph 213, in reference to paragraph 181–188. In the Council Directive 2004/83/EC of 29 April 2004 on Minimum Standards for the Qualification and Status of Third Country Nationals and Stateless Persons as Refugees or as Persons who Otherwise Need International Protection and the Content of the Protection Granted, OJ L 304, 30.9.2004, 12–23, that has been adopted by the Council of the European Union, family members of the beneficiary of refugee or subsidiary protection status, who do not individually qualify for such status, are 'entitled to claim [a residence permit]' (article 23, paragraph 2 compared with article 24). In the earlier proposal for a council directive, Proposal for a Council Directive on Minimum Standards for the Qualification and Status of Third Country Nationals and Stateless Persons as Refugees or as Persons who Otherwise Need International Protection, COM (2001) 510 final, OJ C 051 E, 26.2.2002, 325–334, the dependant family member was 'entitled to a status equal to that of the main applicant for asylum' (article 6, paragraph 1). It appears that the directive that was finally adopted provides for a less stringent reading of the principle than the proposal or the earlier mentioned recommendation B.

33 As will be argued, the 'specific characteristics' that have been described motivate a wider approach to the subject, but there is, in my opinion, reason enough for such an approach in the fact that 'the key to openness lies already in the voluminous and sophisticated

Some legal scholars are of the opinion that aliens law is influenced by politics in a way that makes it uninteresting for people who seek legal doctrine,[34] and indeed even with the new processes of judicial review, this branch of law has a decidedly political character. Furthermore, as argued, the normative content of the rules studied is obscure. The legislator intended it to be so. In this 'normative emptiness' lie the limitations – but also the possibilities. In my opinion, the normative uncertainty and the absence of guiding practice from the highest courts make it an important task for legal scholarship, especially since many decisions in aliens matters may have even more far-reaching consequences for the individual than those made in the criminal process (compare with the systemic conception of criminal law, described by Burman, in this volume).

These legal strategies are, as argued above, central to the aims and methods in the study. They imply, particularly in a legal field where the risk of conflicting interests is apparent, that the rules and their application must be analysed contextually. Furthermore, the character of the legislation seems to set some limits. From the dogmatic point of view the purpose of the study cannot be to 'determine current law', but rather to highlight different legal problems (see for instance Lagerqvist Veloz Roca 2000, 6). According to Hydén, in cases where legislation lacks a more precise content, one has to reconstruct the decision-making process and examine the normative premises which are open or hidden in the decision. By systematizing the decisions one can thereafter identify normative patterns and draw general conclusions from the groups of cases (Hydén 1992, 97). Claes Sandgren advocates a similar approach. He argues that in cases where the legislation is of a pronounced framework character it may be difficult to determine the content in current law in a traditional way and that a 'massive study' of authority praxis or inferior praxis in these cases can supply information about the real application and function of the legislation (Sandgren 1995–96, 742).

Yet, it could also, from a dogmatic point of view, be argued that because of the legal strategy which has been used, 'the law that is made' in each decision should be considered as a 'source of law'.[35] I see *no principal point* in expanding the limits of law in such a way. As described above, feminist legal studies often contain a social constructionist approach to law and legal knowledge, and from a social constructionist position it would be a vain project, both artificial and irrelevant. It would mean acting as if there is a true foundation of law and as if legal science is limited to certain sources of knowledge. It would thus also involve a serious pedagogical problem. Instead, I prefer to see these decisions as sources of knowledge

---

network of means for legal interpretation and application in the doctrine of legal sources [my translation]'. See Westberg 1992, 421, 433, but compare the same author on page 434. See also the discussion by Burman about ways to approach the 'specific characteristics' (the systemic conception) of criminal law and the discussion by Åsa Persson, about the seeming boundaries between law and politics, this volume.

34 See also Lagerqvist Veloz Roca 2000, 5–6. According to Aleksander Peczenik, an increased politicization decreases the influence of legal science. See Peczenik 1998, 484. About the status of aliens law in Sweden, see also Norström 2004, 257.

35 About establishing practice through decisions in single cases, see also description of current order in Prop. 1996/97:25, 155–156, in reference to SOU 1993:24, 5–6.

among others, as it is *not* my purpose to 'determine current law', but to highlight legal problems. Nonetheless, I have to adjust to different conceptions of what the law is, when I am 'sketching the legal terrain', that is *how* the spirit and intentions in the CRC have been implemented in the Aliens Act and its application, in order to identify and understand problems. I am aware that this is a dilemma, having a critical starting point while basing the analysis in part on a dogmatic conception of law. It may also be a dilemma that the major part of my argumentation is based on rhetoric from within the dogmatic paradigm.[36] Whether I reflect upon this quandary and the limited basis for my analysis is, however, crucial when I, as a legal scholar, participate in 'the construction of law' (what it is and what it should be).[37]

One important objective in feminist legal studies is to shed light on problems that are related to legal rhetoric, for instance the significance of the dominance of the image of the child as vulnerable and passive which serves to restrict and silence children's involvement (see for instance Bridgeman and Monk 2000, 6). Analysing the law in this way may even lead to a re-evaluation of parent-child relations. After 'unpacking' it some people may feel uncomfortable with the image of children that it presents and with the relatively powerless position it affords them. This is a form of 'consciousness raising', and one of the aims of what is referred to as discourse analysis (Burr 1995, 43; 2003, 55). As described by Burman, the main focal interest for discourse analysis is the different meanings people give to social phenomena in social interaction and the consequences these meanings might have (see Burman, this volume). As pointed out by Burr, some discourses, or ways of representing the world, are awarded a level of truth or common sense, which raises the issue of power relations as some of these representations appear to have an oppressive or constraining effect upon some groups in society (Burr 1995, 15).

Another important object in feminist legal studies is to shed light on problems related to the practical application of the law, for instance *if* there is a gap between the legislators' intentions (the formal) and the effective implementation (the real), *why* (what is the problem), and *what does it mean* (its implications) (see also Svensson, this volume). Thus, a critical standpoint towards different forms of 'positivism' does not exclude what are defined as empirical studies. On the contrary, feminist legal scholars often champion the need for sound and thorough empirical research (see Ratner and Slaughter 1999, 415, 417). According to Burr, it is valid for social constructionists to use other qualitative or even quantitative methods in their research (Burr, 2003, 150; see also Niemi-Kieseläinen, Honkatukia and Ruuskanen, this volume). Certainly, issues about the 'effective implementation' of the law and its practical function are of importance from a traditional legal, as well as a feminist, perspective. Hence, a study concerning the legal impact may supply important information for an analysis concerning legitimacy.[38] Moreover, a study

---

36 For a discussion about this 'feminist dilemma', see Kouvo 2004, 53, with further references.

37 As noted by Svensson, legal scholarship is considered to be one of the legal sources, in the Swedish doctrine of sources of law, but not highly valued. See Svensson, this volume.

38 Svensson argues that an insufficient coherence between ideology, norm system and reality, constitutes a basis for calling into question the legitimacy of the legal system. See

of the practical function of the law may raise questions about the rule of law: for instance where equal circumstances are determined differently in practice, without it emerging from the explanatory statements of the legislation or otherwise from the relevant documentation, why they do so.[39] A critical starting point, however, involves an awareness of the weaknesses in these methodologies.

Finally, what in this approach to law is a challenge to pessimism? Some feminist theorists may dismiss law reforms as a worthwhile strategy, arguing that this may give undue prominence to law as a site for social change (Charlesworth 1999, 393; see also Kouvo 2004, 52ff.). Some may argue that this, in the main critical and deconstructive, approach to law is a never-ending road and that the possibilities for a positive programme of change therefore seem limited (see Davies with further references this volume; see also discussion in Hydén 2002, 44–45, 212–213, 215).[40] The assumption that the law reproduces values and our concepts of childhood, may – I must admit – lead to pessimism. Challenging the law's fundamental presuppositions may, however, in the long term lead to a change in our image of children and children's rights, and subsequently the position afforded them. I believe that *this is the challenge*: exploiting the given, dichotomies and categories, acknowledging pluralism.

References

National Official Documents: Governmental Bills

Prop. 1988/89:86, *Ny utlänningslag m.m.* [Governments proposal, New Aliens Act etcetera].

Prop. 1989/90:107, *om godkännande av FN-konventionen om barnets rättigheter.* [Governments proposal, On the Consent to be Bound by the UN Convention on the Rights of the Child].

Prop. 1994/95:179, *Ändringar i utlänningslagen. (1989:529)* [Governments proposal, Changes in the Aliens Act (1989:529)].

Prop. 1996/97:25, *Svensk migrationspolitik i globalt perspektiv.* [Governments proposal, Swedish Migration Policy in Global Perspective].

Prop. 2004/05:170, *Ny instans- och processordning i utlännings- och medborgarskapsärenden.* [Governments proposal, New Order of Instance and Process in Aliens and Citizenship Matters].

Svensson 1997, 241.

39 The former is referred to by Sandgren as 'a legal effect analysis' and the latter as a 'function analysis'. See Sandgren 1995–96, 742ff.

40 The disclaiming of the ability to provide 'one answer' does not, however, constrain a reconstruction. Instead, as pointed out by Charlesworth and Chinkin, feminist analysis of international law involves both deconstruction and reconstruction. What it means is that we must 'embrace the permanent partiality of feminist inquiry.' See Charlesworth 2000, 45, 60–61, in reference to Harding 1986, 194.

Government Committees and Other Official Documents

Dir. 1996:15 *Barnkonventionen och svensk rätt* [Committee's Terms of Reference, The Convention on the Rights of the Child and Swedish law].
Dir. 2003:28 *Översyn av utlänningslagstiftningen* [Committee's Terms of Reference, Overhaul of the Aliens Legislation].
Lagrådets yttrande över lagrådsremiss den 6 juni 2002, Utdrag ur protokoll vid sammanträde 2002-10-09 [Council on Legislation, Opinion on Proposal Referred to the Council on Legislation for Consideration the 6th of June 2002, Transcript from protocol at session 091002].
Lagrådets yttrande över lagrådsremiss den 17 mars 2005, Utdrag ur protokoll vid sammanträde 2005-05-09 [Council on Legislation, Opinion on Proposal Referred to the Council on Legislation for Consideration the 17th of March 2005, Transcript from protocol at session 090505].
Rskr 1996/97:80.
SOU 1983:29 *Invandringspolitiken* [Government Commission, Immigration Policy].
SOU 1993:24 *Utlänningslagen – en partiell översyn* [Government Commission, The Aliens Act – A Partial Overhaul].
SOU 1996:115 *Barnkonventionen och utlänningslagen* [Government Commission, The Convention on the Rights of the Child and the Aliens Act]. An English summary of the report has been published: 'The Convention on the Rights of the Child and the Aliens Act. Summary of the interim report of the Committee on the Convention on the Rights of the Child and Swedish Legislation' (Stockholm: Fritzes).
SOU 1997:116 *Barnets bästa i främsta rummet. FN:s konvention om barnets rättigheter förverkligas i Sverige* [Government Commission, The Best Interests of the Child, a Primary Consideration. The UN Convention on the Rights of the Child Implemented in Sweden].
SOU 2003:51 *God man för ensamkommande flyktingbarn* [Government Commission, Custodian for Unaccompanied Refugee Children].
SOU 2004:74 *Utlänningslagstiftningen i ett domstolsperspektiv* [Government Commission, The Aliens Legislation in a Court Perspective].
UD 98/601/MP, *Barnets bästa i utlänningslagen – en praxisutvärdering*, promemoria av Dagerås Wittboldt, Wiktoria [The Child's best interests in the Aliens Act – a Review of Practice, Memorandum by Dagerås Wittboldt, Wiktoria].
1989/90:SoU28 *Godkännande av FN-konventionen om barnets rättigheter* [Committee on Health and Welfare, Consent to be Bound by the UN Convention on the Rights of the Child].
1995/96:KU2y *FN:s konvention om barnets rättigheter* [Committee on the Constitution, UN Convention on the Rights of the Child].
1995/96:SoU4 *Barn och ungdom* [Committee on Health and Welfare, Children and Adolescents].
1996/97:SfU5 *Svensk migrationspolitik i globalt perspektiv* [Committee on Social Insurance, Swedish Migration Policy in Global Perspective].

United Nations Official Documents

Final Act of the United Nations Conference of Plenipotentiaries on the Status of Refugees and Stateless Persons 1951, UN Doc. A/CONF.2/108/Rev.1, 26 November 1952.

UNHCR Handbook on Procedures and Criteria for Determining Refugee Status under the 1951 Convention and the 1967 Protocol relating to the Status of Refugees, HCR/IP/4/Eng/REV.1.

UNICEF, Implementation Handbook for the Convention on the Rights of the Child, Geneva, June 1998, XVII.

European Union Official Documents

Council Directive 2004/83/EC of 29 April 2004 on Minimum Standards for the Qualification and Status of Third Country Nationals and Stateless Persons as Refugees or as Persons who Otherwise Need International Protection and the Content of the Protection Granted, OJ L 304, 30.9.2004,12–23.

Proposal for a Council Directive on Minimum Standards for the Qualification and Status of Third Country Nationals and Stateless Persons as Refugees or as Persons who Otherwise Need International Protection, COM (2001) 510 final, OJ C 051 E, 26.2.2002, 325–334.

Literature

Barnombudsmannen (2000), *Barnets bästa i asylärenden. En studie av Migrationsverkets praxis i asylärenden med barnfamiljer* (Stockholm: Barnombudsmannen).

Bhabha, Jacqueline (2002), 'Demography and Rights: Women, Children and Access to Asylum', 16 *International Journal of Refugee Law* 2002, 227–243.

Bridgeman, Jo and Monk, Daniel (eds) (2000) *Feminist Perspectives on Child Law* (London: Cavendish Publishing Ltd).

Bring, Ove and Mahmoudi, Said (2001), *Sverige och folkrätten* (Stockholm: Norstedts Juridik).

Burr, Vivien (1995), *An Introduction to Social Constructionism* (London: Routledge).

Burr, Vivien (2003), *Social Constructionism* (London and New York: Routledge).

Charlesworth, Hilary (1999), 'Feminist Methods in International Law' in 'Symposium on Method in International Law', 93 *The American Journal of International Law* 1999, 379–394.

Charlesworth, Hilary and Chinkin, Christine (2000), *The Boundaries of International Law: A Feminist Analysis* (Manchester: Manchester University Press, Melland Schill Studies in International Law).

Davies, Margaret (2002), *Asking the Law Question, The Dissolution of Legal Theory* (Sydney: Lawbook Co.).

Eckhoff, Torstein and Sundby, Nils Kristian (1991), *Rettssystemer: Systemteoretisk innføring i rettsfilosofien* (Oslo: Tano).

Gerhard, Ute (2001), *Debating Women's Equality* (New Brunswick, New Jersey and London: Rutgers University Press).

Hacking, Ian (1999), *The Social Construction of What?* (Cambridge, Mass.: Harvard University Press).

Halvorsen, Kate (2004), *Asylum Decisions on Child Applicants, Report on 4-Country Pilot Project* (Stavanger).

Harding, Sandra (1986), *The Science Question in Feminism* (Ithaca: Cornell University Press).

Hollander, Anna (1998), 'Barns rätt att komma till tals – ökat inflytande för barn eller vuxna?', *4 Nordiskt Socialt Arbeid* 1998, 194–200.

Hunt Federle, Katherine (1994), 'Rights flow downhill', 2 *The International Journal of Children's Rights 1994*, 343–368.

Hydén, Håkan (1992), 'Faktorer av betydelse för val av metod', in Basse, Ellen Margrethe and Jensen, Vibeke (eds), *Regulering og styring III, Ett bidrag til den juridiske forskeruddannelse* (København: GEC Gad).

Hydén, Håkan (2002), *Normvetenskap* (Lund: Lund Studies in Sociology of Law).

Juhlén, Karin (2003), *Barns egna asylskäl* (Stockholm: Rädda Barnen).

Kouvo, Sari (2004), *Making just rights? Mainstreaming Women's Human Rights and a Gender Perspective* (Uppsala: Iustus Förlag).

Lagerqvist Veloz Roca, Annika (2000), 'Utlänningsrätt – eller enbart beslut i separata fall?', 5 *Förvaltningsrättslig Tidskrift* 2000, 5–22.

MacKinnon, Catharine A. (1989), *Toward a Feminist Theory of the State* (Cambridge, Mass., London: Harvard University Press).

Migrationsverket. (2001), *Barn i utlänningsärenden. Rapport från Migrationsverket* (Norrköping: Migrationsverket).

Minow, Martha (1986), 'Rights for the Next Generation: A Feminist Approach to Children's Rights', 9 *Harvard Women's Law Journal* 1986, 1–24.

Nilsson, Eva (2005), 'A Child Perspective in the Swedish Asylum Process: Rhetoric and Practice', in Andersson, Hans E., Ascher, Henry, Björnberg, Ulla, Eastmond, Marita and Mellander, Lotta (eds), *The Asylum Seeking Child in Europe* (Göteborg: Centre for European Research).

Norström, Eva (2004), *I väntan på asyl. Retorik och praktik i svensk flyktingpolitik* (Umeå: Boréa).

Peczenik, Aleksander (1998–99), 'Värdenihilismen och den konstruktiva juridiken', 2 *Juridisk Tidskrift* 1998–1999, 462–490.

Ratner, Steven R. and Slaughter, Anne-Marie (1999), 'The Method is the Message' in 'Symposium on Method in International Law', 93 *The American Journal of International Law* 1999, 410–423.

Sandgren, Claes (1995–96), 'Om empiri och rättsvetenskap', 3 *Juridisk Tidskrift 1995–96*, 726–748.

Schiratzki, Johanna (2000), *Barnets bästa i ett mångkulturellt Sverige – en rättsvetenskaplig undersökning* (Stockholm: Juridiska fakulteten, Skriftserien nr 63, Jure).

Strömberg, Håkan and Melander, Göran (2003), *Folkrätt* (Lund: Studentlitteratur).

Strömholm, Stig (1996), *Rätt, rättskällor och rättstillämpning. En lärobok i allmän rättslära* (Stockholm: Norstedts Juridik).

Svensson, Eva-Maria (1997), *Genus och rätt – en problematisering av föreställningen om rätten* (Uppsala: Iustus Förlag).

Svensson, Eva-Maria (2001), *Genusforskning inom juridiken* (Stockholm: Högskoleverket).

Tesón, Fernando R. (1998)., *A Philosophy of International Law* (Colorado: Westview Press).

Wennström, Bo (2003), 'Allmän rättslära och feministisk rättsteori', in Fogelklou, Anders and Spaak, Torben (eds), *Festskrift till Åke Frändberg* (Uppsala: Iustus Förlag), 327–344.

Westberg, Peter (1992), 'Avhandlingsskrivande och val av forskningsansats – en idé om rättsvetenskaplig öppenhet', in Heuman, Lars (ed.) *Festskrift till Per Olof Bolding* (Stockholm: Juristförlaget), 421–446.

Wikrén, Gerhard and Sandesjö, Håkan (2002), *Utlänningslagen med kommentarer* (Stockholm: Norstedts Juridik).

Williams, Patricia, J. (1993), *The Alchemy of Race and Rights* (London: Virago).

Chapter 7

Challenging the Heteronormativity of Law

Görel Granström

Discussions about the meaning of equality before the law have been part of western legal discourse since the 19th century, and for almost all of that period, various groups and individuals have had conflicting opinions about which groups of people are to be regarded as equals. Women were for a very long time, some would say they still are, seen as inferior to men, blacks as inferior to whites, the working class to the bourgeoisie and so on. This perceived inferiority was almost always connected with the idea of difference. Men and women were seen as different, complementing each other, but not alike. The consequences of this way of thinking are still apparent in today's legal discourse and even a striving for gender-neutral legislation cannot change this. But what happens when the legislator acknowledges that gender-neutral legislation can be problematic and tries instead to work with gender-specific laws? This is the case in Swedish criminal law, where the attempt to combat domestic abuse has led to legislation that deals specifically with men who abuse their female partners. This legislation has been seen as a step forward in the struggle against domestic abuse by both women's organizations and politicians (Nordborg and Niemi-Kiesiläinen 2001). However, the legislation has also been criticized for acknowledging only certain kinds of domestic abuse, that is, heterosexual domestic abuse.

This legal construction could be criticized in terms of its deviation from the gender-neutral view of legislation that is current in Sweden. It could also be analysed in the context of theoretical debate about the meaning of 'equality'. The focal point of this chapter is not that, however, but instead the fact that the legislation specifically protects heterosexual women.[1] My hypothesis is that there are underlying assumptions about normality which inform the legislator in decisions about which groups of people are to be protected by law. The assumption regarding domestic violence is then that this is something that more or less only occurs in heterosexual relationships.

To prove my point, I will compare this regulation with the Swedish legislation governing hate crime and specifically homophobic hate crimes. The term 'hate crime' is used to differentiate 'ordinary crime' from crimes of hate and is often taken to mean a crime where the perpetrator's prejudice or bias against a group of people constitute

1 It could be said that the Swedish legislation is a form of positive discrimination legislation, in that it gives special protection to heterosexual women.

a factor in determining who is victimized (Hall 2005, 1–3; Moran 2002, 304; Perry 2001, 7–10). Such groups of people, or the categories of hate that are covered by this definition of hate crime, vary among the legal systems in different countries. In Sweden, hate crime is understood in the context of race, ethnicity, religion or sexual orientation, meaning that hate crimes against people based solely on their gender identity are not regulated in Swedish legislation. I should also point out that, unlike the domestic violence regulation mentioned above, the Swedish regulation regarding hate crime is gender-neutral.

The assumption regarding normality here would then be that hate crime is something connected with a person's sexual orientation, not their gender identity. The question then is why the legislator has chosen to exclude gender in this context and, moreover, whether it is really possible to make a clear distinction between a person's gender identity and his or her sexual orientation. I will try to provide an answer to the first part of this question, but an answer to the second part requires much more space than this chapter allows, so I will limit myself to a problematization of that part of the question.

The Swedish legislation dealing with domestic abuse and hate crimes, will be used as examples in presenting a critical view of the law's ability to protect and provide legal remedies to victims of crime, when these victims do not conform to the notions of normality as constructed by the legal system. My analysis stems from the understanding that the normal, or ideal, victim in these circumstances is presumed to be a heterosexual woman, when it comes to incidents of domestic violence, and a gay man, when a homophobic hate crime occurs.[2]

The following paragraph explains my use of the word heteronormativity: Anti-homosexual bias can be understood to exist on three levels, the individual (homophobia), the cultural (heteronormativity) and the structural or institutional (heterosexism) (Jenness and Richman 2002, 408; O'Brien 2001). Homophobia, as in individual prejudice and hatred against gays and lesbians, is largely omitted from this paper. Instead, the focus is on the cultural and the structural levels. On the cultural level, legal remedies are used to uphold the 'norm' and heteronormativity can be seen as a discursive practice that pervades literature, education and legal language. It could be said that heteronormativity emphasizes the correctness of heterosexuality and traditional family forms. Anti-homosexual bias on a structural level in this context is termed heterosexism. Heterosexism, through for example the law, religion and the economy, legitimizes the violence and discrimination that takes place on other levels. One example of heterosexism is the attitudes that gays and lesbians meet when they come into contact with the legal system as victims of crime.

Heterosexism could also be seen as the institutional discrimination faced by gay and lesbian people as a consequence of entrenched heteronormative assumptions. I would argue that the assumption that the 'normal' family is one that consists of a mother, a father and one or more children is an example of heteronormativity. The

---

2 For a discussion about the concept of the 'ideal victim', see for example Christie 1986.

legal prohibition of same-sex adoption rights or same-sex marriage is an example of a heterosexist structure.

Swedish Legal Reforms Regarding Domestic Abuse

The idea that law in itself, and the legal system, consist of a neutral and objective system of rules has been successfully challenged by feminist legal scholars.[3] One result of these challenges, and also of a more 'woman-friendly' political agenda during the 1990s, is that certain problems facing women have received more attention and led to proposals for law reforms.

In 1998, Sweden changed the criminal law so as to be able to deal more effectively with sexualized violence against women, and one year later the buying of sexual services was criminalized.[4] These are very promising reforms, but there are also some shortcomings. The new legislation on domestic violence, Gross violation of a woman's integrity (*grov kvinnofridskränkning*), focuses primarily on heterosexual domestic violence. This legislation added a paragraph to the general criminal law – the Penal Code – with the aim of criminalizing the systematic abuse and degrading of a person that is the result of violence in a close relationship, violence that can take the form of harassment, threats and various kinds of battering (Larsson 2004, 61–63). The paragraph is structured in two sections; the first dealing with abuse that one person inflicts on another in a 'close relationship', Gross violation of integrity (*grov fridskränkning*). This relationship is defined in the preparatory works as that between a child and its parents or between siblings or other people sharing a household (Prop. 1997/98:55, 132).

The second section of the paragraph deals specifically with abuse that a man inflicts on a woman. The relationship here is defined as one where the man 'is, or has been, married [to the woman] or with whom he is, or has been cohabiting under circumstances comparable to marriage …'.[5] I should point out that the penalty for this crime is the same, regardless of which section is applied. The perpetrator can be sentenced to a prison term that ranges from six months to six years, although most sentences are at the lower end of the range. The difference between the two sections lies instead in that the second deals with close relationships of a sexual nature, that is, the abuser and the victim have to have been living together, either as husband and wife or in cohabitation comparable to marriage. And it is here, in the legislation's definition of a close relationship of a sexual nature, that we can see an example of the law's heteronormativity.

Victims of same-sex domestic abuse have to use the first section of the paragraph, the one which criminalizes abuse between people living together in a shared household, since the second section deals only with abuse that a man inflicts on a woman. By constructing the paragraph this way, it could be said that the

3 See for example Naffine and Owens 1997; Lacey 1998; Cornell, 1998. In a Nordic context, see for example Nousiainen *et al.* 2001.

4 For information about the law proposals, see Prop. 1997/98:55.

5 This translation of the relevant section of the Penal Code (chapter 4 paragraph 4a) can be found in Nordborg and Niemi-Kiesiläinen 2001, 364.

legislator sees the heterosexual relationship as the 'normal' one, even when it comes to violence. Same-sex relationships have been legally recognized in Sweden since 1987, when the law on cohabitation came into force. In 1995 gays and lesbians were able to register their partnerships, leading to a marriage-like legal relationship including, for example, inheritance rights.[6] Why then leave these relationships out of the section that specifically deals with domestic violence?

I would argue that the construction of the paragraph in this manner can be seen as an example of the heteronormativity of the law. The normal relationship is assumed to be that between a man and a woman, the heterosexual relationship, even in the context of domestic violence. In all fairness, I should point out that in one part of the preparatory works, the government commission, it is mentioned (in one sentence) that violence also occurs in same-sex relationships, so there is not total ignorance of the problem.[7] At the same time, it is obvious that neither the government commission that presented the original law proposal nor the government in its bill saw it as such a big a problem as heterosexual domestic violence.

The government bill specifically stated that the legislation on domestic violence was part of an initiative to achieve recognition of the fact that men's violence against women is a great problem in society and should be dealt with accordingly (Prop. 1997/98:55, 21). I am not suggesting that men's violence against women is anything other than an important problem, but I would like to point out that it is not the only one. As I have stated above, domestic violence is not only a problem in heterosexual relationships, it also occurs in same-sex relationships. Victims of same-sex domestic abuse are protected by the same general criminal regulations as heterosexual victims, but this specific paragraph – that has been invoked to show that domestic violence is not acceptable – cannot be used by victims of same-sex domestic violence on the same terms as it can be used by heterosexual women.

By formulating the new legislation on domestic violence – Gross Violation of a Woman's Integrity – in this way, I would argue that the Swedish legislator has made it more difficult for victims of same-sex domestic violence to gain protection from the law, and made it harder for GLBTQ-people (gay, lesbian, bisexual, transgender and queer) generally to feel that the law and the legal system can be used to further their rights. There is a substantial literature that shows the problems that heterosexual women face when trying to leave an abusive relationship.[8] It includes the effects of the normalization of violence that typically occurs in an abusive relationship, where the victim is made to feel that she is worthless, stupid, ugly, and in fact in some way responsible for the abuse that her partner puts her through. There is also the problem of isolation, the fact that family and friends are often unaware of what is going on, which makes it even harder to get help. Finally, if the victim succeeds in leaving the abuser, perhaps by living in a shelter for battered women, the next step includes

6 This was stated in the Registered Partnership Act (SFS 1994:1117).

7 SOU 1995:60, 307. Same-sex domestic violence is not mentioned in the government bill, and in the government commission, there is one sentence that says: 'Violence can also occur in homosexual relationships.' (My translation).

8 For this discussion in a Swedish context, see for example Lundgren *et al.* 2002; Holmberg and Enander 2005.

contact with the police, the prosecutor and the courts. This is a long and difficult journey for any victim of domestic violence, but, as I will outline in the next section, the journey becomes even more difficult if you are a lesbian woman or gay man.

Domestic Violence in Same-Sex Relationships

There are many similarities between domestic violence in heterosexual and same-sex relationships, but also some important differences (Elliot 1996). Heterosexual battering exists in a context of unequal power between men and women, and this relationship model, being the dominant one in western society for hundreds of years, influences all relationships. This model, where one party has greater power and control, also provides the foundation for same-sex battering (Allen and Leventhal 1999). But the cultural context is different. A straight batterer may threaten his victim in various ways, perhaps by saying that he is going to tell everyone that she is a bad mother who cannot take care of her children. A same-sex batterer may threaten her victim on the basis of her lesbianism. A bad mother is one thing; a lesbian mother is quite another. The threat of outing is a reality in a heterosexist society and the isolation of the victim becomes, in this context, even more effective (Gårdfeldt 2003).

The resources for providing help are also different. Many women's shelters do not accept lesbian victims of domestic abuse and a gay man or a transgender person has nowhere to turn (Holmberg and Stjernqvist 2005; Allen and Leventhal 1999, 76–77). Contact with the legal system is another hurdle. There are accounts of how victims of same-sex domestic violence have been mistreated by the police or other legal officials (Pfeifer 2005; Knauer 1999). People in general are, nowadays at least, more ready to accept that women in heterosexual relationships can be the victims of domestic abuse. It is easier to understand that a man can beat up a woman; after all, men are over-represented in crime statistics. But a gay man that tries to file a complaint against his partner may often be met with ridicule or total indifference. Violence between two men living together is not seen as abuse, it is seen as a fight between two equal partners (Gårdfeldt 2003, 18). Culturally in our society, amongst straights as well as queers, there is often a view that men are supposed to be able to defend themselves against violence; they are not supposed to be victims. This is also a problem faced by a straight man abused by his female partner. A 'real' man cannot be abused by a woman. There are very few Swedish studies of female on male domestic violence, and almost no statistics can be found, but domestic violence is also a reality for some straight men.[9]

A lesbian that informs the authorities that her partner abuses her is often not taken seriously (Elliot 1996, 5). Women are not supposed to fight; they are seen as peaceful and cuddly. The concept that two women can have a sexual relationship has historically been very hard to accept (Sorainen 1999, 61). To understand that such relationships exist and that they can even be abusive is even harder to recognize.

9 In a study from the National Council for Crime Prevention (Brottsförebyggande rådet, Brå) 1999 it was estimated that women were responsible for 4 per cent of the domestic violence in heterosexual relationships. BRÅ-rapport 1999:15, 36.

We must also remember that discrimination against and abuse of GLBTQ people has a long historical tradition, where the law and the legal system have been vital parts of the oppression (Jenness and Richman 2002, 404). It is not realistic to expect that these groups will instantly trust the system that used to oppress them. There are also accounts of homophobia – or heterosexism – in the courts, where victims of same-sex domestic abuse are asked very intimate questions about the nature of their relationship. One of the biggest problems, however, is still that so few cases find their way to the courts. The obstacles on the way arc many. The legal rules are insufficient and the attitudes amongst representatives of the legal system towards GLBTQ people leave much to be desired.[10]

I would argue that the heteronormativity that can be detected in the legislation is also repeated in the community, in that same-sex domestic violence is not taken seriously by those institutions or organizations that usually deal with domestic abuse. The ideal victim here is a heterosexual woman, not a gay man or a lesbian woman, or for that matter a transgender person. I will conclude this section with a telling example. As stated above, lesbian women are not always welcome at shelters for abused women, and gay men or transgender persons have nowhere to turn. As a consequence of this, *RFSL* (the Swedish Federation for Lesbian, Gay, Bisexual and Transgender Rights) started their own crime victim's help-line in Stockholm in 1998 (BRÅ-Apropå no. 4-5/2005). This help-line, staffed by professional social workers, caters to both victims of domestic abuse and to victims of homophobic hate crimes.

The help-line's work has been recognized as important and needed, but the organizers have been unable to get public funding. On the contrary, when they applied for public funding from *Socialstyrelsen* [the National Board of Health and Welfare], they discovered that since they did not work with issues concerning violence against women, they were not eligible for funding. This, in my opinion, is a rather narrow and unfortunate view of the scope of domestic violence, but it illustrates the kind of situation I want to define as an example of heteronormativity in this context. Violence against women is seen as something that victimizes heterosexual women and the perpetrators are seen as heterosexual men who have or have had a relationship with these women. When asked by the Swedish newspaper *Stockholms Fria Tidning* whether domestic violence in lesbian same-sex relationships constitutes violence against women, a representative from the National Board of Health and Welfare said: Yes, it does, 'but violence against women is still not RFSL's main area of interest'.[11]

Homophobic Hate Crimes

So far, the focus in this chapter has been on domestic violence. I will now turn to gay and lesbian victims of violent crimes that take place *outside* the domestic context. The example I am going to use is victims of hate crimes, specifically homophobic hate crimes. As I noted earlier, the definition of hate crime is that it is

10 See for example Berrill and Herek 1992, 293–295. For the Swedish context, see BRÅ-rapport 2002:9 and Granström 2006.

11 http://www.ft.fria.nu/modules.php?name=News&file=article&sid=3763

crime motivated by prejudice. The groups of people who are protected vary among different legal systems. Usually, the different legislations target crimes motivated by an individual's bias or hatred of a person's or group's perceived race, religion, ethnicity or sexual orientation.[12]

The term hate crime has a rather short history in a Swedish context (Granström 2006). It is not a legal term, in that there is no category of crime called 'hate crime', and there is no specific paragraph in the Swedish Penal Code that prohibits hate crime. It is, however, possible for the prosecutor to argue for a more severe punishment if it can be shown that a person was motivated by prejudice when committing a crime. In chapter 29 of the Penal Code, on the determination of punishment and exemption from sanction, paragraph 2 states that:

> In assessing penal value, the following aggravating circumstances shall be given special consideration in addition to what is applicable to each and every type of crime: … whether a motive for the crime was to aggrieve a person, ethnic group or some other similar group of people by reason of race, colour, national or ethnic origin, religious belief, sexual orientation or other similar circumstance.[13]

Recent statistics from that part of the Swedish Police Service responsible for hate crime statistics, *SÄPO* (National Security Services), shows an increase in the number of hate crimes in Sweden, especially homophobic hate crimes (Säkerhetspolisen 2005). As many victim surveys show, however, as there is a reluctance amongst gays and lesbians to report instances of homophobic crimes, there is a strong possibility that the numbers of victims and crimes are even higher that the police report.[14]

Still today, even if the victim reports the crime, the chance that the case will be taken to court is not great. There are not many sentences for crimes according to this specific statute meaning that even if a case is brought to court, there is no guarantee that it will be seen as a homophobic crime, rather than an 'ordinary crime'. There is no requirement for the court either to state specifically that the statute has been used or what consequences the use of the statute had in the sentencing (Granström 2006; Tiby 2000, 110).

Another matter that should be taken into account is the homophobic – or heterosexist – tendencies in the courts (BRÅ-rapport 2002:9; Hutchinson 2002). As I noted above in the section on same-sex domestic violence, the legal rules do not sufficiently recognize this type of violence, and the attitudes amongst representatives of the legal system towards GLBTQ people leave much to be desired. The same can be said when it comes to hate crimes. The 'homosexual panic defence' (Ruthchild

---

12 But it should be said that sexual orientation has not been, and in a great many countries is still not, accepted as worthy of protection. See for example Moran 2002, 304; Jacobs and Potter 1998, 65.

13 There is also a special provision in the Penal Code that prohibits hate speech, chapter 16 section 8. The protected groups are religious and ethnic minorities, and since the year 2003 the statute also protects sexual orientation. See Granström 2006.

14 See for example Tiby 2004. Another explanation for this increase could also be the fact that in the past such crimes went completely unrecognized. If reported, they would not be seen as crimes, or not as hate crimes.

1997) is not a valid defence strategy in the Swedish legal system, but I would still argue that this way of thinking about or interpreting violence against gays and lesbians influences Swedish legislators and decision makers. The most obvious example of this is a case that was decided in the Swedish Supreme Court in 1995 (NJA 1995 s. 464). The perpetrator had stabbed his victim 64 times as a result of – as the perpetrator stated – the victim's sexual advances towards him. The Supreme Court, when having to decide if the stabbing should be categorized as murder or manslaughter, focused on the perpetrator's perception of sexual advances from a gay man as a provocation, and sentenced him to eight years of imprisonment for manslaughter.[15]

This case can be seen as an extreme example of what Berrill and Herek (Berrill and Herek 1992), among others, have termed the secondary victimization of gay and lesbian victims of hate crime. This secondary victimization occurs when victims of hate crime come into contact with a legal system that is not prepared, nor especially interested in, dealing with the crimes that they have been subjected to. There is instead a tendency to focus on the victim, on his or her actions, and to accuse the victim of provocation or of inviting the attack (Berrill and Herek 1992, 295).

Is there a Need for a Gender Perspective on Hate Crimes?

In the section on same-sex domestic violence, I argued that one aspect of the heteronormativity of the law is that the legislator in recent law reforms has tended to focus on heterosexual domestic violence as the 'normal' violence. A critical reading of the Swedish legislation regulating hate crime also presents us with one or two interesting points of discussion on what is seen as the norm in this context; first, the lack of a gender perspective when it comes to violence against gay men and lesbian women, and second, the fact that gender-based violence is not criminalized as a hate crime. I will start with the first point of discussion here and conclude my chapter with a problematization of the latter.

Some scholars claim that anti-gay and anti-lesbian violence differs, that is, that homophobic hate crime is not necessarily the same thing for gays and lesbians (Jenness and Richman 2002; Moran 2002; Mason 1997). Jenness and Richman say that:

> Distinguishing between violence directed at gay men and violence directed at lesbian women is crucial insofar as a defining characteristic of violence against lesbians is that it exists on a continuum, from exclusively anti-women to exclusively anti-gay conduct.[16]

---

15 In the Swedish Penal Code, a sentence of murder results in a prison term of ten years or life imprisonment. If there are mitigating circumstances, a person can be found guilty of manslaughter instead, a crime that results in a prison term of six to ten years.

16 Jenness and Richman 2002, 411, with references to Comstock 1991; von Schulthess 1992.

In an Australian study that Mason presents, lesbians were more likely to suffer violence committed by older men, men acting alone and men that they knew. The 'typical' perpetrators of anti-gay violence are often a group of young men. The settings for the types of violence were also different (Mason 1997, 18). Lesbians were more likely to be victims in their homes, or in their work-place, a setting that corresponds to violence against heterosexual women, where the 'private' domain of the crime, and the previous relation to the perpetrator are common aspects. Moran explains it as follows:

> The experience of anti-lesbian violence is intimately connected with but different from violence against women. In simple terms, lesbian brings together sexuality, that might point to distinctions between women and gender that suggests connections between women who might be separated by sexuality. (Moran 2002, 301)

Following the arguments presented above, it is obvious that our understanding of hate crime would benefit from an analysis from a gender perspective. Gender and sexuality are strongly linked in our culture, and it can therefore be difficult to pinpoint whether a perpetrator of a hate crime is provoked by what is seen as a transgression of a gender stereotype or perceived as a sexual aberration (O'Brien 2001, 66–76). Is the butch that is harassed or beaten outside a gay club victimized because she deviates from gender norms of femininity or because she has sexual relations with other women and not with men?

But we must also consider another aspect: whether there is a tendency to focus on the homophobic violence that gay men suffer, and to see that as the 'normal' hate crime. Some lesbians might see this as another example of the 'gay' agenda having more power than the lesbian feminist agendas, as laws concerning vilification on the basis of sexual orientation tend to advantage men more than women. I would argue that we could see this as an example of a gendered power structure even in questions concerning hate crime. It could also be seen as a normalization of the gay man as the victim of hate crime, just as the heterosexual woman is normalized as the victim of domestic violence. Either way, there is no legal recognition of the lesbian woman, as a victim of hate crime, or as a victim of domestic violence.[17]

Perhaps this way of thinking would also give us some insight into the final question for this chapter, that regarding why crimes motivated by prejudice based on gender are not seen as hate crimes in Sweden.

The Private (Straight) Woman and the Public (Gay) Man

As I have noted above, the Swedish regulation on hate crime targets crimes motivated by someone's bias or hatred of a person's or a group's perceived race, religion, ethnicity or sexual orientation. Sweden is no exception here in not including gendered violence or violence against women in its hate crime definition; the situation is the same in most other countries that have some sort of hate crime legislation (Moran

17 I would like to thank one of the editors of this book, Margaret Davies, for reminding me of this aspect of the problem.

4). The arguments for this state of affairs range from maintaining that there dy enough laws and regulations that address violence against women to arguing that the level of violence against women is so high that to define these crimes as hate crimes would reveal too much hatred in society.

This assumes, of course, that there is some discussion at least on why gender-based violence is not considered a hate crime. There has been hardly any discussion in Sweden concerning violence against heterosexual women. The one exception occurred in 1995 when a governmental commission (the same commission that proposed the new crime Gross Violation of a Woman's Integrity) suggested that gender bias should be seen as a hate crime (SOU 1995:60, 295). But the government in its bill in 1998 said that only especially vulnerable groups, such as immigrants and homosexuals, should be protected by the regulation on hate crimes. The argument was that a regulation of this character would run the risk of losing its significance if it was extended to more or less the whole population (Prop. 1997/98:55, 86–87). Furthermore, the government proclaimed that there was really no need for such regulation, since the crime Gross Violation of a Woman's Integrity would lead to more severe punishments for those who abused another person in a close relationship. Based on this argumentation from the governmental bill, it is safe to say that when the question was raised, of whether it is possible to view gendered violence as a hate crime, the answer is no.

In a related issue, namely whether transgender persons should be protected by the legislation criminalizing hate speech, the government stated in its bill that even though transgender persons deserve the same protection as homo- or bisexual persons, the question was whether they were victims in the same way (Prop. 2001/02:59, 39). That is, the government said that the number of violations against transgender persons was still rather low. You could say that what was needed was more evidence of hate speech against transgender persons, before a need to change the law was seen. Here it would seem that transgender persons were judged to be too small a group to claim special protection.

I would argue that the opposite reasoning is used when it comes to women as a group (as seen above concerning the proposal for viewing gendered violence as a hate crime); they are seen as too large a group, not a minority that could claim special protection, or that there is even a need for special protection. So are the sheer numbers, the size of the specific group or minority, the reason why some groups are offered protection and others not?

That might, however, be too easy an explanation. This question could also be discussed in terms of the distinction between the public and the private sphere of society; that is, whether hate crime is seen as something that happens between strangers, and whether women are normally seen as victims in instances defined as domestic violence. Is it really an expression of the normalization of gendered violence that it is almost 'normal' for women to experience violence from the person they are living with? I think the answer might lie somewhere between these lines of discussion. The question of size, that is whether you are part of a legitimized minority group, could be something to take into account, but also the idea of the normal victim has to be considered. As Mason, amongst others, has pointed out there is a tendency to see homophobic violence against gay men as some sort of norm for hate crime (Mason 2002, 39–40; Mason 1997).

Why then is violence against (heterosexual) women not seen as a hate crime? As has been noted above, many cases of anti-lesbian violence are characterized by the fact that it is not always easy to determine whether the woman was attacked because she was a woman, or because she was a lesbian. Was the violence gender based or sexual-orientation based, and is this even a relevant question? The question is relevant in that in posing it, the interaction between gender and sexuality is brought into focus. In the Swedish context, the question is of course relevant because if the violence is seen as based on sexuality, it will fall within the definition of hate crime, whereas it will not if it is 'only' gender-based violence.

It has been debated whether it is in reality possible to separate out violence based on gender from violence based on sexuality (Mason 1997, 15). Moran argues that the theoretical challenge is to try to overcome the separation of the ontological and political connection between identities such as sexuality or sexual orientation, sex/gender, race and ethnicity. We can use the term intersectionality, as the critical race theorists coined it in the 1990s or we can talk about interplay between different aspects of an individual's identity.[18] The result of the use of either concept would hopefully be a deeper understanding of the way that the inter-relationship between different aspects of our identities makes us more complex as individuals, and also more complex as victims of crime. Then again, maybe this is too much to hope for in legislation, since it tends to be a rather blunt instrument.

But one last question remains: What would be the point of defining violence against heterosexual women as a hate crime? I would argue that one reason would be to try and overcome the separateness of different acts of violence against groups of people or individuals. In so doing, we would be able to see more clearly and analyse the process of violence and discrimination against these different victims and through that analysis understand that what connects these victims, be they victims of same-sex domestic violence, heterosexual domestic violence, hate crimes or gender discrimination, is greater than what sets them apart.

As I have tried to show in this chapter, there are disadvantages with both gender-specific and gender-neutral legislation. A gender-specific legislation tends to present a static view, a normalization, of the ideal victim in certain instances; my example has been the Swedish regulation of domestic violence. Here the heterosexual woman is seen as the normal victim, therefore there is a tendency to overlook and belittle the plight of those victims of domestic abuse who are not heterosexual women.

On the other hand, the gender-neutral formulation of the hate crime regulation tends to normalize the gay man as the ideal victim, making lesbian crime victims the anomaly. And in choosing not to see gendered violence as a hate crime, the Swedish legislators are upholding the division between the public and the private sphere in the lives of victims of crime and in society as a whole. There is an unwillingness to see that both sexual orientation-based as well as gender-based hatred is not just an individual, but also a cultural and structural problem.

18 See for example Crenshaw 1995; Moran 2002, 310; Mason 1997, 25.

References

Government Bills

Prop. 1997/98:55, *Kvinnofrid* [Governments proposal, Violence Against Women].
Prop. 2001/02:59, *Hets mot folkgrupp m.m.* [Governments proposal, Racial Agitation etc.].

Government Committees and Other Official Documents

NJA 1995 s. 464 [Supreme Court Decision NJA 1995 s. 464].
SOU 1995:60 *Kvinnofrid* [Governmental Commission, Woman's Peace].

Literature

Allen, Charlene and Leventhal, Beth (1999), 'History, Culture and Identity: What Makes GLBT Battering Different', in Leventhal, Beth and Lundy, Sandra E. (eds), *Same-sex Domestic Violence. Strategies for Change* (London: Sage Publications Inc.).
Berrill, Kevin T. and Herek, Gregory M. (1992), 'Primary and Secondary Victimization in Anti-gay Hate Crimes: Official Response and Public Policy', in Herek, Gregory M. and Berrill, Kevin T. (eds), *Hate Crimes. Confronting Violence against Lesbians and Gay Men* (Newbury Park: Sage Publications Inc.).
BRÅ-Apropå no. 4-5/2005.
BRÅ-rapport 1999:15, *Kvinnors brottslighet.*
BRÅ-rapport 2002:9, *Hatbrott. En uppföljning av rättsväsendets insatser.*
Christie, Niels (1986), 'The Ideal Victim', in Fattah, Ezzat A. (ed.), *From Crime Policy to Victim Policy. Reorienting the Justice System* (Basingstoke: Macmillan).
Comstock, Gary (1991), *Violence Against Lesbians and Gay Men* (New York: Columbia University Press).
Cornell, Drucilla (1998), *At the Heart of Freedom. Feminism, Sex and Equality* (Princetown: Princetown University Press).
Crenshaw, Kimberlé Williams (1995), 'Mapping the Margins: Intersectionality, Identity Politics, and Violence Against Women of Color', in Crenshaw *et al. Critical Race Theory: The Key Writings That Formed the Movement* (New York: New Press).
Elliot, Pam (1996), 'Shattering Illusions: Same-sex Domestic Violence', in Renzetti, Claire M. and Miley, Charles Harvey (eds), *Violence in Gay and Lesbian Domestic Partnerships* (New York: Harrington Park Press).
Gårdfeld, Lars (2003), *Kvinna slår kvinna, man slår man. Homosexuell partnermisshandel* (Stockholm: Nationellt råd för kvinnofrid).
Granström, Görel (2006), 'Rättsväsendets möte med hbt-personer som brottsoffer', in Granström, Görel, Mannelqvist, Ruth and Weinehall, Katarina (eds) *Brottsoffer – ansvar och konsekvenser. Ett viktimologiskt forskningsseminarium i Umeå den 22 November 2005* (Umeå: Umeå Universitet, Juridiska Institutionen).
Hall, Nathan (2005), *Hate Crime* (Cullompton: Willan Publishing Ltd).

Holmberg, Carin and Enander, Viveka (2005), *Varför går hon? Om misshandlade kvinnors uppbrottsprocess* (Ystad: Kabusa Böcker).

Holmberg, Carin and Stjernqvist, Ulrica (2005), *Våldsamt lika och olika. Om våld i samkönade parrelationer* (Stockholm: Stockholms Universitet, Centrum för Genusstudier).

Hutchinson, Darren Lenard (2002), 'Dissecting Axes of Subordination: The Need for a Structural Analysis', in *11:1 Journal of Gender, Social Policy & the Law* 2002.

Jacobs, James B. and Potter, Kimberly (1998), *Criminal Law & Identity Politics* (Oxford: Oxford University Press).

Jenness, Valerie and Richman, Kimberly D. (2002), 'Anti-gay and Lesbian Violence and its Discontents', in Richardson, Diane and Seidman, Steven (eds), *The Handbook of Gay and Lesbian Studies* (London: Sage Publications Inc.).

Knauer, Nancy J. (1999), 'Same-sex Domestic Violence: Claiming a Domestic Sphere While Risking Negative Stereotypes', in *8:325 Temple Political & Civil Rights Law Review* 1999.

Lacey, Nicola (1998), *Unspeakable subjects. Feminist Essays in Legal and Social Theory* (Oxford: Hart Publishing).

Larsson, Monica (2004), 'Slå tillbaka! Har misshandlade kvinnor rätt till nödvärn?', in Granström, Göre (ed), *Den onda cirkeln. Om brottsoffer, genus och rätten* (Uppsala: Uppsala Publishing House).

Lundgren, Eva, Heimer, Gun, Westerstrand, Jenny and Kalliokoski, AnnepMarie (2002), *Captured Queen. Men's Violence against Women in 'Equal' Sweden: A Prevalence Study* (Umeå: Brottsoffermyndigheten).

Mason, Gail (1997), 'Heterosexed Violence: Typicality and Ambiguity' in Mason, Gail and Tomsen, Stephen (eds), *Homophobic Violence* (Sydney: Hawkins Press).

Mason, Gail (2002), *The Spectacle of Violence. Homophobia, Gender and Knowledge* (London: Routledge).

Moran, Leslie J. (2002), 'Lesbian and Gay Bodies of Law', in Richardson, Diane and Seidman, Steven (eds), *The Handbook of Gay and Lesbian Studies* (London: Sage Publications Inc.).

Naffine, Ngaire and Owens, Rosemary J. (eds) (1997), *Sexing the Subject of Law* (Sydney: Sweet & Maxwell).

Nordborg, Gudrun and Niemi-Kiesiläinen, Johanna (2001), 'Women's Peace: A Criminal Law Reform in Sweden', in Nousiainen, Kevät, *Gunnarsson, Åsa, Lundström, Karin and Niemi-Kiesiläinen, Johannal.* (eds), *Responsible Selves: Women in the Nordic Legal Culture* (Aldershot: Ashgate).

Nousiainen, Kevät *et al.* (eds) (2001), *Responsible Selves: Women in the Nordic Legal Culture* (Aldershot: Ashgate).

O'Brien, Jodi (2001), 'Homophobia and Heterosexism', in *International Encyclopedia of the Social and Behavioral Sciences* (London: Elsevier Science Limited).

Perry, Barbara (2001), *In the Name of Hate. Understanding Hate Crime* (New York: Routledge).

Pfeifer, Tara R. (2005), 'Out of the Shadows: The Positive Impact of *Lawrence* v. *Texas* on Victims of Same-Sex Domestic Violence', in *109:4 Penn State Law Review* 2005.

Ruthchild, Carole (1997), 'Don't Frighten the Horses! A Systemic Perspective on Violence against Lesbians and Gay Men', in Mason, Gail and Tomsen, Stephen (eds), *Homophobic Violence* (Sydney: Hawkins Press).

Säkerhetspolisen (2005), *Brottslighet kopplad till rikets inre säkerhet 2004,* Rapport från Säkerhetspolisen (Stockholm: Säkerhetspolisen).

Sorainen, Antu (1999), 'Foreign Theories and Our Histories: The Emergence of the Modern Homosexual and Local Research on Same-sex Sexualities', in 24 *Suomen Antropologi* 1999.

Tiby, Eva (2000), *De utsatta. Brott mot homosexuella kvinnor och män* (Stockholm: Folkhälsoinstitutet).

Tiby, Eva (2004), 'Offer för homofobiska brott', in Lindgren, Magnus *et al.* (eds) *Sårbara och utsatta brottsoffer* (Stockholm: Jure).

von Schulthess, Beatrice (1992), 'Violence in the Streets: Anti-lesbian Assault and Harassment in San Francisco', in Herek, Gregory M. and Berrill, Kevin T. (eds) *Hate Crimes: Confronting Violence against Lesbians and Gay Men* (London: Newbury Park).

Internet-Based References

Stockholms Fria Tidning, (published online 16 April 2005),
<http://www.ft.fria.nu/modules.php?name=News&file=article&sid=3763> (home page), accessed 20 June 2006.

Chapter 8

Social Insurance Law – The Core of Swedish Welfare Law

Ruth Mannelqvist

Welfare is an ambiguous term. It is used to refer both to people's wellbeing, and to systems that are designed to provide for people (Spicker 2000). In economic theory, the term welfare is often described as the good or as the content of preferences. Welfare is regarded as a function of commodities that has a value for people from the perspective of economic efficiency (Hausman and McPherson 2001). In social science, welfare is connected to social policy and is considered as methods by means of which the society can prevent or solve social problems (Korpi and Palme 1997). From a legal point of view, there are no specific definitions of the term welfare. Nevertheless, welfare policies that are found in both economic and social discussions can also be detected in the legal structures of welfare legislation. Welfare law is therefore an obvious outcome of political decisions, made out of both economic and social considerations.

The challenge in this chapter is not to establish current law, but a core of welfare law and to define some typical and distinctive principles which construct the core. The aim is to discuss the underlying principles of Swedish welfare law concerning economic welfare through social insurance. First there will be a sketch of the methodological principles for a broad understanding of welfare law through both the context of state and society and the positive law and legal policy. This is followed by a discussion concerning each of these in more detail in relation to the Swedish welfare state. Finally, some tensions, contradictions and even changes within welfare law are considered.

How to Establish a Core of Welfare Law?

What is welfare law? Is not a definition of the term welfare law necessary in order to establish a core of welfare law? According to Swedish legal tradition, the legal system is divided into private or civil and public law. Each division is separated into subcategories. Private law is considered to be based on the liberal ideology of 'rule-of-law', while public law is often described as an outcome of Swedish welfare-state regulation. Public regulations can be defined as legal regulations linked to the state's striving for equality and welfare, but private law is also embedded in social policy concerning the protection of the less powerful. So even if the law is divided into private and public law, there is no clear boundary between them.[1] This policy and protection may also be considered as the protection of and a striving for welfare. Therefore, welfare law can contain regulations deriving from both private and public law. It is difficult to identify a limit or boundary for welfare law and the definition of welfare law can alter depending on the point of departure. It is not especially meaningful to demarcate this branch of law, since welfare for citizens may concern many aspects, for instance people's ability to work, living conditions or the possibility of providing for themselves, among other things. Drawing a boundary may diminish or limit welfare law. Instead of trying to construct a limit for welfare law, it is more important to establish a core and it is not necessary to identify the branch of law that concerns welfare in order to recognize such a core.

What then is the core of welfare law and how can it be detected? To answer these questions, it is important to look at both the context in which the law exists and the significant role that norms and values play in law.

> As one pulls back further from the detail of the law and policy, one finds a conceptual framework which is traditionally the exclusive domain of social theorists but with which lawyers also ought to engage in order to understand the relationship between the substantive law and its social, economic and political role. (Harris 2000)

First, to clarify the context in which the law exists, the society or the state in which the regulations are instruments for welfare reforms can be used (Vahlne Westerhäll 2002; Mannelqvist 2003). Welfare for people can be secured and provided through welfare states and the state might accordingly be considered an institutional form of social protection (Spicker 2000). The concept 'welfare state' is sometimes used to describe part of the character of the particular state itself, as well as to describe the approach the state has taken to make welfare provisions (Harris 2000). In general, discussion about the welfare state is a question of the extent of the state, and not whether there should be one at all. Therefore, the starting point for revealing the context of welfare law is the various typologies of welfare states that are discussed in social science.

Second, as the context is the welfare state, welfare regulation is influenced by the state regime, within which the law is enacted. Legislation may be viewed as a result of various norms and values in the welfare state, where different types of welfare states provide for welfare in different ways. The norms and values in a society have an influence on law, but at the same time the law affects the ideals in a society (Gunnarsson 1995; Gustafsson 2002; Mannelqvist 2003). Both law and values change over time and in welfare law these changes are swift. It is therefore vital to explore whether there are any norms or values that remain consistent, through legal principles. These principles constitute a core of welfare law.

Legislation changes over time, sometime as a result of a change in society and sometimes as an attempt to change society (Åmark 2005). A central part of welfare legislation consists of social security law, where social insurance has a great significance, and Sweden has a long history of social security. From the beginning

---

1 For further discussions concerning the divisions of Swedish law from a welfare perspective, see Eek 1954; Stendahl 2003, 93; Christensen 2000 amongst others.

of the 20th century, social insurance was the central mechanism for the delivery of modern welfare, and social insurance is still an important part of welfare because its purpose is to sustain economic and social welfare for various groups of people (Hobson *et al.* 2002). In the initial stage, social insurance consisted of low benefits which were supposed to guarantee a minimum income. The benefits were financed by the person insured, payroll taxes and the state. From the 1950s onwards social insurance protection was based on the principle of compensation for lost income and self-support. In addition, the financial burden was mainly borne by the employers through payroll taxes. During the last century the system grew and principles and norms changed over time.

The social insurance scheme has for a long period of time been mostly concentrated around economic compensation and distribution. Legal analysis of social security law is often concerned with details of individual entitlement in specific circumstances. Swedish legal scholars in turn have formerly frequently systematized social law according to established legal structure, seldom considering the underlying principles and norms.[2] But since the legislation is an instrument of government social policy, it is imbued with norms and values. Therefore, it is possible to use social insurance legislation to reveal legal principles. Even though principles can differ in welfare legislation, they can still coexist in what can be described as a pluralistic legal system, due partially to the diversity of regulation. Principles can even be contradictory, but by accepting that law in general is pluralistic, it is possible to strive for normative consistency to a limited extent, for instance in social security law (Mannelqvist 2003; Gustafsson 2002). Consequently, in this pluralistic system, principles in social insurance law can be used to reveal a number of specific features of the core of welfare law. In order to detect legal principles in social insurance law, one has to use both traditional legal sources, mostly focused on preparatory work and legal research, and other research in social science. Thus in this chapter, I intend to discuss those principles and characteristics of the core of Swedish welfare law that can be elicited from social insurance law.

The Context of Welfare Law

The history of most welfare states is a story of transition from relief based on charity and discretion to benefits based on legislation and entitlement. According to Nicola Lacey, the welfare state can be regarded as an institution for social justice, and ideas about the meaning of citizenship have been central to the development of welfare states. There is however, one particular idea that has predominated, and that is the idea of need. Citizens are entitled to, or have a right to, a guarantee that the community will guarantee to meet certain needs. Welfare states also provide people with a possibility of sharing risks, such as illness and poverty (Lacey 1998).

The nature of welfare differs in welfare states, and in social science research such states are divided into different typologies of welfare states. Two well-known schemes for describing welfare states are those introduced by Richard Titmuss and

2 See Vahlne Westerhäll, Eek, Lavin and other Swedish legal scholars in social law.

Gøsta Esping-Andersen. Titmuss distinguished among 'three contrasting models of functions of social policy' (Titmuss 1974; Lødemel 1997). These models were developed to analyse differences in welfare-state provision and the underlying ideas of the role of the state. Welfare states are, according to this model, divided into those that follow: residual model, handmaiden model or institutional redistributive model of welfare. The residual model deals only with people who are unable to help themselves, while the handmaiden model disburses social services on the basis of merit, work performance and productivity. Thc institutional model regards the provision of social welfare as an important activity for the state, organizing universal social services outside the market based on the principle of need. In Esping-Andersen's typology, different welfare states are defined from a political perspective (Esping-Andersen 1990). The main welfare regimes are classified as being social democratic, liberal-residual and corporatist. In social democratic regimes, such as Sweden, welfare is based on general rights that are intended for specific groups of people. Liberal regimes are residual and have limited the role of the state depending instead on the market. Finally, in corporatist regimes the family is held responsible for its own provision and support from the state is therefore aimed at the family.

When a gender perspective is added to welfare-state research, it is obvious that previous research has concentrated on state-market relations. But the welfare state also comprises other relations, such as those between women and men, the family and the labour market. Critical feminist researchers point out, for instance, the lack of consideration concerning the division within the family of paid and unpaid work (Nousiainen 2001; Hirdman 2001). Anneli Anttonen argues that Nordic welfare states comprise two components, namely the social-insurance state and the social-service state (Anttonen 1998).[3] The citizen is protected from income loss, sickness and unemployment in the social-insurance state, while the social-service state provides care for people in need. Anttonen maintains that the social-insurance state mainly supports people who are firmly established on the labour market and, due to the segregation of the labour market, it mostly includes men. In the Nordic welfare model, the possibility for women to combine work and family life has been facilitated, but the actual division of unpaid work between men and women in the family or in care-taking has not changed. According to Anttonen, mainstream welfare research has to consider both sides of the welfare state, in order to bring into focus equality between men and women.

Another typology is made on the basis of the extent of a 'male-breadwinner' model, developed by Jane Lewis and Ilona Ostner (Lewis and Ostner 1995). Lewis and Ostner divide states into 'strong male-breadwinner', 'modified male-breadwinner' and 'weak male-breadwinner' types, and focus on two main elements of welfare provision by the state. The first is the provision of care, especially childcare, and the second concerns tax and benefits policies. Patterns in welfare-state regimes are rooted in the cultural traditions of the family and Sweden can be seen to follow a 'weak male-breadwinner model'. However, Lewis anticipates a change in the models of welfare states and notices a shift towards 'an adult worker model' (Lewis 2002).

3 Vahlne Westerhäll has also discussed a similar division of the Nordic welfare state, in Vahlne Westerhäll 2002.

She emphasizes that there is a re-casting of the traditional male work/welfare model, from 'passive' to 'active', with the stress on responsibilities rather than entitlements. This shift in the welfare state generalizes male labour-market behaviour to women and women's participation in the labour market has, in many respects, become the new norm.

Perhaps influenced by feminist criticism, Walter Korpi and Joakim Palme have defined welfare states from the perspective of class and gender inequalities (Korpi and Palme 1997). The major constellations of welfare institutions can be described by using a combination of these two typologies. This classification indicates that welfare in three of the Nordic countries, Finland, Norway and Sweden, is based on an encompassing and dual earner constellation. The encompassing model combines generality with earnings-related benefits. In Sweden, the pensions system with a general guaranteed pension together with an income-related pension is one example of this encompassing model. The dual-earner, support model reflects the extent to which public policy institutions both enable parents, men as well as women, to combine parenthood with paid work and attempt to redistribute caring work within the family (Korpi 2001).

It is important to recognize that welfare state typology is a statistical analysis and represents a frozen picture of the society as it is, while a description of welfare law contains changes, both in time and interpretation. One standpoint taken in this chapter is that the law is based on values and norms in society and that these can transform into legal principles. Together with legal cultures and social policies, norms and principles are a part of the legal system. At the same time, law in itself can alter norms and values in society or in welfare states. The context of welfare law is mainly the welfare state. However, the concept of the welfare state has different meanings, with a number of definitions. There are, nonetheless, in general three distinctive features of the welfare state: it provides benefits to everyone regardless of contributions; if people have explicit needs, the welfare state provides specific benefits; and the institutions are funded by mandatory taxes or contributions. Collective welfare provisions can be arranged both as a safety net and as a general provision. Provisions conceived of as safety nets presuppose that people in general can provide for themselves and that aid or benefits from society are only forthcoming when that self-support fails. The general provision is in principle accessible irrespective of people's own possibility of providing for themselves.[4] These features serve as guidance in Swedish welfare law (Mannelqvist 2003).

The Core of Welfare Legislation

The Swedish welfare state is described as a social-democratic welfare state in social science with mainly redistributive motives lying behind the welfare policy. This has resulted in a specific Swedish model of welfare that has a number of important features. In Sweden, a belief in state-regulated social welfare and gender equality are two fundamental points of departure.

---

4 Further discussions, see among others, Miller 1989; Lacey 1998.

The public social insurance system is known as the core of the Swedish welfare state. Social protection includes the majority of people and social insurance provides both a high level of compensation for lost income and residence-based benefits. Furthermore, Sweden has a large government sector and the welfare is financed by mandatory taxes and contributions. The significance of work is a further important element in Swedish welfare. Benefits are largely based on the employment strategy, which implies that benefits are connected to earned income from paid work.[5] The employment strategy means that employment always has priority over any measures or payment of cash benefits and the main purpose of the strategy is to encourage people to work. This strong bond between work and social rights signifies that the Swedish welfare state can be regarded as a workfare state (Björklund *et al.* 1998; Gunnarsson and Stattin 2001; Gunnarsson *et al.* 2004; Christensen and Malmstedt 2000).

Another important feature is, as mentioned, the ideology of equality, which is very strong in Swedish welfare policy. For a long time, the abandoning of a class society was an essential task for law and politics. During the 1960s and 1970s, demands arose for equality between women and men, and the principle of gender equality started to become obvious in the preparatory work for social law, among others (Mannelqvist 2003; SOU 1998:6). There has long been a political aspiration to achieve formal equality between men and women and equal treatment of people in Sweden. Perhaps that is one reason why Sweden is considered to be one of the 'weak male-breadwinner models', because women have a greater potential for independence as a result of the social system, the labour market and family structures (Lewis 1992; Sainsbury 2001).

Legal Principles in Social Insurance

As described above, the Swedish welfare state, in which the law exists, influences legal reforms and the provision of welfare reflects the values of the society. Some important characteristics of the Swedish welfare state are redistributive justice, equality and the employment strategy, which serve as normative foundations for social rights and duties. Swedish social insurance law is mainly constructed in the form of collective rights, through individual rights intended for a specific group of people, for instance parents or senior citizens. Furthermore, this legislation is based on a number of legal principles. The following discussion concerning the legal principles in Swedish social insurance legislation is taken from my doctoral thesis, published in 2003 (Mannelqvist 2003).

The public insurance system is general in several senses of the word. It covers the entire population on equal terms. The system is financed largely through proportional contributions and taxes, but the provisions are the same for everyone. This can also be seen as an outcome of one important principle in social security legislation; the principle of solidarity. This principle leads to a public and compulsory social insurance

5 The specifics of the Swedish welfare state have been discussed from many points of view, such as historical, economic and legal perspectives. See for instance, Edebalk 1996; Korpi and Palme 1997; Palme 1996; Sainsbury and Nordgren 1997; Vahlne Westerhäll 2002.

scheme. Everyone, in general, has a right to insurance, but there is a concurrent obligation to contribute to the system. It is impossible not to be part of the system. The presence of this principle can be detected as far back as to the beginning of the 1920s. The principle of solidarity further maintains the 'social contract', meaning that there is an unspoken obligation between different generations in society to take care of each other. For instance, the economic burden of caring for the sick, old or young is shared in this contract. The working population pay for those outside the labour market in a 'pay-as-you-go system' and a very small proportion of the benefits is financed through a funded system.

Another basic principle in social insurance is that of redistribution. Everyone has to contribute to the system but contribution is not a condition for having the right to benefits. Thus, benefits are not connected to contributions and can therefore, legally speaking, be regarded as payroll taxes. As a result, it is possible for the state to impose contributions that are larger than individual benefits. There is a limit to the outcome of benefits, but no restraint on contributions in general. Taxpayers with high incomes pay more into the system then they will get out, which leads to low-income earners receiving benefits to a larger extent then high-income earners. The contributions are paid by the employer but are in principal, for both economic and legal research, considered to be a relinquishment by the employed.

A further important feature in social insurance is the principle of compensation for loss of income. This principle was introduced into social insurance legislation through health insurance in the 1950s, in order to retain the economic welfare that labour work provided. Nowadays, the benefits in the social insurance scheme are largely designed to cover income loss, due for example to sickness, age or unemployment, and only a few benefits are means-tested. The construction of benefits to cover lost income is clearly connected with the overall employment strategy in the Swedish welfare state. It is also one way to secure the financing of the social insurance system, since the income that is compensated for is simultaneously the foundation for the payroll tax.

The principle of gender equality is another important element in social security and the public scheme is designed to consider equality. This principle became visible in the preparatory work at the end of the 1960s and the beginning of the 1970s, and the first changes in the law due to equality came about a few years later. Overall, constitutional law upholds gender equality as an important aim for law and society, and as a result of this, legislation is based on formal legal gender-neutral equality (Svensson 1997; Svensson 2001). In legislation, men and women are seldom divided into different categories. Instead there are other legal categories that can be detected in social insurance law, classified by income, age, maintenance and so on. In social insurance, gender equality is important for instance in parental insurance. This insurance is divided equally between both parents, with a possibility for them to transfer part of the insurance to each other. During a reform in the 1970s, parental insurance changed its name, from maternal insurance, in order to encourage fathers to stay home and take care of their children. This was seen as a way to increase equality between men and women. In another reform at the end of the 1980s, the widows' pension was regarded as unjust, due to the fact that this pension was only designed for women. Since the state did not have the financial stability to extend the pension to include men, the widows' pension was abolished. Instead, a new pension called the survivors' pension was introduced, but it did not have the same favourable conditions as the widows' pension had. Therefore, in order to achieve equality between women and men, women had to give up some of the benefits that they earlier had a right to.

Is the Core Consistent?

Swedish welfare law can in general be described in terms of the principles behind social insurance. As described, this regulation is based on principles of solidarity, redistribution, compensation for lost income and gender equality. In addition, the social insurance system is mainly designed for a specific category of people, such as the sick or the old, in an attempt to equalize economic conditions. As stated, one central principle in the Swedish welfare state and the core of welfare law is gender equality. This 'new' principle shows that it is possible to introduce new principles in legislation which can alter or deepen a normative core. The principle of gender equality demonstrates that the norms and values in society can penetrate already established legislation. The aspiration to achieve gender equality is often obvious in preparatory work, and occurs plainly in legal terms in the form of gender-neutral legislation. One criticism of gender-neutral legislation is that the legislation acquires an objective position in law and does not consider that society, in fact and reality, is different for men and women. The situation of women has not been regarded in law and the law is based on a male norm.[6]

It is, therefore, important to recognize that the principle of gender equality in welfare law does not automatically result in gender equality in welfare issues in Sweden. Again, the pension system can serve as an example of this. Since the beginning of the1900s, there has been an old-age pension scheme in Sweden. Initially, the pension was a state pension which only supported those who were able to pay in to the pension system. The old, the sick and women had only a limited opportunity to pay contributions, and therefore, they derived little support from the pension scheme. During the next couple of decades, the state pension was improved and people were entitled to benefit from the pension plan without having to pay high contributions. However, the pension was low and few could support themselves on it. In the 1950s, a supplementary pension, based on a person's income, was introduced. The supplementary pension was meant to improve the standard of living for old people. At the same time, women's participation in the labour market increased and is today, in principle, as high as men's participation. In the 1990s a new pension system was introduced. But despite the fact that women are taking an active part in the labour market and earn their own income, they are still getting lower pensions than men. There may be a number of explanations for this. One is that some women are part-time workers. In order to take care of children and the household, many women work fewer hours than men. Another reason is that women have a lower income than

6 This has been argued by a number of feminist scholars, both in Sweden and in other countries. In Sweden see for instance, Svensson 1997.

men. The Swedish labour market is segregated according to sex and women work mainly in the public sector where wages are lower than in the private sector. Even if men and women have the same kind of work, education and profession and even the same employer, men still earn more than women. This can also be described as structural discrimination against women. All in all, there are many reasons why women do not get as high a pension as men and from a legal point of view, formal gender-neutral pension legislation does not improve the situation for women. Neutral laws in a discriminatory society only preserve and maintain an unequal reality. Thus, the principle of gender equality can be both invisible and reversed in the legal usage of social insurance law in particular and welfare law in general, and it is, despite the principle being stressed in politics as well as in law. Inequalities in society have a clear impact in formal gender-neutral legislation. Therefore, the present construction of the principle of gender equality in Swedish social-insurance and welfare law may perhaps be questioned.

As stated in this chapter, the features of public social insurance are very specific and cannot be found in private insurance. Even so, social insurance is often compared to private insurance in political discussions and the lack of certain private insurance features is considered a weakness or failure in public insurance. To facilitate the distinctive features in social insurance and illustrate how misleading and confusing this comparison can be, a parallel will be drawn between legal principles in social insurance and private insurance.[7]

In contrast to social insurance, private insurance is based on an individual contract and relies on people's willingness to be a part of the insurance scheme and their ability to pay the fee. Solidarity is therefore not relevant in private insurance in the same way as in public insurance. One other important principle for private insurance is, in contrast to social insurance, the coherence between contributions and benefits. If the insured person does not pay the contribution, he or she has no right to insurance benefits. Coherence in private insurance therefore makes redistribution difficult. Accordingly, redistribution is primarily possible only in the public system. In private insurance, both contributions and benefits are means-tested. For instance, the contribution to sickness insurance depends on the health of the person insured. This implies that private insurance does not secure a person's standard of living by compensating for loss of income, but instead covers those who are able to make large payments. Furthermore, the terms of the agreement in private insurance are based on the principle of mutual understanding. Decisions made by the parties to the contract are binding for the insurance, not principles made in the public interest. In a private contract or insurance, a principle of gender equality is also seldom referred to. As a result of this, private insurance hardly ever takes gender equality into consideration. This is very obvious when it comes to private pensions or pensions paid through collective agreement, where women with low incomes get lower pensions and thereby partly finance the higher pensions of the men (Granqvist and Ståhlberg 2002).

The public social insurance scheme has legal characteristics that differ from private insurance. Nevertheless, these systems are often compared without reflection regarding either legal principles or ideology. It is, in fact, invalid to compare public

7 All this has been done in earlier research, see Mannelqvist 2003.

social insurance with private insurance. They have different principles and aims and the transformation of public social insurance into private insurance would signify a changed view of both social insurance and welfare issues. In spite of this, during the last decade, several suggestions have been made, in various government commissions, about how to make public social insurance more similar to private insurance, in order to improve the former.[8] Few such suggestions have, however, resulted in any change in legislation. Even so, this indicates a possible change in norms and values in society concerning social insurance.

Taken together, without exploring the limits, one may exploit the core of welfare law through legal principles in social insurance law. Fundamental features in the Swedish welfare state, such as solidarity and redistribution, are still essential in social insurance legislation, although one may anticipate a political move toward a public social insurance that includes attributes from private insurance. If these changes gain a hold in legislation, the principles that constitute the core of welfare law would also be modified, but the extent to which the changes will alter the core is hard to anticipate.

References

Government Committees and Other Official Documents

SOU 1996:113, *En allmän och aktiv försäkring vid sjukdom och rehabilitering, del 1–2*. [Final report from the Government Commission on work and sick injuries, with proposals for a general and active insurance]

SOU 1998:6, *Ty makten är din ... Myten om det rationella arbetslivet och det jämställda Sverige*. [Final report from the Government Commission on the distribution of Economic Power and Resources between Women and Men].

SOU 2000:121, *Sjukfrånvaro och sjukskrivning – fakta och förslag*. [Final report from the Government Commission on sickness insurances].

Ds 2002:49. *Den svenska sjukan* ESO-rapport.

Literature

Åmark, Klas (2005), Hundra år av välfärdspolitik. Välfärdsstatens framväxt i Norge och Sverige (Finland: Boréa).

Anttonen, Anneli (1998), 'Den sociala servicestaten som feministiskt kampbegrepp', in Eliasson-Lappalainen, Rosmari and Szebehely, Marta (eds), *Vad förgår och vad består? En antologi om äldreomsorg, kvinnosyn och socialpolitik* (Eslöv: Arkiv Förlag).

Björklund, Anders, Edebalk, Per-Gunnar, Ohlsson, Rolf and Söderström, Lars (1998), *Välfärdspolitik i kristid – håller arbetslinjen?* Välfärdspolitiska rådets rapport (SNS Förlag).

8 For instance in government commissions, SOU 1996:113; SOU 2000:121; Ds 2002:49.

Christensen, Anna (2000), 'Socialförsäkringen i framtiden – från arbetarskap till socialt medborgarskap' in *I väntan på framtiden, report from a research seminar in Umeå*, Januari 2000 fakta nr 2 (Stockholm: Försäkringskasseförbundet).

Christensen, Anna and Malmstedt, Mattias (2000), 'Lex Loci Laboris versus Lex Loci Domicilii – an Inquiry into the Normative Foundations of European Social Security Law', in 2/1 *European Journal of Social Security* 2000.

Edebalk, Per-Gunnar (1996), *Välfärdsstaten träder fram. Svensk socialförsäkring 1884–1955* (Ystad: Arkiv Förlag).

Eek, Hilding (1954), *Socialrätt: föreläsningar* (Stockholm: Institutet för offentlig och internationell rätt).

Esping-Andersen, Gøsta (1990), *The Three Worlds of Welfare Capitalism* (Cambridge: Polity Press).

Granqvist, Lena and Ståhlberg, Ann-Charlotte (2002), *De nya avtals- och tjänstepensionerna: Ökad jämställdhet – men fortfarande sämre pension för kvinnor* (Västerås: Edita Västra Aros).

Gunnarsson, Åsa (1995), *Skatterättvisa* (Uppsala: Iustus Förlag).

Gunnarsson, Åsa and Stattin, Chris (2001), 'Jämställdhetsnormen i skatte- och socialrätten', in Burman, Monica and Gunnarsson, Åsa (eds), *Familjeföreställningar – om familjens betydelse inom juridik, ekonomi och forskning* (Uppsala: Iustus Förlag).

Gunnarsson, Åsa, Burman, Monica and Wennberg, Lena (2004), 'Economic Dependency and Self-support in Family, Tax and Social Law', in Svensson, Eva-Maria, Pylkkänen, Anu and Niemi-Kiesiläinen, Johanna (eds), *Nordic Equality at a Crossroads. Feminist Legal Studies Coping with Difference* (Aldershot: Ashgate).

Gustafsson, Håkan (2002), *Rättens polyvalens. En rättsvetenskaplig studie av sociala rättigheter och rättssäkerhet* (Lund: Sociologiska institutionen, Lunds Universitet).

Harris, Neville (2000), *Social Security Law in Context* (Oxford: University Press).

Hausman, Daniel M. and McPherson, Michael S. (2001), *Ekonomisk teori och moralfilosofi* (Lund: Studentlitteratur).

Hirdman, Yvonne (2001), *Genus – om det stabilas föränderliga former* (Lund: Liber).

Hobson, Barbara, Lewis, Jane and Siim, Birte (2002), 'Introduction: contested concepts in gender and social politics', in Hobson, Barbara, Lewis, Jane and Siim, Birte (eds), *Contested Concepts in Gender and Social Politics* (Cheltenham: Edward Elgar Publishing Limited).

Korpi, Walter and Palme, Joakim (1997), 'The Paradox of Redistribution and Strategies of Equality: Welfare State Institutions, Inequality and Poverty in the Western Countries', in *63 American Sociological Review* 1997.

Korpi, Walter (2001), 'Class, gender and inequality. The role of welfare states', in Kohli, Martin and Novak, Mojca (eds), *Will Europe Work? Integration, employment and the social order* (London: Routledge).

Lacey, Nicola (1998), *Unspeakable subjects. Feminist essays in legal and social theory* (Oxford: Hart Publishing).

Lewis, Jane (1992), 'Gender and the Development of Welfare Regimes', in 2 *Journal of European Social Policy* 1992.

Lewis, Jane and Ostner, Ilona (1995), 'Gender and the evolution of European social policies', in Leidfried, Stephan and Pierson, Paul (eds), *European Social Policy: Between Fragmentation and Integration* (Washington DC: Brookings).

Lewis, Jane (2002), 'Gender and Welfare State Change', in *4 European Societies* 2002.

Lødemel, Ivar (1997), *The Welfare Paradox. Income Maintenance and Personal Social Services in Norway and Britain 1946–1966* (Oslo: Scandinavian University Press).

Mannelqvist, Ruth (2003), *Samband i socialförsäkringen. En rättsvetenskaplig studie av sambandet mellan förmåner och avgifter i socialförsäkringen* (Uppsala: Iustus Förlag).

Miller, David (1989), *Market, State and Community: theoretical foundations of market socialism* (Oxford: Clarendon).

Nousiainen, Kevät (2001), 'Transformative Nordic Welfarism: Liberal and Communitarian Trends in Family and Market Law', in Nousiainen, Kevät, Gunnarsson, Åsa, Lundström, Karin and Niemi-Kiesiläinen, Johanna (eds), *Responsible Selves: Women in the Nordic Legal Culture* (Aldershot: Ashgate Publishing Ltd).

Palme, Joakim (1996), 'Välfärdsstaten som en strategi för jämlikhet', in Palme, Joakim and Wennemo, Irene (eds), *Generell välfärd: Hot eller möjligheter?* (Stockholm: Norstedts).

Sainsbury, Diane and Nordgren, Margreth (1997), 'I nedskärningarnas tecken. Välfärdsstaten och jämställdheten', in *SOU 1997:115*.

Sainsbury, Diane (2001), 'Gendering Dimensions of Welfare States', in Fink, Janet, Lewis, Gail and Clarke, David (eds) *Rethinking European Welfare* (London: Sage and Open University).

Spicker, Paul (2000), *The Welfare State. A General Theory* (London: Sage Publications).

Stendahl, Sara (2003), *Communicating Justice, Providing Legitimacy. The legal practice of Swedish administrative courts in cases regarding sickness cash benefit* (Uppsala: Iustus Förlag).

Svensson, Eva-Maria (1997), *Genus och rätt – en problematisering av föreställningen om rätten* (Uppsala: Iustus Förlag).

Svensson, Eva-Maria (2001), 'Sex Equality: Changes in Politics, Jurisprudence and Feminist Legal studies', in Nousiainen, Kevät, Gunnarsson, Åsa, Lundström, Karin and Niemi-Kiesiläinen, Johanna (eds), *Responsible Selves: Women in the Nordic legal culture* (Aldershot: Ashgate Publishing Ltd).

Titmuss, Richard M. (1974), *Social policy* (London: Allen and Unwin Ltd).

Vahlne Westerhäll, Lotta (2002), *Den starka statens fall? En rättsvetenskaplig studie av svensk social trygghet 1950-2000* (Stockholm: Norstedts Juridik).

Chapter 9

Challenging one Fundamental Norm in Labour Law – the Exception of the Employer's Family and Home

Catharina Calleman

The provisions of the Swedish Employment Protection Act (SFS 1982:80) have been said to give the same protection against arbitrariness in dismissal to female as to male workers (SOU 1978:38 76). This claim is based on the fact that the same rules apply to men and women, a claim which requires reflection on the difference between formal justice and substantive equality.[1] Do the provisions of the act in fact give the same protection to women as to men, when seen in a wider social and legal context? More specifically, does the law protect all kinds of work? Are different work tasks or different conditions of work treated alike? Different treatment for different kinds of work may have strongly gendered effects, as the labour market in Sweden is very much divided according to sex.

When the Act is discussed in such terms, gender equality is more debatable. Already in the first paragraph of the Act we find some exceptions from the application of the law, which have a strongly gendered content. The four exceptions concern employees who are 'in managerial or comparable positions', 'members of the employer's family', 'engaged to work in the employer's household' or 'in subsidized schemes such as relief work or sheltered work'.[2]

The topic of this chapter is the exception of the employer's family and household from Swedish labour legislation. My pre-understanding starting the investigation[3] was that these exceptions would be theoretically interesting from a feminist point of view, but that they would have little quantitative importance. This idea probably stemmed from dealing with Swedish labour law, which focuses on big corporations with collective agreements and many employees. However, contrary to my expectations, the exceptions also appeared to be quantitatively important. It has been estimated that there are currently approximately 200,000 family enterprises in Sweden and the number of small enterprises seems to be growing. This means an increase in the importance of the exception of family members from employment

1 For a discussion on formal and substantive equality see for example Lundström 1999, 28ff.

2 The exception for managerial or comparable positions has been discussed in an article by Fahlbeck 2001.

3 The exception for the employer's family has been treated in Calleman 2004.

protection requirements. The demand for domestic labour has also increased and thereby the importance of the exception for such work. There are several reasons for this, such as the cutting down of care within institutions, increasing demands and stress in working life and increasing wage differences. The effects of both exceptions risk being particularly crucial for immigrant women who are often dependent on domestic work or on work within the family enterprise.

It would probably never occur to many scholars to discuss the exception of family members or of employees working in the employer's household.[4] The topic might not seem to contain much of interest. From a feminist point of view, however, issues of the legal status of working family members and of workers in the household are of interest. The exceptions may be viewed as an example of how the family is constructed as private, pre-legal, and autonomous from the state. The exceptions might appear to be gender neutral, but have the effect of excluding mainly categories that are vulnerable in a society structured by gender, namely women and children. The issue of domestic work is not only gendered but also shows how working conditions are shaped in the intersection of class, ethnicity, nationality and (historically) in the conflict between the cities and the countryside (see Lykke 2003; Mulinari *et al.* 2004).

Historically, nearly all protective labour legislation in Sweden has excluded the family and the household of the employer. Today, the Employment Protection Act is almost the only – but a very important – labour law regulation exempting members of the employer's family who are working in his or her business.[5] Domestic labour in the employer's home, however, is still exempted from most labour legislation, such as the Employment Protection Act, the Working Time Act (SFS 1982:673) and the Work Environment Act (SFS 1977:1160). Instead there is legislation specifically designed to cover conditions in domestic work (SFS 1970:943).

A Feminist Approach to the Limits of Law

In this chapter I will reflect on the exceptions of the employer's family and home from labour legislation using a feminist approach to the limits of law. In my opinion a feminist approach to legal issues has certain specific features, some of which clearly relate to the constructed limits of law. This applies both to the methods used and the issues raised.

One – and perhaps the best-known – feminist critique of law concerns the limit between public and private, both in its analytical and its prescriptive aspects.[6] In labour law this dichotomy[7] appears in the entirely different way that paid and unpaid work are treated, as unpaid work falls outside of the limit of labour law.

4 One exception is Aubert *et al.* 1952.

5 The exception may have both negative and positive effects on family members, depending on their relationship with the employer, see below.

6 For a discussion on the evolution of the idea of a public and a private sphere, see Svensson 1997.

7 For a discussion on gender dichotomies, see for example Lundström 1999, 44 ff.

A feminist approach challenges the limits between law and its social context. It has been said that this implies trying to take back the factual circumstances to the legal field of knowledge. Value and reality, norm and application belong together and cannot be separated (Christensen 1986, 96). In feminist legal studies the social context in which a law appears is important when judging whether legal reforms, purporting to contribute to sex equality, will in fact do so. In labour law the social context is the labour market – the public sphere – but also the private sphere, as this is strongly connected to women's conditions in waged work (Fransson 2000, 30).

Another limit challenged by feminist critique is the limit between academic disciplines. This challenge implies using knowledge, theories and methods from disciplines such as sociology, economics, linguistics, history or philosophy in order to add to, illuminate and fertilize legal thinking and research.

Feminist critique likewise questions and tries to break down the boundaries between established legal areas and legal concepts. It investigates the structure and function of the legal system and is often critical of the legal system as such. Only when legal rules are evaluated in a wider context can we see whether they are really aimed at liberating women or whether they simply displace problems into other fields (Hellum 1979). New knowledge about law is produced by studying the joint effects of family law, labour law and social security law. One example is the myriad rules and policies in fields as diverse as family law, taxation, social welfare policy and healthcare that have a potentially significant impact on the structure and amount of unpaid work performed (Rittich 2002, 130).

In the investigation of the exceptions from labour law of the employer's family and home, I have used material from a variety of disciplines and from different legal areas: historical and economic literature, statistics, preparatory work, case law and legal doctrine.

In order to study the historical development of the exceptions from labour law, I have posed such questions as: What changes in family policies and family law were made in the period studied? Who was considered a member of family and how was domestic work defined? In which industries and professions did women and men work and what kind of work was regulated by labour law?

In order to explore the justifications for the two exceptions I have asked such questions as: Which assumptions about relations within the family and about domestic work have governed the decision to make exceptions from the protection of labour law? What values were addressed in the arguments and what was not mentioned in the legislative process? From which pieces of legislation were exceptions made and when were they not made?

Finally, I have tried to draw some conclusions about the effects and outcomes of the exceptions from employment protection made today. This has been done by placing the exceptions in their social context and in the context of legislation in other legal areas. Some aspects of the exceptions are then discussed in the light of the dichotomy between public and private.

Historical Development

In the early period of Swedish industrialization, most production was carried out within agriculture and within the family household. In the year 1900, approximately 60 per cent of the population was working in agriculture. Work and family life formed an entity, factually as well as legally. The regulation of labour performed in agriculture and by servants – in the so-called *Legostadgan* (SFS 1833:43) – constituted part of family law. A married woman was under the control and guardianship of her husband (according to the *National Code* of 1734). He had the right to demand that she devoted herself to the care of her family and home and she could not dispose of her own labour without his consent. In factories and in agriculture the husband usually settled employment contracts on behalf of the whole family and the wage was paid to him (SOU 1938:47, 74).

The very first protective legislation in Sweden concerned limitations on the work of women and children in factories.[8] No exceptions for the family were made in this legislation. Domestic work was however consistently excluded, as the legislation applied only to factories.

The first protective legislation with a more general scope was the Occupational Safety Act introduced in 1912 (SFS 1912:206). In this Act, work performed by the employer's family was among the exceptions and a labour law family concept was established in the preparatory work of the Act. Not only parents and children were considered to belong to the employer's family, but also other relatives and even people unrelated to the employer such as foster children and wards, if these people shared homes or households with the employer. The spouse of the employer was not mentioned in the enumeration of family members, as two spouses could not enter into an employment relationship because of the husband's guardianship over his wife (Committee on Occupational Safety 1909, 60). Domestic work was initially excluded, but in the later version of the law, the exclusion was considered unnecessary as the law applied only to enterprise (Prop. 1912:104, 187). Domestic work was defined as work which was required in order to maintain the employer's household, such as the acquisition and preparation of food and beverages, cleaning the home, providing heating, illumination etc. (Committee on Occupational Safety 1909, 60).

In 1919 the first limitation of working hours, to eight hours a day, applied to enterprises, where usually fewer than five workers were 'used'. Among the categories of work exempted was work performed by the employer's family (SFS 1919:652). Domestic work was excluded from the regulation of working time, as it was not part of an enterprise.

8 The best known of these pieces of 'protective legislation' is the prohibition of night work for women, the Act (SFS 1909:131) with a ban on the use of women in night work in certain industrial enterprises. This law applied to factories with more than ten employees and therefore never protected the majority of working women. The ban has been much debated. In an investigation in the 1930s it was stated that the ban prevented women from competing with men in some well-paid occupations. SOU 1938:47, 451.

The Marriage Code of 1921 and the abolition of the *Legostadgan* in 1926, saw the revocation of the legal foundation of the reign of the master (Gunnarsson *et al.* 2004). Married women acquired legal capacity and relationships within the family were thereby individualized. Labour law and family law were separated and labour contracts were individualized, but it was still possible to see traces of previous legal conditions. For example, the national collective agreement for agriculture in 1936 contained a provision that a worker could not make an employment contract on behalf of his wife without her consent.

As a consequence of industrialization the relative number of people working in agriculture declined and the population in the cities more than doubled in the forty years after 1900. The number of 'professionals' increased at the expense of the categories of 'helping family members' and 'servants'. Small enterprises abounded. But in spite of industrialization, agricultural work and domestic work remained the two areas of work that employed most females. Most female workers in agriculture were labelled 'helping family members' whose working hours, work tasks and wages were not regulated. Statistically, the wives of farmers were registered as 'wives without a profession', although they were in fact companions in the enterprise and their workload considerably exceeded the norm in other employments (SOU 1938:47, 95 ff).

Gradually, an increasing number of industries, and finally even agriculture, were included in the regulations concerning occupational safety and working hours, but the family, domestic workers and often also small enterprises were still exempted. When the Paid Vacations Act was introduced in 1938, people employed by a close relative were excluded. However, domestic workers were entitled to the provisions of the law (SFS 1938:287).

In the 1930s the figures for marriage and the birth rate were very low and this gave rise to a series of social reforms aimed at increasing marriage and birth rates. Increasing the population and caring for the new generations and their mothers was considered an issue of the greatest importance. A ban on dismissals on the grounds that the employee was engaged, was marrying or was pregnant, was introduced (SFS 1939:727). The employer's family and housemaids were initially exempted from this legislation and so were all enterprises with fewer than three employees. However, some years later, with the explicit purpose of reducing the number of abortions, the ban on dismissal was extended to all employees (SOU 1944:51, 132–133).

When married women entered the labour market in the 1930s and 1940s, the shortage of domestic labour appeared to be a big problem. This resulted in requests for legislation to improve the working conditions of domestic workers. A new act was introduced containing provisions regulating free time, housing and the proper time for paying wages (SFS 1944:461). But the act contained no provisions concerning working hours, as such regulation was considered impossible in housework. Members of the employer's family and also housekeepers, who were mostly employed by widowers and bachelors, were exempted from the act. The new act did not in fact solve the problem of shortage of domestic labour and after the Second World War, many German, Finnish and Norwegian women were recruited as maids or nannies (Lundh and Olsson 1999, 53). The Women's Council of the Trade Union Confederation (LO) tried to direct the attention of the trade unions to the vulnerability of the German housemaids at the beginning of the 1950s, but with no success. The issue of domestic work has been said to concern the lowest ranks of the labour market, where both employers and employees were women and the employees were sometimes foreigners. In the hierarchy of values, which characterized the trade unions in the 1950s and 1960s, domestic work could easily be dismissed as being the concern of limited groups without any immediate relevance to society (Öberg 1999, 188).

Step by step the exception for the employer's family began to be contested. In 1949 amendments were made to the Occupational Safety Act, mainly to adapt Swedish legislation to international conventions.[9] The general exception for the employer's family was then abolished but instead the family was exempted from specific provisions regarding breaks, nightly rest and weekly rest and also from special provisions concerning the work of women and minors. Domestic work was exempted from all provisions of the act, as it applied only to enterprises. In the general Working Time Act of 1970, the employer's family and domestic workers were also exempted. The employer's family was exempted with reference to earlier regulation and domestic workers were exempted with reference to a proposal of a special act on conditions in domestic work in the employer's home. This act, the Domestic Work Act, was introduced in the same year (SFS 1970:943). All kinds of work, which were required for 'the normal care of a private home' were included in the definition of domestic work and it was also expressly stated that caring for children and for sick and old people, who belonged to the household, was included (Prop. 1970:150, 44). The Domestic Work Act in turn exempted family members.

To summarize the development up to the period of intense labour legislation in the 1970s, the most industrialized branches were included first in the protective labour legislation, agriculture came far later and last – if at all – paid work in the employer's home. The least contested exception was the exception for the employer's spouse or for a person who took her place (a housekeeper). It was stated that in the same way it was not possible to regulate the work of a housewife, it was not possible to include housekeepers in the legislation on housemaids (SOU 1939:15, 157-158). The regulation of housework was viewed as almost impossible. The exemption from protective legislation meant that domestic workers and family members were dependent on personal agreements with the employer in all kinds of labour issues, such as working hours, working conditions and occupational safety.

The proportion of the population working in agriculture had been decreasing drastically and in 1970 it amounted to only 6 per cent (SCB 1910–1985). A process of monopolization had started in the Swedish economy, implying the expulsion of many small companies from the labour market. After 1965, increasing productivity led to a decline in the demand for labour in the private sector. Dismissals due to a shortage of work were commonplace and older workers especially often lost their jobs in restructuring processes. Trade union activity had steadily increased and

9 C77 Medical Examination of Young Persons (Industry) Convention, 1946, C78 Medical Examination of Young Persons (Non-Industrial Occupations) Convention, 1946, C79 Night Work of Young Persons (Non-Industrial Occupations) Convention, 1946, C90 Night Work of Young Persons (Industry) Convention (Revised), 1948.

eventually reached a very high level. After some years of political opposition and industrial action, a period of intense labour legislation began. In 1973 there was a proposal for an Employment Protection Act that would apply to all employees. However, the proposal was not accepted as far as the extent of application was concerned. Instead, four exceptions were made and among those exempted were family members and people performing domestic work.[10]

As to family patterns, the 1970s were characterized by an increase in the divorce rate. Cohabitation without marrying also became increasingly common. New taxation rules were introduced which taxed married spouses separately. In 1973 the legislation governing marriage was reformed, the aim being to make spouses more independent of each other. The formalities around entering and dissolving a marriage were also simplified (SFS 1973:645).

In the 1970s family members were included in almost all legislation except the Employment Protection Act. By the mid 1970s new regulations were passed concerning the right to study leave, parental leave and vacation time (SFS 1974:981; SFS 1977:480; SFS 1976:280). It was emphasized that these rights were also to apply to family members on condition that there was a *real* employment relationship.[11] Furthermore, these acts applied to domestic workers.

Recent development has brought contradictory changes in the regulation of work performed by the employer's family and of domestic work performed in his home. In 1994 the Domestic Work Act was made applicable to members of the employer's family working as assistants to disabled persons.[12] In 1996 the regulation concerning domestic work in the Work Environment Act was amended in order to adapt Swedish law to international agreements.[13] This meant that the provisions of the Work Environment Act were made applicable to those employed in domestic work as long as they were under the age of 18. These amendments have slightly widened the scope of labour legislation.

On the other hand, in recent years the exception for the employer's family has been broadened rather than narrowed in the courts. The Labour Court has ruled that it is possible for an employee to have a family tie not only to a physical person but also to an employer in the form of a company, if the related person in question is active in the business and has a considerable influence on the enterprise. This means that the family member of a person who is basically in charge of a company/enterprise might not be protected. The Labour Court has also widened the family concept by equating

10 1 § Act (1974:12) on Employment Protection.

11 The term 'real' in this context has no precise meaning, but presumably means that the work is waged.

12 According to the Act on Support and Service to certain Disabled Persons (1993:387) people with disabilities are entitled to special kinds of services, such as for example the right to engage personal assistants.

13 The UN Convention on the Right of the Child, the Social Charter of the European Council, convention nr 138 of the ILO and the directive 94/33/EG on protection of minors in working life.

cohabitants – heterosexuals as well as homosexuals[14] – with married spouses.[15] In its arguments the court has chosen to refer to a widening family concept in family law while, in my view, it could just as easily have pointed to the increasing protection of family members in labour law, had it wished to narrow the concept.

Justifications for the Exceptions

The exception of the employer's family and household is an example of non-intervention in the 'private' sphere on the part of the state. Feminist scholars have frequently pointed out that non-intervention is just as political as intervention and calls for its own independent justification (Frazer and Lacey 1993, 73; Dahl 1985, 18). However, in the case of the exceptions from Swedish labour law concerning occupational safety, working hours and employment protection, such a justification is not easy to find. The exceptions seem to rely on a value so accepted it does not have to be expressed or explained.

As late as in the preparatory works of the Employment Protection Act of 1973, the legislator referred to discussions concerning the field of application of labour law held at the beginning of the 20th century (Prop. 1973:129, 230). To find the rationalization for the exception you also have to go back to the legislation on occupational safety of 1912. The legislator of that time was of the opinion that limiting child labour and introducing inspection in the employer's home would entail compulsion and intrusion into the private sphere of the family. It was also considered that there was no need to protect family members, as the feelings of belonging and affection within the family would normally replace the protection of law. These feelings were supposed to serve as a guarantee against abuse. In this way the employer was constructed as a good employer/father (*bonus pater familias*) and the home as a peaceful workplace. The exceptions to this picture, were hinted at but never discussed. Family members were also expected to share common interests (Prop. 1976/77:149, 198).

Another argument presented by the legislator was that family members were not usually really employed. The case was rather that the family conducted a business together (SOU 1937:49, 119-120; Prop. 1976/77:149, 198). The possibility that the employer was the sole owner of the business and that power and resources were not evenly distributed within the family was never discussed. Litigations in court between family members were sometimes seen as incongruous and sometimes as something that ought not to exist. Ultimately, in 1973, the argument for the exception from employment protection was that the relationship between the employer and his family members was so 'special', that the employment of family members could not possibly be the subject of legal regulation (Prop. 1973:129, 195).

As to domestic work in the employer's home, it was rarely considered to be in need of the protection of legislation on occupational safety 'because of its own nature'

14 By widening the exception to include homosexual relationships the courts have extended the prerogatives of the employer to a type of relationship where the reign of the master has no tradition.

15 Labour Court ruling 2000 No. 97.

(Committee on Occupational Safety 1909, 60). The tasks of domestic workers were supposed to be of such an individual and varied nature, that working hours could not be fixed in advance (Prop. 1944:217. 40). The employer was assumed to want his or (more rarely) her private life protected and homes were to be free from control by supervising agents as far as possible. One argument presented by the authorities was that the execution of the inspection would be an unpleasant task (Prop. 1963:126, 35).

In the 1970s when the policy was to extend legal protection to all kinds of employees, domestic workers were also considered to be in need of some kind of employment protection. But it was stated that the protection could not be constructed in the same way as for other categories of workers, as domestic workers occupied a special position in relation to the employer. Consequently the Employment Protection Act was not to apply to them (Prop. 1973:129, 195).

The discussions in the legislative process showed inconsistencies and contradictions. On the one hand family bonds were thought to replace legal protection, but on the other hand a large family was said to give competitive advantages to an employer (as more people were able to work outside the restrictions of legal regulation) (SOU 1954:22, 109). It was argued that the work of family members ought not to be restricted by bureaucratic complications and simultaneously it was stated that the compliance with the law would be insufficient anyway. Inspection was considered unnecessary and at the same time undesirable, as it might lead to litigation (Prop. 1948:298, 84).

Values Expressed in the Construction of the Legislation

One value actually protected by the exception from legislation of the family and the home was the employer's autonomy and integrity and his right to make decisions concerning conditions within the family. A value also defended in the construction of the legislation was the issue of avoiding conflicts within the family, at least those visible in public. By making working conditions of family members and housemaids a matter of internal agreements, the legislator avoided litigations in court between members of the same household.

The balancing of values by the legislator may be studied from cases where no exceptions from labour law were made. There are at least two examples of this. The regulation governing employment protection for people doing military service made no exceptions for any category of workers. (This means that all men without exception had the right to leave their job to do their military service without risking unemployment when they came back). This may be interpreted to mean that the mobilizing of men for the defence of the country was a stronger value than the autonomy of the employer. Likewise, in the second version in 1945 of the ban on dismissal due to marriage and pregnancy, all exceptions from the ban were abolished (SFS 1945:844). The argument used was that women fulfilling their duties as mothers should have the right to the same protection as men doing their military service (SOU 1944:51, 132–133). This amendment seems to imply that the value of an increasing birth rate also had a heavier impact than the interests of the employer.

The values of the legislator may also show through the control system and the sanctions chosen. A proposal in 1954 for legislation on working hours for once *did* include domestic workers (SOU 1954:22).[16] In the proposal, however, inspection of the working hours of domestic workers was supposed to be limited to practical advice and to interpretation of the act. Regular inspection was assumed to imply intrusion into the homes and a violation of the integrity of family life. In the proposed legislation on working hours, a provision was introduced stating that a minor offence would not carry a penalty with it. This was made with a reference to domestic work (SOU 1954:22, 105).[17] A similar measure was taken in 1977 when many provisions of the *Work Environment Act* were extended to family members. Once the family was to be included into the act, special rules were introduced concerning the inspection of enterprises where only family members worked. Inspection was supposed to take place only for 'special reasons'. Thus, regulation was rendered ineffective because of the strength of the basic norm concerning the employer's integrity and autonomy. Arguments for this were the limited resources of the inspection authorities and also the interest in avoiding encroachments on personal integrity (Prop. 1976/77:149 261-262). Also the Domestic Work Act of 1970 was restrictive regarding inspection, which was to take place only on request from one of the parties of the contract or if there were special reasons (Prop. 1970:150, 26). Through such construction of the legislation domestic work was probably in fact still exempted from effective occupational safety inspection.

Effects – Crossing the Limit Between Law and the Social Context

Conditions of real life determine whether or not a gender-neutral regulation has gendered consequences. In the case of the gendered effects of the regulation of the work of the employer's family members, one crucial factor is whether men or women are the heads of business. Although this has changed considerably over the years there is still no doubt that in Sweden men are in business to a larger extent than women. According to a recent survey, 82 per cent of entrepreneurs with employees and 70 per cent of entrepreneurs without employees are men (Ds 2003:27). Consequently, family members will most often be women and children.

Similarly a changing social context means changes in the effects of legal regulation. In Sweden there has been a political investment in small enterprise and in the last ten years the number of family enterprises has increased, which naturally means an increase in the impact of the exception for family members. [18]

---

16 The proposal did not result in a widening of the area of application.

17 This part also did not result in legislation.

18 Interest in studying family enterprises has been almost non-existent until quite recently, when some research has been done in the field of economics. In this research, the wife and the children of the entrepreneur are most often seen as an appendix to the male entrepreneur, if they are visible at all. In studies of family enterprises, one single individual is at the centre of the business and the role of the family is to support this individual. Entrepreneurs are usually reluctant to admit that their families are involved in the business. Holmquist 2000.

The Swedish labour market has changed considerably with internationalisation and it can be expected to change even more with the extension of the EU. It has been argued that the domestic tasks of the 'professional household without a wife'[19] have increasingly been relocated to the market; they are bought directly as goods and services or indirectly through hired labour (Sassen 2003, 254). As a result we see the return of the so-called serving classes in all of the world's global cities, and these classes are largely made up of immigrant and migrant women. Although this may not be a typical feature of Swedish cities, women from Poland and the Baltic countries are frequently engaged to perform domestic labour in homes in Stockholm, Gothenburg and Malmö. Another change in the social context is the growing number of people in need of care, who live in their own homes rather than in institutions as a result of cut-backs in institutional care.

Effects – Crossing the Limit Between Legal Areas

The consequences of the fact that parts of labour law is not applicable to the conditions of work for family members, servants and housekeepers, have not been discussed in the legislative process. Family members have been invisible in the process and the exception from legislation has not been discussed from their point of view. The same thing is true of discussions about the exception for domestic workers. (Working conditions of domestic workers were however visible in the process of creating the Act on Housemaids and the *Domestic Work Act*, which were passed with the explicit purpose of making the work more attractive).

The still-existing exception from the provisions of the Employment Protection Act may imply advantages or disadvantages for a family member. Cases in the Labour Court clearly show how the exception may have either positive or negative consequences for the family member in question depending on the character of their relationship with the employer.[20] If the employer wishes to keep a certain person in times of shortage of work, this person may have priority for the remaining jobs, regardless of seniority rules. If a person has fallen into disgrace, e.g. after a separation, she can be dismissed, and there is no protection in law.

Business executives are also exempted from employment legislation. Business executives are however usually compensated for their loss of employment protection through private agreements, sometimes very generous ones, with the employing company. As to family members one would have to carry out empirical investigations to discover whether they are in fact compensated through private agreements for their

19 Sassen (2003) points out that this is regardless of whether its adult couple consists of a man and a woman, two men, or two women.

20 For example in the Labour Court Ruling 1979 No. 145, a stepson of the employer was employed instead of a former employee who would otherwise have had a right to be rehired. The Labour Court ruled that it was not possible to have a right to re-employment before somebody who was not included in the Employment Protection Act. In the Labour Court Ruling 1993 No. 57 the daughter of one of the owners was dismissed. The Labour Court ruled that there was no requirement for 'just cause' for the dismissal, as the daughter was excluded from the Employment Protection Act.

loss of employment protection. The same is true for domestic workers, although it seems less likely that they are generously compensated.

People exempted from labour law may however be compensated through provisions in other legal areas. The question in this case then is whether family members and domestic workers are compensated in other legal areas for their absence in labour law; that is whether there is a balance between their rights and their obligations.[21] As to a married spouse, her marital property may give her compensation in the case of divorce. If, however, a spouse has been working in a business, which constitutes the individual property of the other spouse,[22] she has no right to it in the case of divorce or the other spouse's death. Also, if the parties have been cohabitants, she has no right to a share of the business in the case of separation. Domestic workers have not been compensated by provisions in legal areas other than labour law.

The exception of family members from labour law has the effect of increasing the dependency of family members on the employer and this exception/dependency has been extended to cohabitants. This development is contrary to trends in Swedish family law and tax law, where the general goal has been to make spouses independent of each other; an individualization of relations within marriage has taken place. Within family law, cohabitants have acquired a right to the common household goods, a right which aims to protect the weaker party. The exception of family members from labour law is more a protection for the stronger party. This exception is even more surprising as conditions within waged work have been considered crucial in Swedish strivings for equality.

The Limit Between Private and Public

It has been said that the liberal conception of the limited neutral state carries with it an implicit conception of a private, non-political sphere in which state intervention is inappropriate and where individual autonomy is to be exercised. The discourse of privacy in areas such as sexuality and family life has been said to become a mechanism whereby women's oppression is not only constituted and maintained but also, and most damagingly, rendered apolitical (Frazer and Lacey 1993, 72).

The exception of the employer's family and domestic work in his home from the protection of labour legislation is one example of the private/public divide. Labour law stops at the door of the employer's home. Furthermore, no questioning of this limit has taken place in the labour law debate.

There is no court case concerning the exception of domestic work from the Work Environment Act, the Working Time Act or the Employment Protection Act. With regard to the Domestic Work Act there are only two court cases concerning issues treated in the act.[23] Relative to its quantitative importance, there have been

---

21 I have used gender-specific language because in the majority of cases the 'employee' is the female spouse.

22 The spouses have the option of contracting out of the marital property system, partly or entirely. See Gunnarsson *et al.* 2004.

23 Labour Court rulings 1991 No. 71 and No. 91.

few Labour Court cases concerning the exception of the employer's family, namely seven cases.[24] One reason for this may be that the legal regulation of the exception has been clearly defined in the legislative process. A more important reason, however, is probably that it is seen as 'strange' if a member of a family initiates labour law litigation against another member of the family.

In Sweden, around 85 per cent of employees are members of trade unions. Yet, in neither of the cases concerning the Domestic Work Act was a trade union involved. It is also a well-known fact that domestic workers have had a low level of unionism (Moberg 1978). The same thing was true of the court cases concerning the exception of family members; none of the family members was represented by a trade union. This is probably due to employment conditions also being considered private agreements by the employees, who did not want to be members of the trade union. Then obviously something unexpected happened, a conflict arose or a separation became a fact, and the family member changed her mind about the private nature of the relationship.

The Limit Between Work and Care/Paid and Unpaid Work

The issue of the exemption from labour law of work within the employer's household calls for a discussion on a topic closely related to the public/private divide, namely the paid and unpaid work divide. It has been emphasized that reproductive work is not inherently different from productive work. Its domestic location and the fact that it often involves the care of people with whom the caregiver has an intimate relationship tend to obscure the fact that it is still 'real' work (Rittich 2002, 126). The construction of a limit between work and care is highlighted in a number of ways in the study of the exception from labour law of work in the employer's home. One example is the way in which labour performed by domestic workers has not been considered a profession. This was once thought to be a reason for the shortage of domestic workers and the Domestic Work Act was intended to contribute to the professionalization of domestic work (SOU 1939:15, 30). However, when domestic work was regulated, this legislation differed from other labour legislation regarding its scope, sanctions and provisions on prescription and forum. This was done with reference to the private nature of the relationship and to the economically unimportant nature of the litigations (SOU 1939:15, 165).

Another example of how the legislator has treated the limit between care and work is the discussion around the inclusion of housekeepers in early legislation on working time. Including housekeepers was said to be reasonable, as legislation would considerably improve their working conditions. However, an issue that was considered problematic appeared in the discussions: A number of women, who were called housekeepers, actually lived together with the employer under conditions similar to marriage. The problem was not expressly formulated, but the solution chosen was to emphasize that there must be an employer/employee relationship for

24 Labour Court rulings 1975 No. 42, 1979 No. 145, 1982 No. 135, 1992 No. 84, 1993 No. 157, 1996 No. 139 and 2000 No. 97.

the law to apply. According to the legislator it was sometimes difficult to judge whether or not this was the case, when the relationship was both of a personal and a labour kind. In solving the problem one would have to make a total judgement of the relationship where all facts were to be considered.[25] Obviously the legislator found that working hours were to be limited in an employment relationship, but also that no limit should be set to the same work performed within a personal relationship.

The worker versus non-worker distinction has been said to be highly ideological. It draws upon and develops the messages of the legal culture generally – the public/private distinction, the disjuncture of family and market and the privileging of market activity (Williams 2002, 100). As has already become obvious the Swedish legislator has been upholding a similar distinction. A further example is found in earlier acts on working time in agriculture and in the retail trade. These acts used to contain special statutes, stating that if an employee performed domestic work as part of the employment, this work was to be exempted from protective legislation. Trade unions have reinforced the same distinction by emphasizing that an employer must not circumvent the legislation by using a worker for other work tasks who was formally employed in the household and thereby exempted from labour legislation (Prop. 1974:88, 119).

Recent development has shown how unpaid work is relied upon as a cost-saving strategy and unacknowledged safety net in market reform and restructuring plans. In the middle of the 1990s, measures were taken to involve relatives to a greater extent in the care of elderly and disabled people. The community handed over responsibility to family members through various kinds of legal arrangements. For example family members were given the right to economic remuneration for providing assistance to disabled persons. The assistant then obviously belonged to the family of the disabled person/the employer and also performed labour in the household of the employer.[26] This implied that the Working Time Act would not be applicable, since this act exempted work in the employer's household. It also implied that the Domestic Work Act was not applicable, as this act exempted members of the employer's family. Thus, neither the Work Environment Act nor the Employment Protection Act was applicable to the work in question. At the same time it was not unusual for a disabled person to need and be granted assistance for up to one hundred hours per week. Legislation was amended implying that the Domestic Work Act was also to be applicable to assistants who belonged to the family of the disabled person/the employer. Simultaneously a decision was made not to give economic remuneration for the time exceeding the working time allowed in the Domestic Work Act, namely normally forty hours a week (Prop. 1994/95:77, 1, 5).

---

25 There is an example in case law concerning the right to salary from a man's estate where all witnesses had considered the relationship between the man and his housekeeper, not as 'similar to marriage' but as an employment relationship. The housekeeper was entitled to the right to salary.

26 This was true if the disabled person herself was the employer. If the municipality or a private entrepreneur was the employer, the assistant was not exempted from labour law.

Concluding Remarks

The two exceptions from the Swedish Employment Protection Act discussed in this chapter, have a clearly gendered content, but they differ in character. The exception for domestic work is a reflection of the low value attached to housework, which can be traced in many places in legislation and case law. It may also reflect the fact that both employers and employees are women and that the employees are often immigrant women. On the other hand the exception for members of the family seems to be more controversial when subjected to analysis. It is contrary to legal changes in other areas of Swedish society. It is contrary to the individualization of family relations in family law and in tax law. It is also contrary to tendencies towards intervention in penal law and even in labour law, where the government has tried to push men into caring for small children through regulation of parental leave. The exception is also surprising, as the Government has always stressed the importance of equality in waged work as a basis for equality in general.

References

Government Bills

Prop. 1912:104, *med förslag till lag om arbetarskydd.* [Governments proposal, with a proposition for an Act on Occupational Safety].

Prop. 1944:217, *med förslag till hembiträdeslag.* [Governments proposal, with a proposition for an Act on Domestic Work].

Prop. 1948:298, *med förslag till lag om arbetarskydd.* [Governments proposal, with a proposition for an Act on Occupational Safety].

Prop. 1963:126, *om ändring i arbetarskyddslagen.* [Governments proposal, with a proposition for an Amendment to the Occupational Safety Act].

Prop. 1970:150, *med förslag till lag om arbetstid mm i husligt arbete.* [Governments proposal, with a proposition for an Act on Domestic Work].

Prop. 1973:129, *med förslag till lag om anställningsskydd.* [Governments proposal, with a proposition for an Act on Employment Protection].

Prop. 1974:88, *med förslag till lag om facklig förtroendemans ställning på arbetsplatsen.* [Governments proposal, with a proposition for an Act on Union Representatives].

Prop. 1976/77:149, *med förslag till arbetsmiljölag.* [Governments proposal, with a proposition for an Act on Work Environment].

Prop. 1994/95:77, *Vissa frågor om personlig assistans och om kostnadsansvar för insatser enligt lagen om stöd och service till vissa funktionshindrade.* [Governments proposal, Cost responsibility for measures taken according to the Act (1993:387) on Support and Service to certain Disabled Persons].

Government Committees and Other Official Documents

Committee on Occupational Safety, Report given on the 9th of December 1909 by the Committee on Occupational Safety.

Ds 2003:27, *Företags- och anställningsformer i förändring.* [Series of the Government Offices 2003:27, Changing patterns of business and employment].

SOU 1937:49, *med förslag till semesterlag.* [Government Commission 1937:49, with a proposition for a Paid Vacation Act].

SOU 1938:47, *Gift kvinnas förvärvsarbete.* [Government Commission 1938:47, Married Women's waged work].

SOU 1939:15, *Betänkande angående anställnings- och arbetsförhållanden inom det husliga arbetet mm.* [Government Commission 1939:15, Employment and Working Conditions in Domestic Work].

SOU 1944:51, *Betänkande i abortfrågan avgivet av 1941 års Befolkningskommission.* [Report 1944:51, on the abortion question given by the Government Commission of 1941 on Population].

SOU 1954:22, *Ny arbetstidslagstiftning och partiell arbetstidsförkortning.* [Government Commission 1954:22, A new regulation on working time and a partial shortening of the working time].

SOU 1978:38, *Jämställdhet i arbetslivet.* [Government Commission 1978:38, Equal opportunities in working life].

Literature

Aubert, Wilhelm, Eckhoff, Torstein, and Sveri, Knut (1952), *En lov i søkelyset* (Oslo: Universitetsforlaget).

Calleman, Catharina (2004), Om familjebandet i arbetsrätten –' ett förträffligt korrektiv till missbruk' in *TfR 3/2004*, 318–364.

Christensen, Anna (1986), 'Kvinnorätten och lagpositivismen' in *33 Retfaerd: Nordic Journal of Law and Justice* 1986.

Dahl, Tove Stang (1985), *Kvinnerett I* (Oslo: Universitetsförlaget).

Fahlbeck, Reinhold (2001), 'Firing the boss', in *Festskrift till Hans Stark*, Eklund, Ronnie K. Mikhaël and Sigeman, Tore (eds) (Stockholm: Arbetsrättsliga föreningens skrifter volym V).

Fransson, Susanne (2000), *Lönediskriminering* (Uppsala: Iustus Förlag).

Frazer, Elizabeth and Lacey, Nicola (1993), *The Politics of Community: a feminist critique of the liberal-communitarian debate* (Hemel Hempstead: Harvester Wheatsheaf).

Gunnarsson, Åsa, Burman, Monica and Wennberg, Lena (2004), 'Economic dependence and self-support in family, tax and social law', in Svensson, Eva-Maria, Pylkkänen, Anu and Niemi-Kiesiläinen, Johanna (eds) *Nordic equality at a crossroads: feminist legal studies coping with difference* (Aldershot: Ashgate).

Hellum, Anne (1979), 'Kvinnerett – radikal feministisk fagkritikk', in *Kritisk Juss* nr 3/4 1979.

Holmquist, Carin (2000), 'Företagaren – han, hon eller de?', in Gandemo, Bertil (ed.) *Familjeföretag och familjeföretagande* (Örebro: Forum för småföretagsforskning).

Lundh, Christer and Olsson, Rolf (1999), *Från arbetskraftsimport till flyktinginvandring* (Stockholm: SNS Förlag).

Lundström, Karin (1999), *Jämlikhet mellan kvinnor och män i EG-rätten* (Uppsala: Iustus Förlag).

Lykke, Nina (2003), 'Intersektionalitet – ett användbart begrepp för genusforskningen', in *KvT 1/2003*.

Moberg, Kerstin (1978), *Från tjänstehjon till hembiträde* (Stockholm: Almqvist & Wiksell).

Mulinari, Diana, Molina, Irene and de los Reyes, Paulina (2004), *Intersektionalitet. Kritiska reflektioner över o(jäm)likhetens landskap* (Stockholm: Liber).

Öberg, Lisa (1999), 'Ett socialdemokratiskt dilemma. Från hembiträdesfråga till pigdebatt', in Florin, Christina *et al.* (eds). *Kvinnor mot kvinnor, Om systerskapets svårigheter* (Stockholm: Norstedt).

Rittich, Kerry (2002), 'Feminization and Contingency', in Conaghan, Joanne, Fischl, Richard Michael and Klare, Karl (eds) *Labour law in an era of Globalization – Transformative practices and possibilities* (Oxford: Oxford University Press).

Sassen, Saskia (2003), 'Global Cities and Survival Circuits' in Ehrenreich, Barbara and Russell Hochschild, Arlie (eds) *Global Woman: Nannies, Maids, and Sex Workers in the New Economy* (New York: Metropolitan Books, London: Granta Books).

SCB (1910–1985), Tidsseriehäfte, Förvärvsarbetande, Folk- och bostadsräkningarna 1910–1985 (SCB) (Time series, Employees, Accounts of population and housing 1910–1985, Statistics Sweden).

Svensson, Eva-Maria (1997), *Genus och rätt, en problematisering av föreställningen om rätten* (Uppsala: Iustus Förlag).

Williams, Lucy A. (2002), 'Beyond Labour Law's parochialism', in Conaghan, Joanne, Fischl, Richard Michael and Klare, Karl (eds) *Labour law in an era of Globalization – Transformative practices and possibilities* (Oxford: Oxford University Press).

Chapter 10

Exclusion of Solo Mothers in the Welfare State

Lena Wennberg

This chapter presents part of a research project entitled 'Solo Mothers in the context of active citizenship'. The first stage in the project had as its comprehensive aim to examine and analyse, in a cross-national comparative legal study, social assistance regulations in Sweden, Finland, Norway and Denmark (Wennberg 2004). In the project the theoretical and analytical concept 'solo mothers' is utilized, which challenges both the traditional legal dogmatic position (as explained in the Introduction to this book) and the notion of formal gender equality in law. How maintenance, care and dependency are understood in last-resort schemes, i.e. social assistance, affects their potential to function inclusively or exclusively. This chapter shows how solo mothers are at risk of being excluded from the concept of citizenship when it is understood as 'active' citizenship and argues that a more pluralistic notion of citizenship is required if the EU is to meet its social inclusion objectives. The inspiration to compare social assistance in four Nordic countries arises from the EU policies that have been adopted in the EC Treaty. First, the fight against social exclusion as encoded in article 137 motivates an examination of how 'active' policies are reflected in national regulations.[1] Although there are no regulatory European-level harmonizing measures regarding social assistance, the enactment by the EU institutions of non-binding measures of soft law may encourage the convergence of national practices in welfare provision.[2] Second, gender mainstreaming, which formalizes the importance of promoting equality between men and women, has gained widespread acceptance in the international community as a new approach to gender equality and a policy-making tool in the EU public policy context (see for instance Beveridge and Shaw 2002, 209–212). Mainstreaming has also occasionally been translated into a legal norm.[3] In the field of social protection, mainstreaming requires that all aspects are to be taken into account when setting specific targets

1 Article 137, amended by the Treaty of Nice, signed on 26 February, 2001, Official Journal of the European Communities, *OJ* 24.12.2002/C 325.

2 One of the most explicit statements of European policy in relation to poverty is to be found in 92/441/EEC, Council Recommendation of 24 June 1992 on common criteria concerning sufficient resources and social assistance in social protection systems, *OJ* L 245/46, 26.8.92.

3 The EC Treaty itself has been amended to incorporate a legally-binding commitment to mainstreaming in Article 3(2) EC, introduced by the Treaty of Amsterdam.

or selecting gender gaps where there is a very significant difference in poverty outcomes in general or in some specific aspect of poverty and social exclusion.[4] One such specific aspect is the situation of solo mothers, who are shown throughout the European Community to be vulnerable, both on the labour market and in the welfare state (see for instance Björnberg 1994; Björnberg 1996; Hobson 1994; Hobson and Takahashi 1996, 1997; Bradshaw *et al.* 1996; Duncan and Edwards 1999; Gähler 2001).

The promotion of active policies instead of passive reliance on income maintenance has become one of the key concerns expressed by the European Commission and one of the central elements in the modernization of the European social model. Social assistance is now conceived as a means to achieve social inclusion and active participation and is therefore one aspect of the notion of active citizenship. At the same time social assistance is understood as the most passive form of reliance and most unfavourable form of dependency in poverty and social exclusion discourse.[5] Although the social assistance and minimum income schemes are seen as important instruments in social protection policy, access to employment is emphasized as the best safeguard against social exclusion. Since the Lisbon European Council of March 2000, promoting social inclusion has been a key aim in European social policy. At Lisbon the open method of coordination on social inclusion was adopted with the aim of making 'a decisive impact on the eradication of poverty and social exclusion'. This commitment was subsequently made operational in December 2000 at the Nice European Council, with the adoption of common objectives in the fight against poverty and social exclusion, comprising an agreement that all Member States would draw up two-yearly national action plans to promote social inclusion based on these objectives.[6] The overall objective of modernization was explained as being to strengthen the role of social protection by making it an effective tool for managing change in the EU, while minimizing negative social consequences. A stronger gender dimension was also requested in these National Action Plans against poverty and social exclusion.[7]

'Active citizenship', as a concept, has been interpreted as both conservative, rooted in individualistic and legalistic notions of contract, and radical, emphasizing the potential for participation. Such participation may for example take place in community groups where disadvantaged people, often women, create themselves as subjects rather than objects (Lister 2003, 23-24). One basic assumption in this current research project is that 'social citizenship' contrasts with the notion of active citizenship. Rights and duties, including the distributive principles and participating conditions which enable membership in a society define social citizenship.[8] These

4 12746/02/ (Presse 306) 2454th Council meeting. Employment, Social Policy, Health and Consumer Affairs, Luxemburg, 8 October 2002.

5 For a theoretical discussion on dependencies see Fineman Albertson 2001, 23–37.

6 http://www.europa.eu.int/comm/employmnet_social/soc-prot/soc-incl/index_en.htm. 31 May 2004.

7 12746/02/ (Presse 306) 2454th Council meeting. Employment, Social Policy, Health and Consumer Affairs, Luxemburg, 8 October 2002.

8 For a broader discussion on citizenship, see Gunnarsson this volume.

individual rights and duties balance relations and dependencies, making this a question of equality. This approach is in contrast to the assumption of an active citizen which seems too narrow in its explanation of poverty as merely transitory and related mostly to employment, the age of the person and the citizenship of the head of the household (see Stendahl 2003, 42; who makes reference to Gustafsson and Pedersen 2000, 202). The research also assumes that the granting and legal definition of social assistance may render various groups of women and men more or less vulnerable to social exclusion. The gendered dimensions of law that function as either exclusionary or inclusionary are revealed by the regulation of rights and duties in last-resort schemes and in national constitutions, as well as by the manner in which the principles underpinning these regulations are related to principles in family law. A critical gender perspective enriches the contemporary political and legal discourses on social exclusion by referring to specific gender-based risks and vulnerabilities.

An Analytical Concept for Understanding Gendered Dimensions in Welfare States

The analytical concept of solo mothers has been chosen as one possible strategy for assessing how gender relations are legally acknowledged and understood in the last-resort schemes in place in Sweden, Finland, Norway and Denmark. The concept 'solo' mother in this project differs from a neutral concept of 'single' parenthood, which emphasizes the absence of a relationship with a sexual partner. I have chosen the concept solo mothers rather than lone mothers or single parents, which are common concepts in demographic categorizations, since solo mothers often do not live alone (and are therefore not necessarily 'single') but with children, friends or even lovers (Hobson 1996, 176).[9] From a legal viewpoint, parenthood and maintenance obligations are primarily based on biological ties. 'Solo' is used here to target the assumption of a constant condition of support and care obligations, irrespective of the reason for being solo, and irrespective of new relations, and therefore differs from the frequently used demographic 'single' parent concept. Most single parents are in fact solo mothers, having the primary every-day responsibilities for the child, even though others, especially the biological father, or a step-father, may be involved in some part of the child's subsistence and care.

Solo mothers represent one disadvantaged group in society but could also be interpreted in a sex-neutral way. Such an approach has been taken by Virginia Held. She uses the phrase 'mothering person' rather than 'mother' in the same gender-neutral way as various writers now speak of 'rational contractors'. Held replaces the paradigm of economic man as the dominant representation of humanity with the

9 Hobson (1994) used the same definition in an analysis of income sources and poverty rates of solo mothers in five countries. In her conclusion on gender and social policy she mapped out the dilemma of earning and caring for solo mothers, asking whether it is realistic to imagine a social policy regime that supports equally a mother's wage for caring that would allow her to form an autonomous household, and a system of services and provisions that would allow mothers to be integrated into working life.

paradigm of relations between mothers and children. What she seeks to elaborate is a conception of social relations, based on the experience of both men and women in terms of 'mothering'. Instead of importing principles derived from the market-place into the household, perhaps we should export to a wider society the relations suitable for mothering persons and children (Held 1993).

As I will explain, using solo mothers as an analytical concept brings to a head matters such as the contested issues of particularity versus universality in the designation of social rights, notions of autonomy and dependency and the divide between the public and the private. The manner in which the national last-resort systems are related to assumptions and regulations regarding maintenance obligations in family law has also been examined in order to grasp the gendered nature of relational dependencies and interdependencies.

Women's position *vis-à-vis* power relations in the public, private and symbolic domains, has been identified as exclusionary in feminist analyses. However, a feminist understanding of exclusion has not yet informed mainstream political discourses which have used the concept of exclusion to define individuals and groups living on the margins of society due to some personal or biographical deficit, for example the mentally ill, those with disabilities and so forth. Unlike the concept of poverty, social exclusion has been perceived as better able to reveal the mechanisms causing marginalization and the processes associated with it. This is because the concept focuses on relations rather than average income and does not see wellbeing as primarily financial (Daly and Saraceno 2002, 87). The idea of social exclusion in this version, now adopted by the EU, evokes those who are outside/different, not partaking of mainstream resources and values because of processes within the polity itself. However, in this newer version, the problem of the exclusion of women has not been central. In contrast, it is only or mainly involvement in paid work that is regarded as essential (Daly and Saraceno 2002, 84, 97).

The Nordic Context

In a study of social assistance in the Nordic countries it is important initially to stress the characteristics in Nordic welfare policies that have been crucial for women. Most benefits are individual, not based on family membership. The welfare system is based on an employment strategy and has required workforce participation from women as well as men (see also Gunnarsson; Mannelqvist this volume). Even solo parents, of whom most are solo mothers, have been expected to participate in salaried labour. Since most women work, they have a right to work-related pensions and unemployment benefits. Basic social security is based on residence, rather than contribution, labour or citizenship and is therefore often described as universal. Among feminist legal scholars Nordic women have accordingly been conceptualized as 'Responsible Selves', often bearing the double burden of a job and housework (Nousiainen and Niemi-Kiesiläinen 2001). However, when the general insurance system fails to operate during a cycle in a woman's life, she will become subordinated through discriminatory processes not only in the private sphere, but also in the public sphere of legislative rights. It has therefore been claimed that the equality of rights for women starts and ends within the family (Burman *et al.* 2004, 161).

The Scandinavian Member States have been associated with a version of a radical social justice model based on notions of solidarity, viewing social welfare as a collective activity rather than as the responsibility of individuals (see Hervey 1998). Other typologies of welfare using class and gender inequalities indicate that Nordic welfare is based on an encompassing and dual earner constellation, which combines universalism with earnings-related benefits (see Mannelqvist this volume). The Nordic legal culture has often been differentiated from the Anglo-Saxon and continental in the way that care is understood and how the state and the market are involved. As explained by Kevät Nousiainen, a special feature in the Nordic culture is the notion that individual duties and responsibilities are more important than individual rights. Thus, social protection in the Nordic welfare states has an individual base, in combination with a supportive community when needed, in contrast to other legal cultures that mainly emphasize the family as the caring unit. Nousiainen claims that Nordic legal culture is based on social rights oriented towards 'positive freedom', thereby having the potential to split the private-public divide (Nousiainen 2001, 34, 36).

Nevertheless, interrupted employment patterns and work in low-paid insecure jobs, customarily a woman's position, might still have the effect of excluding solo mothers from the social domain. Women with caring responsibilities are likely to suffer disadvantages in accessing welfare in social protection systems that are based on an employment strategy. In a Swedish context, it is also claimed that services and benefits for low-income families, in which solo mothers are overrepresented, are no longer assured (see for instance Hobson and Takahashi 1997, 121, 136; Vahlne Westerhäll 2002). Single parents, which is the concept most widely used, constitute the group with the greatest risk of falling into poverty in most societies and this is obviously so in the Nordic countries. In Denmark and Sweden one third of all single mothers relied on means-tested social assistance during at least one period every year during the 1990s. The figure in Finland was almost one third of all single parents, most of them single mothers, as in other countries (Puide and Minas 2001, 45). In Norway, probably as a result of changed eligibility rules for special care provisions for lone mothers and fathers, it has become more common for the means-tested housing allowance to be granted to this group and 17 per cent were allowed social assistance in 1999 (Statistics Norway 2002/20, 55–59).[10]

The question of whether a solo mother in need is a worthy citizen in possession of an individual right to live in a manner compatible with human dignity according to European human rights, is certainly an important one to raise. Maja Sakslin in her discussion on social security systems in transition has focused on how we use concepts which create categories that do not only differentiate, but which also privilege and exclude. By using citizenship or work in social security systems as including and excluding concepts, we create a group of citizens, who have rights, and 'margizens' who do not have rights. In defining the personal scope of our schemes,

10 For a discussion on care and social rights in Norway: see also Brækhus 2004, 91–106.

Sakslin advocates that we should consider the possibilities of using a 'more-active/less-active' scale instead of 'worker/non-worker' for inclusion/exclusion judgements (Sakslin 1998, 160–163). The increasing demand on solo mothers to be independent through fulfilment of the societal duty to perform on the labour market or rely on household or family members for their maintenance, reflects the need for laws that respect diversity.

The assumption of a continuously disadvantaged position for solo mothers questions a one-dimensional view that, in discussing the impact of welfare regimes on poverty dynamics in the EU, mainly explains poverty as the result of deficient labour-market participation (see for instance Layte and Whelan 2002). Such an explanation fails to recognize that dependency is relational. As Eva-Maria Svensson points out in her contribution to a problem-oriented approach to the notion of law, the logic of separation is used to make women's experiences invisible in law (Svensson 1997, 53–69).

Solo mothers belong to a group which, both historically (see for instance Florin and Kvarnström 2001) and in contemporary society, has been and is particularly economically vulnerable. They are women who in general earn less than men, and they are family providers, bearing the main economic responsibility for others (Gähler 2001, 87–91). Moreover, they are dependent in relation to a new partner or an ex-husband through a divorce proceeding, dependent on the other parent's provision for the child and dependent on a more or less supportive or demanding welfare state. Therefore, a one-dimensional view of poverty, explaining paid labour as the central determinant of poverty, is not sufficient to explain and reveal the gender dimensions that create dependency. Here, a notion of gender that comprehends the relational dependencies between the sexes and between the citizen and the state is therefore adopted.

Methodological Considerations

The limitations of the dogmatic approach to legal analysis are revealed by a contextualized study of law, which focuses on difference and diversity in citizenship and which uses the notions of inequality and disadvantage as opposed to an abstract notion of formal equality. In the cross-national comparison of four Nordic countries legal 'craftsmanship' in the traditional dogmatic sense has been needed in order to define current law and reveal the principles and the systematization of law. At the same time, the dogmatic approach has had to be combined with a more pluralistic notion of law and its sources, of the citizen and of social rights.

The last-resort safety nets are administered on local municipality level in all of the nation states under consideration. The last-resort assistance is given varying legal definitions in each country which are of great importance in grasping the normative principles and values encoded in the last-resort schemes. Social assistance is, however, used as a central concept in my discussion of the last-resort safety nets.

As social assistance is constructed more or less as policies and statutory rules, the sources of knowledge in the study have been both legal and political. Law, as exemplified by the soft law processes in the EU, seems today to be more dependent on policy norms than ever before. As the Finnish legal scholar Lars D. Eriksson has shown, policy norms presuppose an argumentation about goals and means alien to the normal interpretation of rules and principles. According to Eriksson these norms evade all the traditional methods of interpretation that lawyers use when interpreting rules and principles (Eriksson 2003, 21). Collective objectives such as combating social exclusion and fighting poverty are certainly neither rules, nor principles. Therefore, in a situation when law, ethics and politics seem to be increasingly intermingled, getting beyond the dogmatic notion of law is of importance in legal scholarship. A dogmatic method appears to be deficient and poorly adjusted to my project which, instead of merely analysing conformity to law, is diachronic in that it is future-focused and seeks new directions and processes of development as part of the emerging EU polity and law. The area of study is critical and emancipatory, as the aim is to challenge the perception of who in a society is in possession of social rights.[11]

Social Assistance in Sweden, Finland, Norway, and Denmark

The gap between the legal rhetoric of formal sex equality and the inequalities which can be seen in practice is an inbuilt conflict in welfare state regulations concerning obligations and rights. In the study referred to here, equality has been conceived contextually in order to define what differences are legally relevant and how they are relevant, and not as a demand for formal similarity.[12] Are there multiple and not always internally consistent outcomes in law, that in legal practice can lead to exclusion from the enjoyment of rights? Written law, decrees and government guidelines have been interpreted by questioning the texts as to the nature of social assistance in the light of the vulnerable situation of solo mothers.

The relationship of social assistance to family law has been examined in each country in order to address the question of dependency and its interpretation in normative terms. How is the legal unit constructed in the various branches of law? How are maintenance obligations for social assistance recipients regulated within the unit solo mothers are part of, in relation to children and in relation to a previous or a new partner? The relation between the solo mother and the authorities administering and granting social assistance has also been examined by evaluating the extent to which both eligibility for, and the content of, social assistance are constructed as legal rights in acts of parliament and in constitutions, or as policies without the force of law.

The use of framework laws in Nordic welfare legislation has given rise to a strong belief in law governing change in society, and has led to a wide-ranging debate (see for instance Andenæs 1992; Tuori 1993; Hollander 1995; Hydén 1998). Framework laws aim to promote material justice, laid down in general statutory objectives. Such laws stand in contrast to the traditional rule of law, which is more

---

11 For a broader discussion on academic legal knowledge and its demarcations: see Svensson this volume.

12 This approach has been espoused by Nousiainen and Pylkkänen in the project 'Including Differences in Legal Subjecthood'.

<http://www.helsinki.fi/oik/tdk/tutkimus/naistukimus/frontpage.html.>

suited to a detailed law with a formal notion of justice. From an individual point of view, benefits and services can only be defined as genuine claim-rights when they are regulated as clear and predictable formal rights, granted by the welfare state to the individual. The legislative strategy (i.e. framework laws vs. detailed statutory regulation) chosen in each country is of interest because it determines the location of power in decision making. How incomes in various units are estimated can reveal something about both dependency on others and what possibilities there are for solo mothers to overcome their economically vulnerable situation. This relationship has also been examined by asking what obligations and activating demands, and what corresponding sanctions, exist in each country. To encompass both universal and particular aspects the question has been raised of whether the schemes consider and take into account gendered difference and diversity.

These factors and results from the comparison of social assistance in Sweden, Norway, Finland and Denmark are presented in the table on page 179.[13]

The cross-national examination of legally constructed social assistance shows how all the countries in the study have in recent years moved towards a notion of the active citizen, an entity who is poorly adjusted to the living conditions of solo mothers. Apparently, social assistance legislation in Sweden, Finland, Norway and Denmark have the same objectives i.e. to further an autonomous citizen independent of public support, through waged work or support from the family or the household. The employment strategy in combination with general social protection through the solidarity principle is still visible in social assistance schemes. However, all of the examined countries are seemingly moving closer to the notion of an active citizenship that underlines work-related social protection. The objective of eliminating dependency on public support seems to be a formal understanding of gender equality that does not take seriously the vulnerable situation of solo mothers. This also applies in the Nordic countries examined in the study.

New activation requirements for entitlement to social assistance have been introduced in all the countries but to varying extents. In Norway the demands are reminiscent of a poor relief discourse in strengthening the powers of the administrative body. In addition, economic support under the Norwegian Social Services Act is an entirely discretionary benefit. In contrast, in Sweden, there is a statutory right to maintenance support under The Social Services Act, however this is combined with a general demand on the recipient to actively strive for independence through paid work. Individuals below the age of 25, students and others in special need of further qualification measures are targeted as having the greatest number of obligations in order to be entitled to social assistance. In Denmark a workfare policy is especially visible, both in the Act on an Active Social Policy, which regulates the Danish last-resort scheme, and in the constitution, where this policy is expressed as a duty

13 In Sweden social assistance is regulated in Socialtjäntlagen, *Social Services Act* (2001:453), in Finland Lag om utkomststöd, *Act on Social Assistance* (1412/97), in Norway: Lov om sociale tjenester m.v, *Social Services Act*, Lov 1991-12-13 nr 81, and in Denmark Lov om aktiv socialpolitik, *Consolidated Act on an Active Social Policy*, LBK nr 709 af 13/08/2003.

Table 10.1 Social assistance in Sweden, Finland, Norway and Denmark

Social Assistance	Sweden	Finland	Norway	Denmark
Legislation strategy	Unified framework social law	Differentiated social law	Unified framework social law	Differentiated employment laws
Constitutional protection	No	Yes	No	Yes, but in combination with a duty
Legal status	Legal right with a corresponding duty for certain indicated groups	Legal right	Non-legal right with a devolving general duty	Legal right with a corresponding legal duty
Contents	Statutory maintenance support for fundamental needs, discretionary reasonable costs	Statutory minimized livelihood support necessary for a life with human dignity, basic benefit and supplements	Discretionary economic support for a defensible living	Statutory cash benefit, start-up benefit and activation. Provisions for necessities to prevent a need for support
Supplements	Discretionary way of life in general for a reasonable standard of living	Discretionary preventive livelihood support	Discretionary expenses necessary for core living	Discretionary special support, reasonable non-recurrent for unforeseeable expenses
Legal unit	Individual and household	Person and family	Individual and family	Adult person and family. Differentiation
Unit for maintenance	Household contract	Marriage contract but *de facto* household	Marriage contract but on equal footing extended to household	Marriage contract Household for recipients of the start-up benefit
Estimation of incomes	All incomes and assets	Share of monthly income, certain allowances, and assets necessary to ensure an uninterrupted living statutory exempt	Wage earnings and economic rights	Certain incomes, benefits, revenues, capital and compensations statutorily exempt
Activation demands	Yes, for indicated groups	Yes, obligatory but differentiated according to age and duration of receipt. Exemptions for certain groups	Yes, for all persons fit to work	Yes, a pre-condition for assistance. Caring activities and a spouse practising domestic work exempted
Sanctions	Reduced or terminated assistance	Reduced assistance	Assistance terminated or distributed as goods or services	One-time benefit. Reduced and terminated assistance. Repayment

to participate and to be active. The workfare policy is also underlined by the fact that regulations are issued by the Ministry of Employment. The Danish last-resort scheme is no longer constructed as a social task, but rather as belonging to the labour-market ministry. In contrast, the Finnish constitution focuses on the right of the citizen to subsistence and care necessary for a life with human dignity: total exclusion from entitlement to livelihood support under the Act on Social Assistance is prohibited.

Norway, and (in part) Sweden, retain a framework legislation strategy and therefore still rely on the notion of an assessment of individual needs, rather than a legislative determination applying to all regardless of individual needs. In Sweden there is a mix of statutory individual rights and discretion within the municipality. Social assistance is meant to ensure a reasonable standard of living regarding fundamental needs. The fundamental needs explicitly protected in the statutes have been curtailed in recent amendments to the Social Services Act. All possible individual needs other than the enforced fundamental ones are made discretionary, and are based on assessment of reasonableness. The guidelines and supplementary recommendations issued by the National Board of Health and Welfare (SOSFS 2003:5(S); *Socialstyrelsen* 2003) can function as a tool for identifying the tensions between law and politics, administration and individuals in how the application of the Act should function. The recommendations contain a larger number of exemplifications than previously, however they are not binding on the deciding authorities.

The trust in the 'good' state, which is presumed as a guarantee for fulfilling social needs, is still very much alive in the regulations. In Norway, as in Sweden, there are no inherent guarantees of social protection in the social assistance scheme. Economic support in Norway refers to a defensible living and reality-based considerations of individual needs. Norway seems to be the country with the least legal certainty, as the Norwegian legislation is entirely discretionary, supervised by legally non-binding government guidelines (Rundskriv SOS – 1/34/2001).[14]

In contrast to the situation in Sweden and Norway, in Denmark and Finland the framework strategy has been abandoned in social assistance legislation in favour of an explicit rights discourse. In Denmark the statutory regular cash benefit aims to prevent exclusion from the labour market and is meant to be an economic safety net for the provision of necessities. The assumption of an active citizen is reflected in the precondition for eligibility. This precondition has undergone changes that have resulted in it being expressed as an inability to provide the necessities of living for one's self and one's family. Thus, a low income *per se* does not constitute entitlement to a benefit. Eligibility for the cash benefit also requires that the applicant has been residing in the country for at least seven of the last eight years. Staying abroad for more than two months during a year results in exclusion from eligibility for the benefit. If an applicant cannot authenticate the residence demands the lower start-up benefit can be allowed. The Danish strategy of using regulations to explicitly enforce rights and duties gives little scope for assessing reality-based needs that are not specified in detail. However, the administering body also has the competence to permit help for reasonable non-recurrent expenses, implying that such needs can be considered. In contrast, in Finland social assistance is expressed as protecting

14 This circular is complemented by more recent supplementary circulars.

what is necessary for a life with human dignity and aims to have a wider task than merely maintaining life. Social assistance in Finland is meant to cover costs other than those that are necessary in qualification measures aimed at social inclusion. The constitutional interpretation protects the needs of the individual or family. The basic benefit that refers to a minimized consumption level is complemented with a statutory supplementary benefit. In Finland, the discretionary powers of the authorities are limited to a special preventive livelihood support, which is aimed at expanding the use of preventive social assistance [15]

The care responsibilities that form part of the situation of solo mothers are not adequately acknowledged in legislation. The traditional dual-breadwinner family or dependency on household members, in combination with paid work, is still the guarantee for social security. In Denmark, Finland and Norway care has been a criterion for special arrangements regarding national social insurance.[16] However, none of the systems have elaborated effective strategies for providing for solo mothers in need. Seemingly, Home Care Allowances for the domestic care of children have mainly been constructed to suit a traditional dual-earner family. In Norway the special lone parent benefit has not been sufficient to reach the levels indicated in social assistance schemes (see Brækhus 2004, 91–106). In Denmark, special care provisions for families with children cannot be received in combination with other public provisions. This indicates that these provisions are not an option for a caring Danish solo mother with caring responsibilities. Sweden is the only country in the study that has no specific social insurance benefits geared to solo mothers. Hence, the legislation is general and gender-neutral without any particular interests being visualized. A Swedish solo mother seems the least noticed in social insurance schemes, in comparison to her Nordic counterparts.

In the regulations on social assistance, dependency in the family is assumed in all the countries examined but it is legally constructed in different ways. Similarly, the construction of the legal entity varies. In Finland the legal entity is a person, with or without a traditional family, and in Sweden it is a single individual or cohabitee, with or without children of different ages, forming a joint household. In Norway the legal entity is an individual with or without a family. In Denmark the legislator differentiates among people depending on their parental, marital and national status. Sweden seems to be the country where social assistance constructed as a last resort has gone furthest. The household, which is conceptualized as the unit in social assistance regulations, is understood as gender neutral. Regardless of marital and parenthood status, individuals who form a household from the starting-point of a sexual relationship, are obliged to maintain the other members of the household.

In addition, in Sweden social assistance is subsidiary (means-tested by reference) to all kinds of incomes and disposable assets of members of the household. This also applies in Norway where social assistance is subsidiary to wage earnings and other

---

15 The Finnish Ministry of Social Affairs and Health issues recommendations for the legal application and hearing of cases in municipal social services in a handbook; Handbook 2002:2.

16 An overview of the attitudes taken to care responsibilities by the various nation states within social security is presented in the study referred to but omitted from the table.

legally enforced economic rights. The legally enforced discretionary powers of the authorities in Sweden and Norway, however, leave the decision in the hands of the authorities. In contrast, in both Denmark and Finland, certain incomes and assets are statutorily exempt in the estimation of the assistance. Sweden seems to be the country that also uses a gender-neutral understanding of human needs to the fullest extent without any particular interest in the need for special legal protection in last-resort schemes. In contrast to Sweden, the significance of marital status for maintenance obligations (a 'marriage contract') is still visible in the Norwegian, Danish and Finnish regulations; now however maintenance obligations have gradually been extended to cohabiters (a 'household contract'). In Norway the significance of marital status for maintenance obligations in the matter of allowing economic support under the *Social Services Act* has recently been abandoned whereas in Finland *de facto* maintenance will be decisive for eligibility for a separated solo mother. In Denmark marital status has turned out to be decisive only for those who have qualified for the cash benefit. A spouse in a family who is granted the cash benefit and who chooses domestic work is released from the societal duty to be active on the labour market. For those who are allowed the lower start-up benefit the household is assumed to be the unit to be relied on in situations where there is a need for economic assistance. This kind of differentiation in the Danish regulations seems to have had as its main outcome the ethnocentric exclusion, rather than inclusion, of poor people. Whether the use of the Danish start-up benefit, which differentiates between national citizens and EU/EEC citizens and other foreigners, protects the necessities of life with human dignity, on the precondition that other demands are complied with, is open to question. In addition, Denmark is the only country that in principle deprives children of the status of legal entities in the last-resort scheme.

At a time when welfare has become increasingly constructed as workfare combined with an employment strategy, constitutional protection of subsistence and care for a life with human dignity might become important for vulnerable groups. The Finnish constitutional protection of subjective social rights prevents total exclusion from social assistance. Consequently, sanctions are limited in time and range, while a reduction of social assistance is not allowed to the full extent and, in principle, the statutory right to a dignified life can only be changed in favour of the recipient. In all other countries in the study constitutional protection is lacking or is vague. In Denmark the right to social assistance is strongly connected to employment as a duty. A recipient and her family can lose the benefit, partly or totally, for non-compliance with the demands of active participation. In comparison to the other countries in the study, the protection of children's social security seems to be most developed in Finnish social assistance regulations, and also supplemented by the Act on Children's Welfare.

Activation Strategies in the EU

The Social Protection Committee, established by the European Council in December 2000,[17] is meant to be a forum for exchange regarding policy development, aimed at promoting social inclusion as one of the objectives endorsed by the Council to enhance policy cooperation in the area of social protection. Article 144 of the TEC as amended by the Treaty of Nice expands the task of the Committee to include monitoring the social situation and the development of social protection policies in the Member States. In the first report adopted by the Social Protection Committee, progress is evaluated most strongly in the domain of social inclusion (European Commission 2002). Social exclusion is now perceived as a multi-dimensional problem, requiring an integrated policy approach. A stable job providing a steady source of income is recognized as the key factor in preventing social exclusion. Addressing the sex neutral concept of 'lone' parents, improvements in childcare support and parental leave arrangements are seen to be significant social inclusion policies in the Member States. Improvement in minimum-income guarantee schemes is also regarded as an important step in the inclusion process.

As I have indicated, active participation is the main theme of labour-market policy reforms in the Member States, extended beyond those officially registered as unemployed to other people who are out of work, for example lone mothers with young children. Increased pressure on those receiving benefits to participate in active labour market programs, and a tendency to tighten rules governing the entitlement to benefit, are also shown to be converging in the Member States (European Commission 2002, 7-9). For instance, in a recent communication from the European Commission Member States are requested to review and modernize their social protection systems to make them more employment friendly by removing barriers and disincentives to work and to create the right conditions to make work more attractive. However, as part of the efforts to improve incentives to work, the Commission underlines the importance of avoiding stricter conditions, particularly imposed on social assistance benefits, which may put disadvantaged people in particular at serious risk of poverty and social exclusion (European Commission 2002, 22). In the mid-term review of the Social Policy Agenda, the European Commission stresses that a high level of social cohesion is based on the principles of solidarity and social inclusion (European Commission 2003). The belief is expressed that 'the European Union must continue to underpin fundamental social rights and develop effective policies and measures to combat discrimination and eliminate barriers to participation on the grounds of race, ethnic origin, religion or belief, age, disability and sexual orientation' (European Commission 2003).

---

17 Council Decision 2000/436/EC of 29 June 2000 setting up a Social Protection Committee. later repealed by Council Decision 2004/689/EC, <http://ec.europa.eu/comm/employment_social/social_protection_commitee/index_en.htm>.

Feminist Critique of Welfare Models

Feminist critiques of Scandinavian welfare states have brought woman-friendliness into question and made use of the term 'public patriarchy'. By integrating both gender-sensitive notions and mainstream models of welfare regimes, the vision and idea of a woman-friendly welfare regime can be developed into an analytical model. Ulrike Liebert has articulated the principles of 'degendering of care' and 'engendering of freedom' as basic norms for a gender-sensitive welfare regime and as the basis for a redefinition of citizenship. In such a work–carer model applied to both men and women, unpaid caring work would be given the same recognition as paid work with regard to entitlements to benefit (Liebert 2001, 261, 263, 269). What feminist scholars have called woman-friendly policies[18] have been policies that have enabled solo mothers to be heads of households without the risk of poverty. Such policies have traditionally been a feature of Nordic welfare states.

The triangular relation, evolved by Tove Stang Dahl, between the family, the state and the market, has been one tool for evaluating the relational aspects of maintenance and care from a gendered perspective. Kirsten Ketcher has described these relations in a model of *two* triangular relations, of which the first represents money and the second care in the maintenance relationship. The model has contributed to bringing to light the importance of the connection between maintenance relations in reality and structures in distributive welfare law (Ketcher 1998, 60–68). However, to me it seems that maintenance as a gendered issue, and the problems of the combination strategy which is an attempt to reconcile care work and wage work, have mostly been analysed from the perspective of a marriage contract. Gendered dimensions on maintenance and care have mainly been based on an assumption of either the bread-winner or the dual-earner family. The special conditions for solo mothers, in the approximation of their dual role of earners and caregivers, have not been fully recognized in these analyses.

It is interesting to include the terms and conditions in which people engage in families – and the extent to which they can maintain an acceptable standard of living independent of the family – in the concept of the 'defamilialisation' of welfare state policies as a criterion for evaluating social rights. In a comparative study, Diane Sainsbury has discussed solo mothers' entitlements as a challenge to the male breadwinner model (Sainsbury 1996, 39, 45–46, 74–75). As single parents solo mothers must often fulfil dual roles as earners and caregivers. If solo mothers actually perform these twin tasks, they approximate the division of labour of the individual model of social policy rather than the highly gendered division of tasks in the family as prescribed by the breadwinner ideology. On the other hand, the ways in which the male breadwinner model and female caregiver model are encoded in legislation affects both solo mothers' ability to fulfil these roles and the quality of their social rights. In addition, according to Sainsbury, solo mothers expose basic contradictions and limitations in Gøsta Esping-Andersen's reasoning on de-commodification (Esping-Andersen 1990). This concept has been used in determining

18 The notion of a woman-friendly welfare state was first introduced in Hernes 1987.

the de-commodifying potential of policies, asking whether they do in fact provide a genuine work-welfare choice, allowing individuals and families to uphold a socially acceptable standard of living, independent of market participation. In her analyses comparing the social entitlements of solo mothers, Sainsbury uses both criteria: the de-commodifying and the de-familializing effects of welfare policies. She concludes that social rights based on citizenship or residence showed fewest stratifying effects, while welfare entitlements do have stratifying influences on women depending on whether women's access to benefits is granted to them primarily as wives, as mothers, or as workers with a given labour-market status.

Discussion

As long as poverty and social exclusion are realities in society there will be a need for ultimate safety-nets functioning as a means of ensuring a life with human dignity. How then can social assistance function inclusively in relation to solo mothers and their children who are already more or less excluded? A more pluralistic notion of the citizen than that now perceived seems to be a necessity for preventing marginalization, poverty and exclusion. On a national level, dependent solo mothers need other measures than the largely restrictive eligibility rules in the last-resort schemes. In order to include solo mothers, difference has to be understood as relational, dependent upon circumstance and particularity. The idea of the autonomous citizen therefore needs to be questioned. As long as society is structured by gender with gender inequalities, restrictive measures in last-resort systems, aimed at fostering active citizens, risk intensifying existing inequalities related to gender, ethnicity and class. Dependency, if seen as a human condition in caring relations between citizens, has to be acknowledged and justified. Solo mothers, as well as other 'mothering persons', need to be evaluated as worthy citizens, owning the personal right to live a dignified life, regardless of gender and regardless of whether they are married, cohabiters or are living with a partner.

The proclaimed active citizenship in the European Community has emphasized citizenship obligations over rights appealing to the common good in identifying engagement in paid work as the prime obligation on welfare recipients for the support of their families. How solo parents are treated certainly has gender implications that raise questions about the status of care as a citizenship responsibility. In the new politics of active citizenship the state provides social assistance in return for which it can require individual citizens to fulfil certain obligations, most notably the obligation to seek and to undertake paid work. Whether this should be understood as primarily a way forward by enhancing participation in society or as a discriminatory structure that denies the relational gender dimensions of citizenship seems to be a legal as well as a political and ideological issue.

A feminist notion of citizenship committed to the principle of inclusion cannot be halted at the borders of the nation states. Obviously, the solo mother's vulnerable situation shows that the Nordic strategy of combining labour-market work with family life is too narrow a concept for long-term improvements in gender equality for all citizens. Notwithstanding, social citizenship as conceptualized in the Nordic countries has functioned as a general protection with both de-commodifying and de-familializing effects, which have made it possible for solo mothers to form a household of their own, without being stigmatized or excluded by society. There are lessons here to be learned for gender mainstreaming as conceptualized in the EU, and for a review and modernization of social protection systems. At the same time, the Nordic countries should learn from the European objectives by critically examining law and discourse on a national level. Such an approach could reveal selectivity and collective and structural discriminatory practices within national systems that have become invisible in gender-neutral regulations which emphasize formal equality. An approach which is open-minded to difference and diversity among social citizens, could tell us which norms are privileged and how individual and collective entitlements and obligations are constructed and could therefore be useful in emancipative legal scholarship.

As part of the European integration process and mainstreaming efforts, legal studies need to take on such things as the important question in Europe today about whether social assistance is to become a human right to be claimed by some citizens, and a request for poor relief for others. Furthermore, an important issue for future legal studies would seem to be how human rights instruments, on both a regional European level and a global level, can be compared to and function within a Nordic legal culture in order to develop principles for the protection of pluralistic welfare needs. Given that law is not an isolated phenomenon in society and that scholarly legal studies are not just an internal matter, new strategies seem to be needed that will encourage legal scholars to participate in the development of a Citizens' Europe in a broader sense than simply in relation to the market. The Nordic welfare states' adjustment to European objectives in the field of social policy is in danger of increasing inequalities if principles of solidarity are abandoned in favour of principles based on the notion of an active and autonomous citizen.

The study referred to here can say nothing about social consequences and the social justifications of legal decisions in reality, but could function as a legal-strategic tool for evaluating the protection of one economically and socially disadvantaged group. One conclusion drawn so far from a legal point of view is that social rights, suited to a differentiated and a pluralistic notion of the citizen, on both a national and European level, seem to be of decisive significance for preventing exclusion and poverty. Another conclusion – not new but still worthy of great emphasis – is that the concepts underlying legal constructions and techniques need to be the subject of constant discussion if solutions are to be found that correspond more closely to human needs in a changing and pluralist context.

References

Official Documents – National

Handbook 2002:2, *Recommendations for the legal application and hearing of cases in municipal social services*. [Finnish Ministry of Social Affairs and Health].

Rundskriv SOS – 1/34/2001, Statlige veiledende retningslinjer for utmåling av stønad til livsopphold etter sosialtjenestelovens § 5–1 tredje led m.v. [Norwegian Ministry of Social Affairs, Circular, Government instruction on guiding principles for the allowance of livelihood support under Social Services Act Chapter 5 section 1, third subsection].

Socialstyrelsen (2003), *Ekonomiskt bistånd. Stöd för rättstillämpning och handläggning av ärenden i den kommunala socialtjänsten.* [Swedish National Board of Health and Welfare, Economic Assistance. Support for the legal application and hearing of cases in municipality social services].

SOSFS 2003:5(S), *Socialstyrelsens allmänna råd. Ekonomiskt bistånd.* [The National Board of Health and Welfares' general guidelines, Economic Assistance].

SOU 2001:54, *Ofärd i välfärden.* [Research anthology of the Government Commission on a balance sheet for welfare of the 1990s, Poverty in Welfare]

Statistics Norway (2002), *Økonomi og levekår for ulike grupper trygdemottakere 2001.* (Statistics Norway, 2002 /20).

Official Documents – EU/EC

COM (2003a) 842 final, Brussels, 30.12.2003. 'Communication from the Commission to the Council, the European Parliament, the European Economic and Social Committee and the Committee of the Regions'.

COM (2003b) 312 final, Communication from the Commission to the Council, The European Parliament, The European Economic and Social Committee and the Committee of the Regions, Mid-Term Review of The Social Policy Agenda.

European Commission, Employment & Social Affairs, '*Social Protection in Europe 2001*', May 2002.

92/441/EEC, Council Recommendation of 24 June 1992 on common criteria concerning sufficient resources and social assistance in social protection systems, in *OJ* L 245/46, 26.8.92.

Literature

Andenæs, Kristian (1992), *Sosial omsorg i gode og onde dager* (Oslo: TANO).

Björnberg, Ulla (1994), 'Ökad press på alltfler ensamstående mödrar', *Kvinnovetenskaplig tidskrift,* Nr. 2, 12-–5.

Björnberg, Ulla (1996), 'Ensamstående mödrar i Sverige – med utblick mot Europa', *Zenit* Nr.132/133, p. 34.

Brækhus, Hege (2004), 'Care and Social Rights in Norway', in Svensson, Eva-Maria, Pylkkänen, Anu and Niemi-Kiesiläinen, Johanna (eds) *Nordic Equality at a Crossroads. Feminist Legal Studies Coping with Difference* (Aldershot: Ashgate), 91–106.

Bradshaw, Jonathan, Kennedy, S., Kilkey, M., Huttong, S., Corden, A., Eardley, T., Holmes, H. and Neale, J.. (1996), *The Employment of Lone Parents: A Comparison of policy in 20 Countries* (London/York, Family Policy Centre/Joseph Rowntree Foundation).

Burman, Monica, Gunnarsson, Åsa and Wennberg, Lena (2004), 'Economic Dependency and Self-Support in Family, Tax and Social Law', in Svensson, Eva-Maria, Pylkkänen, Anu and Niemi-Kiesiläinen, Johanna (eds) *Nordic Equality at a Crossroads. Feminist Legal Studies Coping with Difference* (Aldershot: Ashgate).

Daly, Mary and Saraceno, Chiara (2002), 'Social exclusion and gender relations', in Hobson, Barbara Lewis, Jane and Siim, Birte (eds) *Contested Concepts in Gender and Social Politics* (Edward Elgar Publishing Limited).

Duncan, S. and Edwards, R. (1999), *Lone Mothers, Paid Work and Gendered Moral Rationalities* (Macmillan Press Ltd.).

Eriksson, Lars D. (2003), 'En legalstrategi för 2000-talet', *100 Retfærd: Nordic Journal of Law and Justice* 2003, 21–31.

Esping-Andersen, Gøsta (1990), *The Three Worlds of Welfare Capitalism* (Cambridge: Polity).

Fineman Albertson, Marta (2001), 'Dependencies', in Hirschman, Nancy J. and Liebert, Ulrike (eds). *Women and Welfare - Theory and Practice in the United States and Europe* (New Brunswick, New Jersey, and London: Rutgers University Press), 23–37.

Florin, Christina and Kvarnström, Lars (eds) (2001), *Kvinnor på gränsen till medborgarskap: genus, politik och offentlighet 1800–1950* (Stockholm: Atlas).

Gähler, Micael (2001), 'Bara en mor – ensamstående mödrars ekonomiska levnadsvillkor i 1900-talets Sverige', in SOU 2001:54 *A Balance Sheet for Welfare of the 1990s: Ofärd i välfärden.*

Gustafsson Björn and Pedersen, Peder J. (eds) (2000), *Poverty and Low Income in the Nordic Countries* (Aldershot: Ashgate).

Hantrais, Linda (2000), *Social Policy in the European Union* (Basingstoke: Macmillan Press Ltd).

Heikkilä, Matti and Keskitalo, Elsa (eds) (2001), *Social Assistance in Europe. A comparative study on minimum income in seven European countries*. Synthesis Report from the project, 'The Role of Social Assistance as a means of Social Inclusion and Activation' (Helsinki: Stakes).

Held, Virginia (1993), *Feminist Morality. Transforming Culture, Society and Politics* (Chicago: University of Chicago Press).

Hernes, Helga (1987), *Welfare State and Power. Essays in state feminism* (Oslo: Norwegian University Press).

Hervey, Tamara (1998), *European Social Law and Policy* (London and New York: Longman).

Hirschmann, Nancy J. and Liebert, Ulrike (eds) (2001), *Women and Welfare. Theory and Practice in the United States and Europe* (New Brunswick, New Jersey, and London: Rutgers University Press).

Hobson, Barbara (1994), 'Solo Mothers, Social Policy Regimes and the Logics of Gender', in Sainsbury, Diane (ed.), *Gendering Welfare States*, Sage Publications, 170–187.

Hobson, Barbara and Takahashi, Mieko (1996), 'Genusperspektiv på det sociala medborgarskapet: En studie av ensamstående mödrar', in Palme, Joakim and

Wennemo, Irene (eds) *Generell välfärd – hot eller möjligheter?* (Välfärdsprojektet, Stockholm: Socialdepartementet).

Hobson, Barbara and Takahashi, Mieko (1997), 'The Parent – Worker Model: Lone Mothers in Sweden', in Lewis, Jane (ed.) *Lone Mothers in European Welfare Regimes Shifting Policy Logics* (London and Philadelphia: Jessica Kingsley Publishers).

Hobson, Barbara, Lewis, Jane and Siim, Birte (2002), (eds), *Contested Concepts in Gender and Social Politics* (Cheltenham: Edward Elgar Publishing Limited).

Hollander, Anna (1998), *Rättighetslag i teori och praxis* (Uppsala: Iustus Förlag).

Hydén, Håkan (2002), *Rättssociologi som rättsvetenskap* (Lund: Studentlitteratur).

Ketcher, Kirsten (1998), *Almindelige Pricipper Retssikkerhed og administration* (København: Gadjura).

Lewis, Jane (ed.) (1997), *Lone Mothers in European Welfare Regimes Shifting Policy Logics* (London and Philadelphia: Jessica Kingsley Publishers).

Layte, R. and Whelan, C.T. (2002), 'Moving in and out of Poverty: The Impact of Welfare Regimes on Poverty Dynamics in the EU', EPAG Working Paper 30 (Colchester: University of Essex).

Liebert, Ulrike (2001), 'Degendering Care and Engendering Freedom. Social Welfare in the European Union', in Hirschmann, Nancy J. and Liebert, Ulrike (eds) *Women and Welfare. Theory and Practice in the United States and Europe* (New Brunswick, New Jersey, and London: Rutgers University Press).

Lister, Ruth (2003), *Citizenship: Feminist Perspectives* (New York: New York University Press).

Nousiainen, Kevät (2001), 'Transformative Nordic Welfarism: Liberal and Communitarian Trends in Family and Market Law', in Nousiainen, Kevät, Gunnarsson, Åsa, Lundström, Karin and Niemi-Kiesiläinen, Johanna (eds) *Responsible Selves, Women in the Nordic Legal Culture* (Dartmouth: Ashgate).

Nousiainen, Kevät and Niemi-Kiesiläinen, Johanna (2001), 'Introductory Remarks on Nordic Law and Gender Identities', in Nousiainen, Kevät, Gunnarsson, Åsa, Lundström, Karin, Niemi-Kiesiläinen, Johanna (eds) *Responsible Selves, Women in the Nordic Legal Culture* (Dartmouth: Ashgate).

Nousiainen, Kevät, Gunnarsson, Åsa, Lundström, Karin, Niemi-Kiesiläinen, Johanna (eds) (2001), *Responsible Selves, Women in the Nordic Legal Culture* (Dartmouth: Ashgate).

Palme, Joakim and Wennemo, Irene (eds) (1996), *Generell välfärd – hot eller möjligheter?* (Stockholm: Socialdepartementet).

Pieters, Danny (ed.) (1997), '*Social Protection of the Next Generation in Europe*' (EISS Yearbook: Kluwer Law International).

Puide, Annica and Minas, Renate (2001), 'Recipients of Social Assistance', in Heikkilä, Matti and Keskitalo, Elsa (eds) *Social Assistance in Europe. A comparative study on minimum income in seven European countries*. Synthesis Report from the project, 'The Role of Social Assistance as a means of Social Inclusion and Activation' (Helsinki: Stakes, 2001).

Sainsbury, Diane (ed.) (1996), *Gendering Welfare States* (Cambridge University Press).

Sakslin, Maja (1998), 'Worker versus Citizen? – Why not forget them both?', in Pieters, Danny and Stendahl, Sara (eds) (2003), *Communicating Justice, Providing Legitimacy. The legal practices of administrative courts in cases regarding sickness cash benefit* (Uppsala: Iustus Förlag).

Svensson Eva-Maria (1997), *Genus och rätt, en problematisering av föreställning om rätten* (Uppsala: Iustus Förlag).

Svensson, Eva-Maria, Pylkkänen, Anu and Niemi-Kiesiläinen, Johanna (eds) (2004), *Nordic Equality at a Crossroads. Feminist Legal Studies Coping with Difference* (Aldershot: Ashgate).

Tuori, Kaarlo (1993), 'Lagstiftningsstrategierna inom social- och hälsovården', in *62 Retfærd: Nordic Journal of Law and Justice* 1993, 5–18.

Vahlne Westerhäll, Lotta (2002), *Den starka statens fall? En rättsvetenskaplig studie av svensk social trygghet 1950–2000* (Stockholm: Norstedts Juridik).

Chapter 11

Gender Equality and the Diversity of Rights and Obligations in Swedish Social Citizenship

Åsa Gunnarsson

This chapter is one of three contributions in this volume that reflects on how and why a comprehensive welfare state like Sweden, with far-reaching egalitarian commitments, still reproduces inequalities between men and women. The gender perspective adopted in the chapter concerns both the politics of sex equality between men and women, and the legal constructions of gender relations. Formally, social participation in the welfare state, implemented in terms of equal, individual eligibility for social entitlements and individual tax obligations, seems to go hand in hand with equal opportunities. Welfare regime provisions governing the distribution of social rights and tax obligations are mainly linked to individuals and there is also a strong state involvement in the care of children. Nevertheless, in times of budget cuts in expenditure the distributive principles in what can be defined as a normative Swedish model of social citizenship have been put to the test. One important outcome, and a point of departure for this chapter, is that a large number of women have suffered disproportionately from cutbacks in public welfare provision. This is probably a symptom of a gendered dimension to social power within the legal structures that regulate the right to receive social welfare and the obligations to participate in generating public welfare. One frame of reference for scholarly analysis is that a normative model of individual rights and obligations creates an imaginary concept that all citizens are equal under a neutral law. Such a uniform approach to social citizenship is incapable of identifying those legal structures in which the patterns of social power reside, and which reproduce sex inequalities between men and women together with stereotyped gender constructions. In contrast, taking a gender perspective on welfare-state regulations highlights the diversity of possible legal strategies for achieving sex equality drawn from social, economic and political contexts. The aim of this chapter is to explore, from a Swedish perspective, why a transformed conception of social citizenship is needed in order to achieve a more inclusive social welfare regime from a gender perspective.

Applying a Concept of Social Citizenship to the Legal Framework of Welfare Provisions

The theoretical concept of *social citizenship* is commonly used in contemporary research, not always explicitly but in substance, as an instrument for analysing gender, equality, and welfare regimes (Lister 2003; Hirschman and Liebert 2001; Kittay 2001; Orloff 1993; Sainsbury 1993, 1996, 1999; Montanari 2000). Social citizenship is not a mainstream legal definition of the relation between state and individual, based on the legal discourse of classical, constitutional freedoms and rights (Gustafsson 2002, 207–209). Instead, the use of the concept aims to highlight the scope of social inclusion through distributive rights and obligations constituted in the welfare state in the division of responsibilities between individuals and the state and between individuals per se (Liebert 2001, 261). The rights and duties, including the distributive principles and participatory conditions which constitute membership in a society, define one form of social citizenship (Wennberg 2004, 36). This emphasizes the human need for social security and how society provides for social protection. From this perspective social rights and obligations are the lowest common denominator for membership in a community. This perspective points out the core idea of the citizen's social entitlements in welfare states, namely that the meeting of certain needs should be guaranteed by public provision. The political consensus concerning need is assessed in relation to the social balance of power in a welfare regime. Conflicting interests emerge in the political process of modifying the social consequences of the market economy in order to achieve greater equality. State intervention in the market economy is always restricted by the interest of individual economic and political freedoms (Orloff 1996; Lister 2003; Lacey 1998).

One central aspect of what the state becomes as an outcome of political processes is expressed in social justice. What the state conceives as legitimate principles for distributing social goods corresponds to the principles governing participation in generating the wealth needed. The legitimate principles that construct social citizenship set the standards of normality, in which legal norms of justice regarding distribution and participation are incorporated. The expressed and reproduced assumptions of what welfare-state law conceives as the normal model for citizens' contributions to society, creates a boundary between those who are included and those excluded from full social membership in a society (Tronto 2001, 65).

Eligibility and responsibility of both an individual and collective nature are decisive for how citizens share the burdens and the benefits of a comprehensive welfare state. Social entitlements, constituted as general rights, services or benefits in welfare state law, are formally equally available to all. The responsibilities for taking part in fiscal obligations such as paying taxes, social contributions and fees, are also formally neutral in relation to the ability to pay or consume. Nevertheless, the Swedish welfare regime still reproduces inequalities between men and women.

The obvious problem is that access to social entitlements as well as to the possession of means from income and capital are commonly structured along gender patterned lines (Lacey 1998, 59–61). The Swedish legal framework for the distribution of welfare seldom explicitly intervenes in this structural inequality between men and women. The legal constructions of the Swedish welfare state, to which a theoretical concept of a social citizenship can be applied, are based on the employment strategy (referred to by Ruth Mannelqvist this volume) and the dual-breadwinner family model. The politics of sex equality are promoted within the framework of the reconciliation of work and family life. What this welfare regime fails to see, however, is that workers require care if they are to remain capable of work. When the employment strategy, sometimes also referred to as an ideology of workfare, develops a citizen-worker concept, care work becomes an invisible prerequisite for, and constitutes a gendered separation of, public and private. The existence of gendered diversity and difference in social citizenship, which arises from human functions connected with labour, care, responsibility and time are basic theoretical issues for gender research into legal reforms in the welfare state (Sevenhuijsen 1998, chapter 1).

The gap between formal sex equality and the practice of sex inequalities represents a conflict of interest in welfare state regulations concerning distributive obligations and rights. Such a gap is clearly a normative problem beyond the scope of a formal principle of equal treatment. Therefore, in order to define what differences are legally relevant and in what ways, equality, as well as justice, should be conceived dynamically and not as a demand for similarity (Nousiainen 2004). Such a theoretical approach to law comprises several elements. First, the simplified world of legal analysis has to be questioned (Minow 1991, 2). Legal paradigms have to grasp the idea that legal orders are not closed normative systems (Gustafsson 2002, 84–87). This intellectual and empirical standpoint emphasizes that legal research is about all aspects of legal norms (Hydén 2002, 132). In contrast to a legal formalist perspective, where legal norms are seen as being detached from the social and economic values that shape the conditions of life, these legal norms should be regarded as a comprehensive concept.[1]

Second, traditional legal assumptions about the self and society have to be challenged. The boundaries of normality in law are, in a traditional setting, constructed on a hidden normative standard of the self as an autonomous, competent individual. Matters of relational dependency are defined as different and are excluded from legal discourse. The abstract concept of the individual has shaped the idea of privacy, not in the sense of integrity, but as a contextual value of a private sphere, free from public intervention. On the other side of the dichotomy, the public sphere has been the scene of politics and the intervention of law. This normative argument has been much debated. Nevertheless, looking at the normative structures of law and the legislative prerequisites for what should or should not be regulated, there is often a divide present between public and private life in various welfare-state regulations. A well-established, internationally recognized, feminist critique of mainstream legal studies has shown that women from any background may be neglected by legal rules, given their traditional exclusion from public processes (Lacey 1998, 71–124; Minow 1991, 7–11; Svensson 2001, 95–97; Fineman 2001, 24–30).

1 This theoretical approach to law is shared with Mannelqvist and Wennberg.

Third, questions about law other than those based on the traditional[2] view of 'law as fact' have to be addressed. Asking questions about sex inequalities in law, at the neutral level of formal equality of social rights and obligations, neglects the possibility that the substantive pre-conceptions of legal forms, rules and principles in welfare provisions can be to the social disadvantage of women (Okin 1989, 113; Lacey 1998, 27–28). The task of investigating the premises for gender justice in the normative substance of equal opportunities in welfare state regimes, has its legitimate foundation in the legal doctrines of gender mainstreaming in Sweden and the EU (Svensson 2001). However, substantive elements of equality, the requirements for equality of resources, capabilities, and results are also significant for gender perspectives on welfare states in general (Fraser 1994, 591). Without a social context it is impossible to analyse whether the substance and the material outcome of legal reforms will promote sex equality or if sex equality is supported in the practice of law (Lacey 1998, 66–70).

Fourth and finally, the theoretical limitations of a dogmatic position have to be tackled. It is obvious that notions of social justice legitimate the welfare state in both political theory and socio-political typologies. Distributions of responsibilities, rights, favours, goods, or power, are always a potential source of justice and injustice. Concepts of social justice are used to legitimize state intervention for the common good (Okin 1989, 114; Orloff 1996, 52). However, traditional legal studies do not provide for a set of general implications for theorizing either social justice or gendered dimensions in law. Thus, one way of moving beyond the scope of dogmatics is to apply an outside perspective on law. It is important to find a concept that has the potential to dissolve both the boundaries of normality and the limits of the public and private divide.

Applying Gender Equality on the Principles of Social Justice in Tax and Social Security Law

The recognition by the welfare state that certain social needs are legitimate creates a legal framework for social access. The controversial issues are, of course, to reach a basic political understanding of the idea of need, and the extent to which the needs accepted by a political legal body should be fulfilled. An introductory remark has already been made about the conflicts of interest that restrict equality-oriented state intervention. It is in this context that social justice becomes an important instrument for gaining legitimacy for distributive principles concerning the distribution of responsibilities and goods among citizens (Lacey 1998, 47–52, 59).

Thus, the manifestation of distributive principles through law is based on the dominant political conception of social justice. From a theoretical standpoint, these principles are the main source of social constructions in welfare-state law. The conception of social justice expresses and reproduces assumptions of normality about the self and society. Legal concepts are reflections of these assumptions, but

2 A further explanation of the traditional view as a dogmatic approach to legal scholarship is presented in the Introduction.

the underlying values and modes of life shaping the assumptions are rer The separation between values and law produces apparently neutral and incl… legal concepts of fair principles for distributing legitimate needs (Lacey 1998, 148, 229–230). This illusion of neutrality in law makes it difficult to see the links between the levels of equality achieved through welfare-state arrangements and the discriminatory boundaries of normality in the politics of social justice.

The gendered nature of the welfare produced and distributed in a triangular, institutional relationship between state, market and household (family) has remained unacknowledged in Swedish welfare-state arrangements (Gunnarsson and Stattin 2001). The lack of knowledge about how gender relations have impacted on the distribution of power and resources in this social-welfare triangle has proved to be a common problem in all western welfare regimes, regardless of variations. As the substance and material outcome of law reflects the basic normative foundations in social-welfare reforms, it is important to deconstruct the legal concepts emanating from welfare provisions from a gender perspective. It needs to be recognized that both private and public institutions produce welfare, which emphasizes the fact that welfare is a broader set of activities and possessions than that which is embraced by welfare-state regulations. Applying a gendered dimension to welfare state law challenges the conditions for becoming eligible for inclusion in social insurance schemes that offer income protection or need-based support, such as housing allowances or social assistance. It also challenges the prerequisites for recognized contributions that constitute a participating and thereby entitled citizen. Obviously, the stratification shaped by welfare arrangements in terms of equal or unequal access to resources has a blind spot where the outcomes of living conditions do not change gender relations (Liebert 2001, 268; Orloff 2001, 134–135; Tronto 2001, 66–70).

One key issue for eliminating the blind spot is to analyse the context of the social location of the household, i.e. the family. Women's living conditions are largely bound up with family life. Normative and structural patterns that shape these living conditions emerge from the traditional gendered functions within the family, in combination with how the family as an institution is organized in society. The general picture of unequal distribution of power and resources between men and women shows that women's economic dependency resides and is reinforced in the exchange of time, care and economic resources in the triangular relation of state, market and family (Stang Dahl 1988; Ketscher 1998, 60–68). In other words, family life constitutes economic and social subordination for women, but in mainstream social and legal science, as well as in political notions of social justice, the presumption is made that family institutions are just. However, the unequal distribution of responsibilities, financial resources, powers and time within the family is closely related to inequalities in the society outside the family institution. Welfare is produced in a cyclical process across the state, the market and the family, that, in structural terms, reinforces the dominance of men over women, from home to work, to the welfare regime, and thence back home again (Gunnarsson 2003, 22–23; Nyman 2002, Article 3; Okin 1989, 21–22, 92, 95, 113).

The above analysis is argued from a sex-equality-oriented basis. A gender perspective inevitably comprehends issues of sex inequalities, but is primarily about gender relations, and the constructions of gender (Svensson 1997). Thus, if the gender dimension is taken seriously, social welfare has to be regarded as a broad concept that includes the aspect of social power within legal structures. It ought to include both the right to receive welfare, and the obligation to participate in generating public welfare. The basis of entitlement to social provisions should be tested from the perspective of how social benefits and services contribute to women's autonomy or reinforce their dependency. Such a test ought to include the range of benefits and services, and underpinning criteria such as coverage (including eligibility requirements), duration, benefit levels, etc (see Orloff 2001, 135–136; Sainsbury 1996, 44–45). From the perspective of the social welfare triangle it is also important to investigate how tax regulations can promote sex equality by creating incentives and disincentives regarding work decisions and family formations.

When systematizing law from these perspectives, it is important to realize that this theoretical approach incorporates the question of social power in law. Depending on the perspective chosen, a different emphasis will be given to the range of legal criteria and the structural legal conditions for receiving welfare, and the participation in the obligation of giving welfare. Compared to a gender perspective, a positivist perspective will result in a legalistic and formal understanding of welfare-state law as it excludes the issue of social power. When welfare-state law is approached from a gender perspective, questions about sex inequalities in social entitlements and tax incentives and disincentives will produce knowledge about social positions in welfare-state law (see Davies and Svensson this volume). The pluralism of what can be understood as social citizenship in the Swedish legal welfare structure will also inevitably be constructed on different concepts of social justice.

Social Entitlements Categorized on the Basis of Citizenship/Residence, Work Performance and Means-Tested Need for Financial Support

The comprehensive scope of the Swedish welfare state, with respect to the range of publicly provided benefits and services, the population coverage, and the high level of benefits, can be divided into two parts. One part has the features of a 'social service state', which is a definition used to emphasize the general welfare services and benefits strategy, and the centrality of public services. Compared with other models or typologies for welfare states, this has been regarded as an inclusive policy. The other part of the Swedish welfare regime can be defined as 'the social insurance state' protecting income loss, under which benefits based on earnings-related schemes should be categorized (Sainsbury 1996, 31–32; Vahlne Westerhäll 1996; Vahlne Westerhäll, 2002, 640–641; Mannelqvist this volume with further references to Anttonen).

Within the structure of a social service state, the most inclusive regimes are regarded as those which provide flat-rate or in-kind benefits and services structured as programmes for active measures and entitlements based on residence (Sainsbury 1996, 45–46, 86–87). Social services covering various types of care are mainly based on residence. Good healthcare should, at least as stated formally, be provided on the same conditions for the entire population. The right to child care is not stipulated with the same generality since it is conditional, albeit rather generously, on the parents' or the children's need for child care. The major part of flat-rate benefits is directed to households with children. Criteria for eligibility based on residence are relevant for child allowance, guaranteed levels of parental insurance, advance maintenance allowance, children's pension allowance, allowances for international adoptions, and financial aid to children attending upper-secondary schooling. Housing allowance is means tested, conditional on the family income, the size of the family home, and the number of children (Gunnarsson 2003, 131–132). Residence-based social entitlements make no distinction between paid work and unpaid work. Hence eligibility becomes neutral vis-à-vis the gender inequalities in the social-welfare triangle (Gunnarsson *et al.* 2004).

It is therefore easy to come to the conclusion that when entitlements are solely based on citizenship or residence they are less likely to reproduce gender relations. Benefits and services in-kind or at a flat-rate for which one criterion for eligibility is residence have the potential to alter gender relations. When benefits and services are not affected by marital status, the sort of dependency that exists in a family relationship becomes weaker for those in both care-taking and care-giving positions. In contrast, the eligibility of an individual to means-tested benefits and services is often affected by the income and assets of the other spouse or the cohabitating partner when they are assessed on the basis of household income. Normally, means testing aims to target the legitimate needs of various categories. The whole point of such targeting is to exclude everyone who does not fulfil the criteria for legitimate need for a specific welfare programme. Families or households are used as the benefit unit to target those without the means to support or care for themselves, subsidiary to a maintenance principle within the family. If maintenance principles are of vital importance in a welfare state, which is not the case in Sweden, a common structural effect is for the benefits and services to become differentiated between husband and wife (Sainsbury 1996, 44–45, 86–87; Gunnarsson *et al.* 2004).

Social entitlements, following the public insurance principle, derive from labour market status and constitute a public, social insurance system providing income compensation when an individual is incapable of work. Eligibility for the public insurance system is based on an assessment of qualifying income from the performance of paid work, and on past employment-related social contributions. One basic idea behind public social insurance is to protect the working citizen from the social risks induced by income loss due to old age, sickness, occupational injury, unemployment and parenthood (Mannelqvist 2003, chapter 5; Stendahl 2003, chapter 6).

Benefits stemming from the social insurance part of the welfare state modify dependency on market forces for the recipients. However, the degree of accretion of rights to benefits such as state earnings-related pensions and unemployment benefits are very unequally distributed between men and women because of the difference in gender relations. Referring back to the social-welfare triangle, inequalities are reproduced because on average men still earn more. The reasons are to be found both in the private sphere of the family and the public sphere of the market place. Domestic responsibilities are unequally shared between the sexes, men more often than women have unbroken career paths, and part-time work is much more common among women. Moreover, women suffer from income discrimination on the labour market, on both an individual and a structural level, more often than men. Whilst eligibility is based on work performances and income from paid work the gendered division of labour will continue to be transmitted into social rights (Gunnarsson 2003, 34–37).

Social Rights or Discretionary Assistance from the Perspective of the Individual

It is important to note that constructing typologies or models for eligibility to welfare provisions from categories consisting of needs, work performance and citizenship/residence would not be considered valid in a positivist legal analysis. Even if the Swedish Social Insurance Act makes a distinction between social benefits based on work and residence, which is similar to the categories above, the concepts have a somewhat different meaning; one major difference being that need is not an independent category. Need is an ongoing requirement mostly for residence-based benefits, but also for some of the benefits based on work performance (Mannelqvist 2003, 80–87).

From an individual, gender-neutral perspective, some benefits and services can be defined as genuine claim rights when they are regulated as clear and predictable rights, given by the welfare state to the individual. For such types of social rights, the authorities' responsibility is not discretionary, meaning that the state-individual relation has almost the same characteristics as it does with classical, liberal freedoms and rights. From this legalistic perspective a social benefit has the status of a claim right when it is independent of public budget restrictions, subordinated to control from a governmental body, and sanctioned. Soft law characteristics in the form of policies, guidelines and goal-orientation do not have the this status (Hollander 1995, 35; Gustafsson 2002, 235–248).

Following an individual perspective on social rights in Swedish welfare regulations, three categories emerge. The first group is defined as genuine or legal rights, closest to the legal structure of claim rights. The second group can be called quasi-rights or service rights, with a much weaker limited legal strength. These rights are often addressed to the authorities in terms of it being their duty to enforce them, without a correlative right for the individual to claim. The functions of service rights are mainly upheld by control from governmental bodies. The third group is often called goal-oriented social rights, which have the legal structure of a framework for goal-oriented means of distributive social justice. Here, the responsibility for raising the necessary economic resources to guarantee that those social needs to which citizens are entitled, is mostly placed on local authorities (Westerhäll 1994, 87–90). The experience is that giving unconditional rights to the citizen encroaches on the constitutional principle of municipal self-government and local democracy. Of these three categories, the genuine rights or claim rights are seen as the strongest, with respect to giving the individual the rights to have specific needs met, as they are correlated to comprehensive duties for the municipalities (Gustafsson 2002, 453).

Historically, from 1950-1960, the distribution of supplementary public economic support in relation to earnings was based on a kind of equality of treatment between those in need of support and those without the same need. One important objective was to give need-based maintenance to those who lacked the means to support themselves. From the aspect of formal, individual justice those in need and those not in need were thus treated equally. Later on, the dominant idea of substantial justice, meaning solidarity and redistribution, also affected reforms concerning individual need for financial support. Today, the definition of social justice for different categories of need-based support, such as the income-tested housing allowance, or maintenance support for basic needs, should be placed on a scale of rights ranging from social service and discretionary assistance to claim rights (Vahlne Westerhäll 2002, 490–491, 526–537).

Parallel to the system of need-based benefits there was an early system of social insurance rights, as a result of a combination of a public insurance principle and a maintenance principle of self-support. When the public insurance principle became the predominant influence, it was formally characterized in the basic value of collective justice (Vahlne Westerhäll 2002, 225–227, 539–542). In the 1970s, solidarity principles, such as the social contract between generations which Mannelqvist refers to (Mannelqvist this volume), had an impact on social insurance reforms where elements of substantial social justice were introduced. Social insurance benefits are earned rights. The qualification for income compensation is work performance.

Another effect of the emphasis on the solidarity dimension was goal-oriented legal reform, particularly in the area of social assistance and social services. The values governing the reforms were of a distributive, commutative, and corrective nature. The dominant idea of justice was more substantial than formal (Vahlne Westerhäll 2002, 490–491, 527–527). Social assistance for income support is the last social safety net for those who cannot provide for themselves. One part of the qualifications for receiving social assistance is constructed as an individual claim-right, the so-called right to maintenance support. However, this is largely discretionary, and depends on what society defines as social needs in terms of a reasonable standard of living, which is in turn closely related to what public budget restrictions allow. History has shown that at times of economic recession, the comprehensiveness of social assistance is curtailed (Vahlne Westerhäll 2002, 182; Wennberg 2004, 64–73, 119).

The right to essential medical care and treatment originally had no legal framework. The state only regulated the administrative obligations of the healthcare authorities to provide medical care for those in need. The social-service characteristics of the regulations did not change when the Health and Medical Care Act was introduced as duty-imposing legislation, outlining the responsibilities of the healthcare providers. This goal-orientated framework for access to health and care service rights can be defined as a 'service state' regulation. The legislation is not based on principles of rights or justice on an individual or a collective level. In the eyes of the individual, the rights have the characteristics of an individual quasi-right (Vahlne Westerhäll 2002, 613–614).

When analysing the development of cash-transfer benefits, in particular during the 1990s, the economic crisis in the welfare economy has to be considered. The large deficit led to budget cuts in expenditure, on such a scale that it has been labelled 'welfare-state retrenchment' (Sainsbury 1996, 198). Principles of social justice in family politics, social security politics and the politics of social assistance proved to be largely discretionary. Access to various parts of the system was tightened for individuals in vulnerable positions during the 1990s. The number of non-eligible individuals grew (Stendahl 2003, 366–369). As I have indicated, until the 1980s the Swedish welfare-state arrangements followed a principle of substantive justice. Under the influence of the solidarity principle a range of benefits were clearly redistributive, mainly from childless households to families with children, and with some emphasis on low-income families. Conversely, welfare-state retrenchment during the structural economic crisis of the early 1990s made family support less comprehensive. Criteria for income assessments, levels of compensation, and duration were tightened, which hollowed out income maintenance programmes for family support (Gunnarsson 2003; Gunnarsson *et al.* 2004).

When principles of social justice are regarded as discretionary when policy is reviewed, the uncertainty of the legal status of various social rights becomes obvious. One analysis is that the legal strategies used during the era of welfare-state retrenchment resulted in the use of more quasi-rights for social entitlements in all categories, a sign of the fall of the strong state (Vahlne Westerhäll 2002, 582–583, 635–639). This may well be the case, but one has to consider that social justice, throughout the history of Swedish welfare-state regimes, has probably been discretionary, and determined largely by the level of social expenditure. The fall of the strong state also implies a shift in responsibility for providing welfare from the state to the market. Looking at the changes initiated during the 1990s from a narrow Swedish perspective, it is true that such a shift can be seen in some areas of welfare provision. However, in comparison with other OECD countries, the characteristic features of the Swedish welfare model have remained relatively unchanged. We have, like the other Nordic countries, retained a high degree of universalism in public services and basic social security benefits covering all residents (Kautto *et al.* 2001; SOU 2000:83). Commonly used retrenchment strategies such as the promotion of private sector involvement and a shifting to means-tested benefits and increased targeting, have not been adopted in Sweden (Sainsbury 1996, 199-224). So, perhaps the strong state still stands, but the downsizing of welfare-state programs has highlighted how randomly social entitlements can become eroded.

Tax Obligations

In theory, the basic obligation of citizens in a welfare state is to share the burdens of benefits, through both collective and individual, direct and indirect taxes and social contributions. The recognition of citizens' social rights ought to correlate to the obligatory common responsibility to generate the wealth needed. In that way, the obligation of the citizen is based on the legitimate demand to support certain basic needs (Lacey 1998, 50–52). In public finance, the concept of generating wealth is centred in the obligation to pay taxes and social contributions, which constitute the main sources of revenue. The total tax ratio for Sweden has for many years, with few exceptions, been the highest among the OECD countries. Tax ratios among countries are difficult to compare due to several factors of which various differences in the existence, levels and structures of social security contributions and taxes are the most pronounced (see for example Messere 1993, chapter 3; Messere *et al.* 2003, 33; Riksskatteverket 2003). Even so, the Swedish welfare state is strong when the tax obligations of the citizens are measured. According to theory, the presumption is that the correlation between obligations and legitimate needs ought also to be strong, in order to achieve the dominant political conception of social justice expressed in distributive principles of equality and solidarity. However, such normative coherence does not exist between tax and social security law. The justification for tax fairness is based on somewhat different distributive principles in relation to social security law.

Taxation has many sources such as real estate, wealth, capital, beneficial transfers consumption, goods, services, production, labour and income. The Swedish tax system draws, directly or indirectly, on all of these sources, except for beneficial transfer which has just recently been abolished as a tax base. In effect, most economic activities are taxed. One basic problem is that the tax system operates with a very diverse set of distributive principles. How 'tax citizens' come to share a common tax burden is, therefore, not particularly transparent.

When structuring taxation in relation to the economic circulation in society, one can see that the flow of incomes has three main sources. Production is the original source from which income springs, the next step is transfer of the incomes of production to the households, and the third step is the use of incomes for consumption. The circle is then closed as the incomes from consumption return to production.

On the level of production, the sum of the employees' gross incomes, the payroll in a company, constitutes the basis for the assessment of the employer's social security contributions. These contributions are structured as payroll taxes for employers, and could easily be classified as a tax on investment in the productive factor, labour. The early system of social security rights for income losses was financed by income taxes and individual social contributions. The shift from financing social insurance schemes through general income taxes and individual social contributions to a payroll tax for employers, was based on the recognition that production should carry the burden of social insurance, not the individual employees (Mannelqvist 2003, 87–88). The social insurance reforms equalized the burdens of the benefits by collecting the social contributions from a collective of employees. As mentioned above, when the insurance principle became predominant it was grounded in a basic value that can be defined as formal justice on a collective level (Vahlne Westerhäll 2002, 225–227, 539–542). So, the correlation between social security contributions and social security benefits, which can be defined as claim rights, is not constructed as a correlation between duty and right for the individual, apart from a smaller part of the old-age pension scheme.

The incomes from employment also constitute the tax base for income tax, for which the employees are the tax subjects. This is an individual, direct tax on the basis of the net income from earnings. The personal income tax base includes in principle all incomes and fringe benefits from work performances of all kinds. It also includes a large part of public, social transfers. In general, benefits based on residence, and social assistance in the form of maintenance support are exempted from income taxation.

Savings from earned income become capital, and income from that capital also constitutes a separate tax base. Certain capital possessions also constitute a tax base for a wealth tax. When using earned or saved income for private consumption, an indirect consumption tax is added to the consumer price for services or goods. The pluralism of the taxation sources, comprehensiveness in the use of broad tax bases, and the combination of both direct and indirect taxation of individuals, makes the concept of obligation to pay tax wider than the qualifications for social entitlements. In short, to become a taxpayer is much easier than to become a social beneficiary. The subjects of obligations do not need to meet demands for eligibility such as residence or active citizenship.

Social justice in income tax law has traditionally been defined by the principle of ability to pay. Over several decades the principle developed into a concept of the individual's ability to pay under a progressive income tax rate schedule. Joint taxation of spouses and various tax reductions for support of dependants within the household, normally the wife and the children, have been abolished on the grounds of sex equality aims. The abolition of joint taxation of spouses was based on knowledge of the correlation between the labour market participation of women, married or living in partnerships and the income of their husbands or partners. When individual taxation was first introduced the incentives for the wife to participate in the labour market increased. The effective marginal tax rate (the tax paid on the last Swedish Krona of earned income) was higher for married men in relation to the generally lower marginal tax rates for women, and an increase in working hours for women was more beneficial for the households (Gunnarsson 2003, 61).

Since the tax reforms at the beginning of the 1990s, the theoretical definition of the ability-to-pay principle has become vague because of political pragmatism about its core meaning. In the early 1990s, the tax system was redesigned in a comprehensive reform based on the principles of tax neutrality and horizontal fairness or equity. The idea of neutrality was designed to avoid unwanted welfare losses by adjusting taxation to promote what is understood to be an efficient allocation of resources in the market economy. Horizontal equity was introduced as an equality-oriented interpretation of the ability-to-pay principle, implying horizontal equality of treatment. Both principles were invoked to justify broader income and consumption tax bases and a flattening of the income-tax-rate schedule. As a result of these changes, more incomes, goods and services became taxable and income tax became less progressive.

The reform had multiple objectives, but the focus was on cutting the effective marginal tax rates on earned income. Those income earners with the highest incomes had the highest effective marginal tax rates, as the income-tax-rate scale had a redistributive, progressive profile. The sex equality problem of the significant cross-over effect between the marginal costs for women's paid work and the income of their husbands or partners was unfortunately not considered. Not surprisingly, the cuts in the effective marginal tax rates had a moderating impact on women's paid work as the marginal net of taxed salaries increased for men (Aronsson and Palme 1994). The shift from income tax to consumption tax had a side effect that also contributed to the moderating impact on women's labour supply. Value Added Tax (VAT) at a rate of 25 per cent was introduced for the first time on several services that could be regarded as substitutes for the type of household maintenance that is traditionally produced by women. It became more expensive for the households to buy these services instead of producing them (Wennemo 1997, 18–19).

The equality-oriented interpretation of the ability-to-pay principle has yet another problematic side. As the predominating idea of tax neutrality has justified broader income and consumption tax bases, at the same time as the income taxes have become less progressive, the equality of treatment has shifted from subject to object. The principle has transformed from equality of treatment of tax subjects with equal economic capacity into an equal treatment of equal incomes. Equal treatment of all incomes by broad tax bases has become synonymous with the definition that all incomes constitute an equal ability to pay. The shift from subject to object is manifested in the change from a global to a schedular income tax. In schedular systems each source of income is treated as a separate tax regime, in contrast to a global system where all sources of income are taxed under the same regime. That means that the ability to pay is no longer judged on the basis of the individual tax subject's cumulative ability to pay, based on the net incomes from different sources (Gunnarsson 1995, 1999, 2001).

The manner in which principles of horizontal tax fairness and tax neutrality have shaped the Swedish tax system allows no space for a social dimension in tax law. However, this attitude has proved to be impossible to uphold. After the 1990s tax reform several changes have been made to adjust the taxation to the individual tax subject's overall collected ability to pay. This has not been done by shifting back to a global taxation, instead tax reductions have been used to adjust the tax burden for certain categories of taxpayers with very low incomes. Single parents have had a standardized reduction for a period of some years, and those senior citizens who are paying high taxes for real estate are today entitled to a reduction when their incomes are low (Gunnarsson 2003, 62, 126).

The aim of cutting effective marginal income tax rates was in line with the employment strategy that operates as a basic principle in social security law. High marginal tax rates are an obstacle to the willingness to work, at least if the analysis is based on the narrow economic perspective of the relation between the income tax system and work supply. The taxation on earned income is still over 55 per cent on the margin for those with the highest incomes. However, for most employees income tax is less than 35 per cent, as they only pay the proportional local tax in the municipalities. Because we had a tax shift from income tax to VAT the general consumption tax on most goods and services is 25 per cent today. One interesting effect, from the perspective of participation in the contribution of welfare, is the relatively small gap between income tax and consumption tax for those with low or moderate incomes. In this respect the tax reform from the beginning of 1990 contributed to economic incentives that reflected the employment strategy. However, in a somewhat different way, the same problem concerning the reproduction of inequalities through social entitlements based on work performances was reinforced by the tax reform. The reform in effect created incentives for married men, or men living in a partnership, to work more hours or take better paid work.

The Construction of Dependency and Autonomy in Welfare Provisions

Using an individual approach when analysing social rights and obligations is formally correct, but it provides an incomplete picture of the substance of social justice from a gender perspective. The wide range of benefits and taxes creates a complicated pattern of dependency between households and the state, and within households. These patterns of dependency stem from normative structures both inside and outside the law. Obviously, the traditional division of paid and unpaid work between men and women in families permeates social provisions. The greater extent of women's unpaid work is the major historical explanation for why women in general have lower salaries than men through having low-paid or part-time work, predominantly in the public sector. As is known from comparative studies, one of the most important welfare state variations is the extent to which the gendered division of labour is protected or confronted in tax and social security law. If a welfare regime emphasizes the need to support the male breadwinner it is based on the ideology of a strict division of paid and unpaid work in a family. The recognition of maintenance obligations on the part of the breadwinner in relation to the carer and other dependants becomes the distributive principle. Consequently, the legal system rests on a normative model where the family or the marriage is the unit of assessment for entitlements and taxation, in which the carer has only supplementary and no individual rights. A male bread-winner regime is of course distinctively sexually segregated – the earner is the husband and the carer is the wife (Sainsbury 1996, 44–45; Sainsbury 1999, 77–80; Orloff 1993, 314).

The opposite of the normative model of a breadwinner is the individual model of social entitlements and income taxation on the basis of work performance and citizenship or residence. This is where the Swedish welfare regime can be placed. The lack of sex equality produced by the division of labour is recognized by the Swedish welfare state and is officially resisted by a combined strategy for the reconciliation of paid work and family life in a dual breadwinner family. Individual obligations via income tax, and individual social rights based on earnings-related social security schemes are measures that, as one of several objectives, aim to increase economic autonomy for married women. Parallel to individualization, and the ambition to achieve gender neutralization of social rights and tax obligations, there has been a growing realization that public intervention needs to equalize the burden of caring and unpaid work between the sexes. Caring, principally in the form of parenting, as the basis for entitlements has become an individual right, not a supplementary right, and the financial costs of children are shared by public childcare and general child allowances available to all families (Gunnarsson 2003; Sainsbury 1999, 77–80).

Parenting qualifies an individual for several benefits and services. Parental insurance covers both paid parental leave for the care of small children and temporary leave to care for sick children. These benefits are individual and part of a social security scheme constructed as social insurance to cover income loss, apart from the guaranteed levels, at a fixed rate. Parental leave insurance gives both parents the same legal right, based on a conception of parents as free agents with an equally shared obligation to support, care and contribute economically in the family and in the labour market. Even if this last assumption has turned out to be wrong, it is interesting to note that parenting is a prerequisite for eligibility for these benefits. Parents also receive the service of public childcare for small children, which is a substitute for their own responsibility for social care (Gunnarsson 2003, 139–145; Gunnarsson *et al*. 2004).

Nevertheless, even though gender equality in welfare distribution has improved, Sweden has not managed to overcome all gender equality problems emerging from the traditional division of paid and unpaid work. The structural patterns do not follow the theory. To some extent, the division is directly reproduced in tax and social law when means testing is based on the economic ability of a larger unit defined as marriage, cohabiting couples or households. The collective incomes of cohabiting parents is the unit for assessment for some parts of family support benefit, and the rates for public childcare are in general assessed on an income unit which also includes the income of a step-parent. Due to the above-mentioned income differences between men and women, this type of regulation acts to disqualify far more women than men from access to benefits. Thus, the provisions construct a dependency similar to the male breadwinner model.

However, this is just a small part of the problem. Looking at the outcome of social inclusion, it seems that there is a much more illusive, normative conflict within the Swedish welfare system. One striking example is the social exclusion of solo mothers and their children that Wennberg emphasizes in her chapter (Wennberg this volume). Considering the claim structures of work, need and parenting solo mothers constitute a demographic group with the highest risk of falling into poverty and becoming social assistance recipients. When women are left with the principal family responsibility for providing economic welfare and care for their children, they suffer disproportionately from retrenchments in welfare provision.

In the years after the implementation of the extensive tax reform in 1991, budget deficits and inflation escalated. One effect was the previously mentioned erosion of social justice in the principles of social security law. A personal social contribution was introduced at the same time as the tax bases for income taxes and consumption taxes were broadened, once again. Benefits such as child and housing allowances and compensation levels for income losses due to sickness and parental leave were reduced. Municipalities increased fees for childcare. The combined effects of these poorly co-ordinated reforms in tax and social law made the system as a whole more progressive, especially for families on low incomes. As a result, an increase in gross income leads, at best, to a very modest increase in disposable income, and sometimes even to a reduction for low-income families. The tax paid on the last Swedish krona of earned income and the loss of benefits that occurs directly or indirectly because of that last krona consumes the increase in gross income. This is a kind of adverse effective marginal tax-rate problem as it gives a progressive profile to low income households that creates disincentives in the form of poverty traps which influence work and study decisions related to income. The more targeted the means and income testing becomes, when also conditional on family income, the more women can become trapped into 'choosing between work and welfare'. For a family with small children and where the parents have traditional gender roles, it is seldom beneficial for the family if the woman modestly increases her salary (Gunnarsson 2003; Sainsbury 1996, 86).

On the level of principle, one consequence of these changes in both tax and social welfare law is that the dichotomy of dependency and autonomy is highlighted. Theoretically, the construction of entirely individual social duties and rights is rooted in an underlying assumption of the individual as autonomous. On the other hand, needs-based benefits rest on an assumption of the existence of an obligation to support, and a corresponding dependence on support among family members. The individual who claims a social right is seen as a part of a larger unit, a family or a household. The problem is not merely a question of using different principles for social justice in the public distribution of welfare and taxes. The big problem is that most welfare reforms overlook the fact that relational dependency is always present in welfare distribution. Dependency is more a matter of degree, not a one-way relationship in which dependency is traditionally assumed to be a question of 'either, or'.

In effect we have a conflict between the normative model of sex equality and the practice. Sex equality in tax and social security law rests on the employment strategy. The ideal family is constituted of dual breadwinners, where work and family life for both women and men have been reconciled, and where the adults in a family are self-supporting individuals. In reality, the general structure of the exchange of time, care and economic resources in the triangular relation of state, market and family shows that the life patterns of families with small children do not correspond to the normative ideal. The standard for a Swedish nuclear family with small children consists of no more than one and a half breadwinners, where normally the woman is not self-supporting because of the unequal division of paid work and unpaid care work, when it comes to both money and time.

How to Challenge the Social Power that Reproduces Gender Inequalities by Revising what is Included and Excluded in Social Citizenship

As shown, the inequalities reproduced in the Swedish welfare regimes emanate from not recognizing the gendered division in the production and distribution of welfare in the cyclical process across the state, the market and the family. It is a common problem for all western welfare states, but it is more intriguing when the welfare arrangements are both comprehensive and strongly committed to achieving sex equality. The existence of benefits and services for parenting, which women receive to a greater extent than men,[3] in line with their social positions and responsibilities, can only have had a marginal impact on the vulnerable role of a caregiver when it comes to economic independence in relation to family, state and market. Such a conclusion is not at all unique. Benefits for caring are normally isolated from the principles for the welfare system as a whole.

From a gender perspective the question of benefits and services for social caring is very ambiguous in the context of social citizenship. The dilemma is whether upgrading care so that it becomes an integrated part of social citizenship is a constructive strategy for sex equality objectives. To challenge the normative welfare model of social citizenship based on work performance and earned claim rights is, as Pateman put it already more than fifteen years ago, a strategy which is unpromising (Pateman 1989). The workfare ideology that seems to rest upon an employment strategy on the one hand and a tax neutrality strategy on the other, results in a concept of social justice that is connected to work. Consequently, the right to claim full citizenship is based on the concept that you have to earn your living and pay your taxes. Working and paying for social rights sends a strong message concerning

3 See the annual sex equality appendix to the Swedish Public Budget Proposal.

the obligations to participate and to contribute. Care, representing women's special contribution and relationship to the welfare state, is seen as economically valueless. Even if the normative model may be both unattractive and impossible for many women, an alternative that would recognize care as an activity for eligibility to social entitlements could very well undermine equality of rights.

However, the liberal discourse of freedom is not at all applicable when care makes the caregivers dependent on maintenance support, irrespective of whether it is organized as a private or public arrangement. As long as secondary or derivative dependency for the caregiver resides in distributive rights and obligations, welfare policies become simply delusional when they proclaim liberal assumptions about self-sufficient, independent individuals with a free choice. One way to change the patterns of dependency could be to reconceptualize the normative model so that care-giving activities are resourced in correlation with what they contribute in value. Value can be calculated in terms of time, money, and emotional sustenance. A care-giving activity such as 'mothering', which represents the traditional responsibility of mothers to care for their children, can be performed by men as well as women. The upgrading of care would equalize the social location of the 'mothering person' in the welfare regime, with the normative standard of the self as an autonomous, competent individual. The concept replaces 'mother' as a sexed subject, and should be considered gender-neutral in the same sense as the concept of the 'autonomous individual'. Such a principle of the value of care could hopefully attenuate inequality, in the sense that provision of care would provide disadvantaged or unequal individuals with resources that would make them more equal (see Held 1993; Hirschman and Liebert 2001, 10; Tronto 2001; Kittay 2001; Fineman 2001).

Nevertheless, when we ask for the upgrading of care in social policies it would be quite disappointing if we were to arrive at a dichotomy of two normative models of welfare arrangements that are mutually excessive as they promote either the traditional life patterns of men or those of women. Borrowing the terminology of Fraser the two contrasting models could be labelled the universal breadwinner model and the caregiver parity model. When the normative concept of universal breadwinner is emphasized, equality between men and women is promoted through an employment strategy in combination with extensive services, especially for care work, that enable women to participate in paid work. Such a model is similar to the Swedish welfare system at present. The caregiver parity model represents the opposite stand, as it highlights the idea that sex equality can be accomplished through an extensive programme of caregiver allowances that support informal care work performed in the households. Both models deliver gender equality concepts that are conditional. In the universal breadwinner model those women who can adapt to the traditional life patterns of men benefit from the welfare arrangements. Welfare support in a caregiver parity model is beneficial for women with significant care work responsibilities (Fraser 1994, 601–610).

Social justice in welfare support ought to be more than 'either, or' when promoting sex equality. Accepting social differentiation between men and women in the construction of subjects of welfare has proved to be a dead end for substantial equality. The intervention of public provision must be more pro-active in relation to the context of the socially vulnerable role of caregiver. By challenging the conceptualization of women as caregivers, social construction allows us to call into question the fundamental assumptions. From this standpoint care ought to be interpreted as a human activity in which all people are engaged both as givers of care and as receivers, and as such a fundamental criterion for determining social citizenship (Hirschman 2001).

This critical, deconstructive process produces new knowledge about law. It contributes to a transformation in how we understand law, and hopefully will ultimately be a part of shaping a legal culture which is more consistent with a comprehensive human rights culture. Concentrating on the care of children, the pro-active measures should be occupied with finding principles for the distribution of rights and obligations that enable the mothering person to form and sustain an autonomous household. An outcome worth striving for is legal requirements that construct a genderless family with the clear objective of protecting the welfare of all children. A more favourable environment for rearing citizens of a just society will, as one of its many advantages, have the potential to improve the social position of solo parents and their children (Okin 1989; Orloff 1993; Held 1993; Gunnarsson 2003; Wennberg 2004).

This view of social justice is of course very demanding and at present there are, not surprisingly, no well-packaged solutions to choose among. Nevertheless, when applying a concept of social citizenship to the Swedish legal framework for welfare and tax distribution, it is possible to identify some strategies that will improve gender equality. Some of these strategies already reside in law, which probably sounds contradictory to the critique delivered above. Even though the combination of comprehensive welfare arrangements and the strong influence of sex equality politics have not dissolved the remaining barriers to achieving gender equality, there are several features within the legal framework that already recognize some aspects of social power in gender relations. By systematizing those parts of welfare law that construct social citizenship from a gender perspective, in contrast to a positivist perspective, it has been possible to identify a plurality of normative patterns. At a first level of normative structures it seems that the most important boundary for gender differentiation in social entitlements can be drawn between the legal frames of social insurance benefits, and residence-based services and benefits. Within the frames of a social insurance state, claims to benefits are based on the division of labour between men and women, which reproduces inequalities. In contrast, within the frames of a residence-based system claims to benefits and services seem to be more inclusive from a gender perspective as they modify this reproduction of inequality. However, when the construction of dependency and autonomy are added into the analysis of welfare provisions a new level of normative patterns occurs. The major part of residence-based benefits consists of family support, which only contributes to modify the reproduction of income inequalities between parents of young children. Residence-based benefits are of course inclusive when they are of a general character, but most of these benefits are targeted. Targeting means-tested benefits and services assessed on the basis of household income reinforces the subsidiarity to a maintenance principle within the dual income family, as long as the exchange of paid and unpaid work is not recognized. On the other hand, one part of the social insurance scheme recognizes parenting as a qualification. Parenting may well become the most important distributive principle if the aim is to enable all parents to form and sustain an autonomous household in the best interest of the children.

References

Government Committees and Other Official Documents

SOU 2000:83, *Two of a Kind?* [Report from Governments Commission on the Balance Sheet for Welfare of the 1990s].

Literature

Aronssson, Thomas and Palme, Mårten (1994), 'A Decade of Tax and Benefit Reforms in Sweden – Effects on Labour Supply, Welfare and Inequality', *3 Tax Reform Evalutaion Report* 1994 (Stockholm: Ekonomiska rådet).

Fineman, Martha Albertson (2001), 'Dependencies', in Hirschman, Nancy J. and Liebert, Ulrike (eds) *Women and Welfare. Theory and Practice in the United States and Europe* (Brunswick, New Jersey and London: Rutgers University Press).

Fraser, Nancy (1994), 'After the Family Wage: Gender Equity and the Welfare State', *22 Political Theory* 1994.

Gunnarsson, Åsa (1995), *Skatterättvisa* (Uppsala: Iustus Förlag).

Gunnarsson, Åsa (1999), 'Equity Trends in Taxation – with Examples from Swedish and New Zealand Tax Reforms', in *Liber Amicorum Leif Mutén* (Amsterdam: Kluwer).

Gunnarsson, Åsa (2001), 'Familjen – genusforskningens utmaning', in Burman, Monica and Gunnarsson, Åsa (eds) *Familjeföreställningar. Om familjens betydelse inom juridik, ekonomi och forskning* (Uppsala: Iustus AB).

Gunnarsson, Åsa (2003), *Fördelningen av familjens skatter och sociala förmåner* (Uppsala: Iustus Förlag).

Gunnarsson, Åsa and Stattin, Chris (2001), 'Jämställdhetsnormen i skatte- och socialrätten', in Burman, Monica and Gunnarsson, Åsa (eds) *Familjeföreställningar. Om familjens betydelse inom juridik, ekonomi och forskning* (Uppsala: Iustus AB).

Gunnarsson, Åsa, Burman, Monica and Wennberg, Lena (2004), 'Economic Dependence and Self-Support in Family, Tax and Social Law', in Svensson, Eva-Maria, Pylkkänen, Anu and Niemi-Kiesiläinen, Johanna (eds) *Nordic Equality at a Crossroads. Feminist legal studies coping with difference* (Aldershot: Ashgate).

Gustafsson, Håkan (2002), *Rättens polyvalens. En rättsvetenskaplig studie av sociala rättigheter och rättssäkerhet* (Lund: Lund Studies in Sociology of Law).

Held, Virginia (1993), *Feminist Morality. Transforming Culture, Society and Politics* (Chicago: University of Chicago Press).

Hirschman, Nancy J. (2001), 'A Question of Freedom. A Question of Rights? Women and Welfare', in Hirschman, Nancy J. and Liebert, Ulrike (eds), *Women and Welfare. Theory and Practice in the United States and Europe* (Brunswick, New Jersey and London: Rutgers University Press).

Hirschman, Nancy J. and Liebert, Ulrike (2001), *Women and Welfare. Theory and Practice in the United States and Europe* (Brunswick, New Jersey and London: Rutgers University Press).

Hollander, Anna (1995), *Rättighetslag i teori och praxis. En studie av lagstiftningen inom social- och handikappområdet* (Uppsala: Iustus Förlag).

Hydén, Håkan (2002), *Normvetenskap* (Lund: Lund Studies in Sociology of Law).

Kautto, M., Fritzell, J., Hvinden, Björn, Kvist, J., Uusitalo, H. (2001) (eds), *Nordic Welfare States in the European Context* (London: Routledge).

Ketscher, Kirsten (1998), *Socialret. Almindelige principper. Retssikerhed og administration* (Köpenhamn: GadJura).

Kittay, Eva Feder (2001), 'From Welfare to a Public Ethic of Care', in Hirschman, Nancy J. and Liebert, Ulrike. (eds) *Women and Welfare. Theory and Practice in the United States and Europe* (Brunswick, New Jersey and London: Rutgers University Press).

Lacey, Nicola (1998), *Unspeakable Subjects. Feminist Essays in Legal and Social Theory* (Oxford: Hart Publishing).

Liebert, Ulrike (2001), 'Degendering Care and Engendering Freeedom: Social Welfare in the European Union', in Hirschman and Liebert. (eds), *Women and Welfare. Theory and Practice in the United States and Europe* (Brunswick, New Jersey and London: Rutgers University Press).

Lister, Ruth (2003), *Citizenship: Feminist Perspectives* (New York: New York University Press).

Mannelqvist, Ruth (2003), *Samband i socialförsäkringen. En rättsvetenskaplig studie av sambandet mellan förmåner och avgifter i socialförsäkringen* (Uppsala: Iustus Förlag).

Messere, Ken (1993), *Tax Policy in OECD Countries. Choices and Conflict,* (Amsterdam: IBFD Publications BV).

Messere, Ken, de Kam, Filip and Heady, Cristopher (2003), *Tax Policy: Theory and Practice in OECD Countries* (Oxford: Oxford University Press).

Minow, Martha (1991), *Making all the Difference* (Ithaca and London: Cornell University Press).

Montanari, Ingalill (2000), *Social Citizenship and Work in Welfare States. Comparative Studies on Convergence and on Gender* (Stockholm: Swedish Institute for Social Research).

Nousiainen, Kevät (2004), 'On the Limits of the Concept of Equality: Arguments for a Dynamic Reading', in Svensson, Eva-Maria, Pylkkänen, Anu and Niemi-Kiesiläinen, Johanna (eds), *Nordic Equality at a Crossroads* (Aldershot: Ashgate Publishing Limited).

Nyman, Charlott (2002), *Mine, yours or ours? Sharing in Swedish couples* (Umeå University: Doctoral thesis at the Department of Sociology).

Okin, Susan Moller (1989), *Justice, Gender, and Family* (New York: Basic Books Inc. Publishers).

Orloff, Ann, Shola (1993), 'Gender and the Social Rights of Citizenship: The Comparative Analysis of Gender Relations and Welfare Sates', 58 *American Sociological Review* 1993.

Orloff, Ann Shola (1996), 'Gender in the Welfare State', 22 *Annual Review of Sociology* 1996.

Orloff, Ann, Shola (2001), 'Ending the Entitlements of Poor Single Mothers: Changing Social Policies, Women's Employment, and Caregiving in the Contemporary United States', in Hirschman, Nancy J. and Liebert, Ulrike (eds) *Women and Welfare. Theory and Practice in the United States and Europe* (Brunswick, New Jersey and London: Rutgers University Press).

Pateman, Carol (1989), 'The Patriarchal Welfare State', in McDowell, Linda and Pringle, Rosemary (eds), *Defining Women. Social Institutions and Gender Divisions* (Cambridge: Polity Press).

Riksskatteverket (2003), *Skatter i Sverige. Skattestatistisk årsbok, 2003* (Riksskatteverket utgåva 6).

Sainsbury, Diane (ed.) (1993), *Gendering Welfare States* (London: Sage Publications).

Sainsbury, Diane (1996), *Gender Equality, and Welfare States* (Cambridge: Cambridge University Press).

Sainsbury, Diane (ed.) (1999), *Gender and Welfare State Regimes* (Oxford: Oxford University Press).

Sevenhuijsen, Selma (1998), *Citizenship and the Ethics of Care. Feminist Considerations on Justice, Morality and Politics* (London: Routledge).

Stang Dahl, Tove (1988), *Women's Law* (Oslo: Norwegian University Press).

Stendahl, Sara (2003), *Communicating Justice Providing Legitimacy. The legal practices of Swedish administrative courts in cases regarding sickness cash benefits* (Uppsala: Iustus Förlag).

Svensson, Eva-Maria (1997), *Genus och rätt – en problematisering av föreställningen om rätten* (Uppsala: Iustus Förlag).

Svensson, Eva-Maria (2001), 'Sex Equality: Changes in Politics, Jurisprudence and Feminist Legal Studies', in Nousiainen, Kevät, Gunnarsson, Åsa, Lundström, Karin and Niemi-Kiesiläinen, Johanna (eds), *Responsible Selves. Women in the Nordic Legal Culture* (Aldershot: Ashgate Publishing).

Tronto, Joan C. (2001), 'Who Cares? Public and Private Caring and the Rethinking of Citizenship', in Hirschman and Liebert (eds), *Women and Welfare. Theory and Practice in the United States and Europe* (Brunswick, New Jersey and London: Rutgers University Press).

Vahlne Westerhäll, Lotta (1996), 'Rättigheter som grund för social trygghet', in *Retfaerd 75.*

Vahlne, Westerhäll, Lotta (2002), *Den starka statens fall? En rättsvetenskaplig studie av svensk social trygghet 1950–2000* (Stockholm: Norstedts Juridik AB).

Wennberg, Lena (2004), *Social Assistance for Solo Mothers in Sweden, Finland, Norway and Denmark*, (Umeå: Umeå Studies in Law no 8/2004).

Wennemo, Irene (1997), 'Hushållsarbedtets organisation och tjänstesektorns utveckling', in SOU 1997:17, *Skatter tjänster och sysselsättning. Betänkande av Tjänstemannautredningen.*

Westerhäll, Lotta (1994), *Sociala trygghetslagar* (Stockholm: Norstedts Juridik).

Chapter 12

Notes Towards an Optimistic Feminism: A Long View[1]

Margaret Davies

The title of this anthology refers to a crisis of confidence or state of 'pessimism' in contemporary feminist legal thought. Although it might be overstating the issue to say that feminist legal thought is presently dominated by various forms of pessimism, it is certainly true that a number of factors in the recent history of legal feminism and in the changing political climate have given cause for reflection about the direction of critical thought in the legal academy. In some instances, such reflection has led to an apparent impasse for feminist engagement with law and uncertainty about the available directions for promoting change. This chapter examines briefly some of the sources of pessimism in feminist legal thought, and considers the possible 'challenges' to such pessimism. I characterize the challenge to pessimism as a form of pluralism, in that it involves recognition of a pluralistic and responsive feminism as well as a pluralistic understanding of law. While I do not and cannot offer a Swedish feminist approach to this issue, my objective is to reflect upon its general theoretical dimensions and, hopefully, offer useful commentary on the distinctive Swedish intervention in the debate which this anthology represents.

Sources of Pessimism in Feminist Legal Thought

To begin then, what are the sources of pessimism in current feminist legal thought? A review of recent literature shows that legal feminists have identified a number of issues which can appear to be standing in the way of progress.

---

1 This chapter was originally presented at the Hemaven seminar, hosted by Umeå University, March 2004, and was subsequently presented to the School of Accounting and Commercial Law, Victoria University of Wellington in March 2005. Many thanks to the Swedish feminist community for inviting me to participate in this project, and to the participants at both seminars for their feedback and comments. I would also like to thank Reeta Randhawa and Debbie Bletsas for excellent research assistance. Research for this chapter has been funded by an Australian Research Council Discovery Grant (DP0451107), and my research visits to Sweden were funded by the Swedish Foundation for International Cooperation in Research and Higher Education. I would like to thank both organizations for their assistance.

The Level of 'Progress'

First, and perhaps most obviously, is the perception by many legal feminists that we have not, after all, made much progress in the arena of law, or that we have not made as much progress as we would like. Despite legislative reform in many areas designed to recognize harms to women and improve equal opportunity, feminists seem to be going constantly over the same ground. Of course, as I will indicate later, 'progress' is a very complex and relative idea: in the feminist context, 'progress' is relative to feminist goals, which vary substantially according to political positioning. We should remember that even something as uncontroversial in the contemporary context as the right to vote was not always universally supported by feminists: Emma Goldman argued against women's suffrage on the grounds that it only co-opted women into the machinery of the state, a corrupt system which would not change simply because of women's participation (Goldman 1910, 195). If Goldman were alive today, she would perhaps say that while women have made progress in relation to our position in state hierarchies, we have not achieved freedom from the sexual determinism imposed by the state and society.

Within a more conservative paradigm (that is, conservative of the concepts of law and state), there are perhaps some measures of feminist progress which are fairly uncontroversial. We would like to see a measurable increase in the rate of successful prosecutions for sexual violence, a breaking of glass ceilings, the alleviation of female poverty, and universal recognition of women's human rights. To take one very specific matter dear to the hearts of feminist legal academics, in many countries there is still a very obvious under-representation of women in the higher ranks of the legal profession – this is especially evident in the judiciary.[2] Increased numbers of women studying and practicing law has not led to a proportionate increase in the numbers of women in the upper ranks of the legal hierarchy. Those who thought that equality is a matter mainly of access, assumed that the numbers of women students would gradually trickle up into the higher arenas of the profession. After two decades of roughly equal access this assumption is beginning to wear thin as it becomes evident that males are still progressing at a faster rate and to higher levels than women. Of course we are aware of a number of reasons for this lack of change (for instance, the absence of child care facilities and flexible work arrangements), meaning that there is still more work to be done by feminists (Hunter 2002). However, it would be surprising if this lack of progress did not result in some feelings of pessimism. Of course, as many feminists have pointed out, having women in the judiciary and among the senior advocates or barristers, does not necessarily translate directly into better experiences for women under the law, although it seems probable that, over time, a more diverse judiciary will be less likely to rely on damaging stereotypes in their reasoning (Kenny 2002). This may point to yet another source of pessimism, which has been only too evident in the political sphere as well as in law, which is that women leaders do not always have a feminist consciousness, even in the

2 In common law countries, the judiciary is the pinnacle of the legal profession: judges are generally appointed from senior barristers. There have been a few examples of judges being appointed from the academic community, but this is very rare.

minimal sense of trying to promote formal equality. For some feminists, of course, an important reason for having women on the bench, independent of any 'difference' women may make, is to achieve a 'genuine integration of women into all aspects of decision making' (Kenny 2002; Malleson 2003).

Scepticism Concerning Law Reform

A second and related source of pessimism for legal feminists is the argument that change in substantive law does not necessarily result in an improved situation for women. Feminists have argued persuasively that the dominant values of Western positive legal systems tend to reflect the values stereotypically associated in the cultural sphere with masculinity, and that we need to be cautious about taking action which tends to legitimate those values. As long ago as 1989, Carol Smart said that feminists 'need to engage with law for purposes other than law reform and with a clear insight into the problems of legitimating a mode of social regulation which is deeply antithetical to the myriad concerns and interests of women' (Smart 1989, 164). In other words, we cannot simply look towards law as a source of social change, because as it currently stands law reproduces the values which pose problems for women collectively and individually in the social and political spheres. We need to find ways of challenging law's fundamental presuppositions, rather than merely expect that change will flow from legislative reform.[3]

The need to look beyond law reform has been especially clear in the law of rape and sexual assault where, despite legislative changes such as those designed to prevent the victim being systematically discredited on account of her previous sexual history, there are still a great many obstacles to a successful prosecution. Only in the last decade have feminist scholars begun to think about this issue in terms of courtroom culture and discourse rather than the heavy-handed mechanism of legislative change (Larcombe 2002; Young 1998; Burman this volume; Niemi-Kiesiläinen *et al.* this volume).

There are signs that some legal regimes may be ready to adopt a more holistic approach to gender, possibly providing hope that the system as a whole can change: for instance, 'gender mainstreaming' has been adopted in the development of European policy. Whether this will make a significant difference to the fundamental culture of law (and therefore meet at least part of Smart's objection) or simply add another layer of gender-oriented bureaucracy is yet to be seen.[4] There is a temptation to say that gender mainstreaming *must* be better than piecemeal legislative reform which takes no account of the ways that different areas of law interact; on the other hand surely a great deal also depends on the local contexts in which mainstreaming takes place (Liebert 2002) – we know that any amount of law reform or mainstreaming

3 For instance, Martha Fineman says, 'I have lost faith. Feminism, it seems, has not – and perhaps cannot – transform the law. Rather, the law, when it becomes the battleground, threatens to transform feminism.' Fineman, cited in Armstrong 2004.

4 See generally *Feminist Legal Studies* 2002, 209–328 (special issue on gender mainstreaming in Europe).

bureaucracy does not necessarily change the underlying attitudes which make reform necessary in the first place (see generally Charlesworth 2005).

The perception that simply opting into law as a mechanism for change may involve a misplaced faith in law, and hence could result in disappointing outcomes is not necessarily in itself a pessimistic argument: indeed, to my mind, it is a positive argument which identifies the depth and complexity of gender relations in society, indicating that we cannot expect change to flow simply from modest alterations in formal law, which is only one part of the socio-legal culture. To feminists who have been trained as lawyers, however, and trained to put faith in law as a mechanism of social change, the realization that law reform may not make much difference without broad cultural and political change could certainly be a source of pessimism.

A specifically Swedish twist on the theme of the limits and limitations of law is identified by this anthology (and discussed at more length in the Introduction). The Swedish difficulty does not arise from the general perception that engaging with law involves the legitimation of an essentially patriarchal institution: Swedish feminists have not, on the whole, seen law and the state in this light but rather as the agents of useful social engineering operating to reinforce broad communitarian values (Nousiainen and Niemi-Kiesiläinen 2001, 12–14). It is true that in recent years, there has been a growing appreciation within the Nordic countries that state intervention has not always been successful (Svensson and Pylkkänen 2004, 19). More importantly though, as indicated in the Introduction, the dogmatic understanding of law in Sweden has meant that law and legal scholarship have emphasized a relatively inflexible and formalistic view of law, making it difficult for legal feminists to engage broadly with matters traditionally identified as being beyond the legitimate concern of legal scholarship and legal methods. Thus, as Eva-Maria Svensson argues, while Swedish legal feminism sometimes operates from within a dogmatic perspective, it is also often to be found at the margins of legal discourse, explicitly contesting its boundaries (Svensson this volume). Thus, to simplify, the Swedish emphasis has become the definition of law in both its practical and academic settings – the traditional domain of legal theory. Rather than ask *whether* as feminists we should be engaging with and relying upon law, the Swedish question reflected in this book is 'what *is* this concept of law which we are engaging with and relying upon?' How can we re-figure law so that it has a more responsive and less formalistic character? Feminist legal studies have therefore become involved in the project of transforming the boundaries and the concept of law and the legal discipline through specific engagements, as well as through theoretical interventions.

The Perception of 'Post-Feminism'

Third, feminists have noticed a widespread perception that feminism has run its course and that we are in an era of 'post-feminism' (Hawkesworth 2004; Thornton 2004). As Mary Hawkesworth explains, there are a number of quite different factors influencing such a view: for instance the 'narrative of [feminist] dissolution' sees the movement of feminism from a strongly focused and singular political movement to a highly dispersed, somewhat segregated, array of interests and approaches, as evidence of decline (Hawkesworth 2004, 963–965, 968). A further basis in legal discourse for such a conclusion is a singular focus on formal equality – if the goal of feminism were to achieve equal rights merely as equal formal rights (an absence of explicit discrimination), then the main goals of legal feminism would have been achieved in the 1980s in most countries (Thornton 2004, 7). Feminists realize that mere formal equality is not a satisfactory basis upon which to judge the success of feminism, however, pessimism may spring from the existence of a social and political perception that formal equality is sufficient, and the apparent resistance of the idea of formal equality as the sole indicator of social equality. Another basis for the perception that we are in an era of 'post-feminism' is the fact that policy-makers are undoubtedly more sensitive to feminism now than even a decade ago: does this lead to a notion that feminism is 'redundant'? (Conaghan 2000, 355.) There is even a perception by many (non-feminists) that the climate has swung too far in favour of women in certain areas – the most obvious one being in family law.

Postmodernism

Fourth, pessimism arises from the ascendency of postmodernism, which has a controversial place in feminist theorizing. A number of feminists feel that postmodernism has done a disservice to feminism by its endlessly critical interventions – the possibilities for a positive programme of change seem limited, if not entirely stifled. For instance, Catharine MacKinnon has stated bluntly that postmodernism is not about reality, and that feminists need theory which addresses real conditions, real social structures, and the physical nature of the gender hierarchy (Mackinnon 2000). Anne Barron says that

> postmodernism seems to yield a wholly negative approach to politics which is corrosive not only of liberal political and legal norms, but in principle of every normative framework – including that of feminism itself. (Barron 2000, 276)

According to Barron, this 'negativity' about postmodernism has led to a

> palpable reluctance on the part of feminists now to formulate political programmes or proposals for legal reform that purport to articulate the interests and needs of women for fear of 'essentializing' the feminine in the process of doing so. (Barron 2000, 276; see also Cooper 2001, 122–124)

Certainly postmodernists have critiqued the idea that we can map out a normatively certain programme of change in the way that Marxism attempts to map out a programme of social and economic change. But this is very far removed from arguing that no change is possible, and as I will indicate shortly, there is a much more positive and a more practical reading of postmodernism (Cooper 2001, 122–124). Another angle on this issue flows from the perceived disengagement of academic feminism from political feminism. As Joanne Conaghan points out, feminism has become more accepted in the academic setting, but has this been at the expense of connection with political and social engagement (Conaghan 2000)? Despite general academic controversy about postmodernism, it may be that abstract theoretical approaches do contribute to the academic acceptability of feminism – but do these necessarily remove feminism from the sphere of ordinary life? (See Thornton 2004).

Critique of Essentialism

A fifth source of pessimism is to be found in the widespread critique of essentialism. The critique of essentialism is often mentioned in connection with postmodernism (Barron 2000, 276) and, although postmodern thought certainly does challenge essentialism in theory, the critique of feminist essentialism arose independently from postmodernism in a much more practical setting: women whose identities were being ignored or excluded by white, middle class, educated, heterosexual feminists. The most visible face of feminism in the 20th century was the face of the privileged white woman concerned with the effects of male dominance. A feminism drawn from the experience of such an élite group of women surely cannot expect to command the attention of all women. One example of the exclusionary effects of dividing people into broad categories of male and female is provided by Görel Granström (Granström this volume): replacing gender-neutral laws on domestic violence with gender-specific laws goes some way towards recognizing that this is a crime mainly perpetrated by men against women. However, such a reform may mask less pervasive forms of domestic violence which do not fit this model, in particular violence within same sex relationships.

In its more postmodern form, the critique of essentialism has often been raised by queer theorists who challenge the very idea of the two-sex system, and emphasize that sex/gender is not fixed or stable in the binary pair of female and male. Of course the difficulty is that feminism seems to depend on a stable notion of 'woman' as a political identity (Conaghan 2000, 367). The earliest expression of feminism was the challenge to sexual inequality, not to white racial dominance, or heterosexual privilege, or the duality of sex. Arguably, a more inclusive, more diverse, concept of 'woman' is needed, at the same time as it is under the more radical challenge that it is not, after all, a fixed biological category but a construct which – in collusion with 'man' – represses more fluent and diverse expressions of sex/gender. Some feminists have seen the questioning of the concept so that it is no longer singular but multiple and inherently unstable, as representing a threat to feminism's ability to consolidate around a political position, leading to debates about whether to adopt a position of 'strategic essentialism' (Conaghan 2000, 366–374).

Neo-Liberalism

Sixth, at an ideological and political level, the discourse of social justice, including feminist discourse, is taking second (or third, or fourth) place in the neo-liberal market climate, which subordinates issues of social power to economics. As Margaret Thornton argues

> The social justice environment that engendered Second Wave Feminism has become passé. The shift to the right is so pronounced that it has enabled the discourse of the market to become the metanarrative of our time. (Thornton 2004, 7)

In recent years this trend towards neo-liberalism has been supplemented conservative climate of xenophobia – thus national security and border prote are higher on the political agenda than social and political rights of citizens.[5] In s a context, as Iris Marion Young has argued, feminist concerns may be selectively appropriated by fear-invoking governments in an effort to justify war: she gives the example of the urgent need for women's liberation in Afghanistan being used by the US government in its defence of military intervention on humanitarian grounds (Young 2003, 16–20). Needless to say, prior to the perception of a raised security threat to the US posed by the Taliban, little interest was shown by either the Bush or Clinton administrations for the cause of women's human rights in Afghanistan. As Young says '[a]ppeal to women's rights was thus a cynical attempt to gain support for the war among the citizens of the United States and other liberal countries' (Young 2003, 18).

This climate of neo-liberalism is very evident in the United Kingdom and Australia at present and possibly increasingly evident in Sweden as a result of the process of economic integration with the European community (see generally Svensson *et al.* 2004). It has led to a generalized disillusionment among left-wing and progressive thinkers, given that principled political discourse has been more or less abandoned by major political parties in favour of popularism, xenophobic concepts of national security, and persistent obsession with economic growth.

One of the differences between the Swedish context and the context of other (non-Nordic) Western democracies is the existence and undoubted strength of Swedish 'state feminism': (Nousiainen *et al.* 2001, 14) in Sweden feminism has been able to promote its objectives through the mechanism of the state, in contrast to more liberal regimes where the state and its 'femocrats' have often been regarded with scepticism by academic feminists. The rise of neo-liberalism in Western democracies justifiably enhances this sceptical attitude. However, as indicated by several of the chapters in this collection, the process of 'Europeanization' has also led to an increasing liberalization of policy in the Nordic context (illustrated for instance, by an increased emphasis on individual rights over systemic sources of inequality) to the detriment of the traditional Nordic focus on more communitarian values (Wennberg this volume; Gunnarsson this volume). In discussing this issue in *Responsible Selves*, Kevät Nousiainen uses the phrase 'distribution of liberal and communitarian principles' to indicate that it is not really a question of ideal or extreme forms of liberalism and communitarianism which actually exist in particular states, but rather a range of values which are balanced in different ways (Nousiainen 2001, 25, 45). Thus, in certain areas of law, particularly those associated with social welfare, the 'liberal' principles are at present gaining the upper hand. In other, more limited contexts, communitarianism may be becoming stronger,[6] but the overall

5 As Graeme Austin has pointed out to me, the erosion of certain fundamental protections, as well as the rise of conservative religious discourse, may be symptomatic of a 'retreat from modernism' in certain contexts which exists alongside the ultra-modernism which neo-liberalism might be said to represent.

6 Nousiainen identifies contract law as an area which is possibly adopting more communitarian values in Finland (Nousiainen 2001, 27; See also Svensson and Pylkkänen

trend is towards increasingly liberal, individualist, self-consciously neutral (though often effectively biased) types of regulation.

The Challenge to Pessimism

To summarize then, potential sources of pessimism include the following: reflection over the rate of progress in achieving gender equality, debate over the uses of law reform, a perception that feminism is outdated as a political movement, the postmodern critique of universalism, the critique of essentialism and the resulting politics of diversity, the individualizing consequences of neo-liberalism, and the distance between academic feminism and activism. All of these components add up to a potential fragmentation of feminist goals, and the perception that feminism has reached an impasse in terms of substantive political and legal projects.

There are probably other sources of pessimism within legal feminism. My rather simplified list is an attempt to capture what I see to be some of the issues making it difficult for feminist lawyers to know how to proceed, given that the central goal of feminism is promotion of practical social change for women. We certainly need to remain conscious of the very real political and theoretical issues facing feminism today. However, as the title of this book suggests, the 'challenge to pessimism' is a core concern of the contributors, and I would like to sketch some of the foundations of such a challenge before turning to the question of the limits of law.

Feminism and Change

First, optimism is to be found in the recognition that change does not necessarily flow only from intentional, positive change in law, policy, or social structures. Certainly we do not have a clear programme for promoting change at a general level – we do not have, as it were, a blueprint for progress – and the issues outlined above constitute some of the reasons for the lack of a blueprint. They are possibly insurmountable difficulties as far as an extensive *programme* of change is concerned, although this is not to say that specific reform proposals cannot be successfully pursued.

While feminists may not be enthusiastic about finding a key which will unlock a clearly-defined and large-scale legislative or policy direction, that certainly does not mean that broad change is not possible. As Davina Cooper argues, 'social pathways' created through repeated usage – 'multiple tramping of the same soil' – offer possibilities for 'enduring change' (Cooper 2001, 129). Such change may be gradual and the consequence of a number of intersecting social movements. They may not even be directly attributable to a definite political movement. For this reason, I would want to qualify Joanne Conaghan's claim that feminism 'gains its legitimacy through its ability *visibly* to bring about political change' (Conaghan 2000, 355 emphasis in original). It is certainly true that academic feminism may be *perceived* to be legitimate only if there is a direct causality between it and political and social change, and moreover, that this relationship must be visible. Regardless

2004, 20).

of visibility though, is it not possible that feminism could contribute to unexpected and unmotivated change, change which is indirect and a consequence not only of feminism but of broader intersecting social movements of which feminism is just one part? Is it not further possible that such change can happen invisibly in the sense that there might be no obvious intervention leading towards a particular change, but rather merely an accumulation of changing discourses and values? In many instances, 'visibility' is a high standard, given the delay between feminist demands for change and political action on a particular issue.

One very clear example of feminist work which may not always have direct political or social results is the boundary work identified by Eva-Maria Svensson (Svensson this volume). As she argues, feminist legal scholars are continually contesting the limits of academic propriety in their subject areas: in the Swedish context this means challenging the dogmatic scholarly insistence that academic knowledge of law ought to follow the contours of the law in its practical settings. In order to make claims about, for instance, the effect of welfare law on women, feminist legal scholars must in the first instance challenge the traditional limitations of legal knowledge (Gunnarsson this volume; Mannelqvist this volume). In itself, such 'boundary work' may not have an entirely evident outcome although, as numbers of the chapters in this work illustrate, it is often combined with scholarly analysis with very practical implications. Whether or not a body of feminist legal scholarship leads to any direct or visible change, the ongoing work of challenging the boundaries of scholarship arguably contributes to a climate of greater flexibility and responsiveness in legal discourse, possibly leading to other, as yet un-envisaged political and social changes. Of course, we may never fully comprehend the eventual results of our theorizing and activism: it may backfire or succeed in ways we have not imagined. The point is that, as feminists have increasingly recognized, our political projects are often processes, and not necessarily defined end-points.

If indirect, unexpected, broad-based alteration in values were all that feminism achieved then in my mind it would still be a legitimate social movement. In the Nordic context, as in other Western democracies, feminism *has* visibly influenced the direction of policy and law, and these changes are supplemented by a less obvious but possibly more enduring transformation in values and in the culture of knowledge-production.

Pluralistic Feminisms

Second, far from illustrating the increasing introspection and disarray of feminism, matters such as the critique of essentialism and the responses to that critique show a movement which is highly responsive, able to modify itself, and able to re-evaluate its own theoretical foundations. Efforts to singularize feminism will necessarily fail for the very reason that feminism is not a monistic philosophy but a social movement with pluralistic foundations in communities of workers, activists, policy-makers, and academics. Reduction of feminism to a single phenomenon would be a first step in the denial of this social basis. Moreover, it seems reasonably well-established that feminism need not occupy a defined political space, to promote a single position, or even to avoid internal contradictions. As Eva Nilsson points out, feminist analysis is strengthened by its diversity (Nilsson this volume). For a social movement diversity and contradiction are clearly unavoidable and should be a source of strength, producing not division but dialogue, reflection and re-invention.

In the domain of academic scholarship, the absence of an analytical basis to feminist thought would traditionally be seen as a sign of weakness or theoretical incoherence. This philosophically conventional view is no longer as persuasive as it once was: thus, as Wendy Brown argues, we do not necessarily need to make a choice between the resistant social concept of woman whereby our biology is seen to determine our identity, and the view that sex/gender is an unstable and fluid construct which should continually be challenged (Brown 2003, 367).[7] Rather than 'either/or', we can have 'both/and'. Moreover, although the demands of the moment are very significant, and in some cases urgent, a long historical view shows that social movement does not always occur immediately in the direction we might like. What is clear, then, is not so much that feminism is suffering from an anxiety attack, but rather that it is important for feminism as a movement to remain self-reflective and responsive to changing conditions (such as the rise of neo-liberalism).

Pragmatism and Idealism

A third reason for optimism flows from the ability of feminist thought to adopt elements of both idealism and pragmatism. Thus, to use the example provided by Wendy Brown feminists necessarily engage with normative constructs of femininity and conventional notions of woman: we presume an identity 'woman' as we critique the social expectations and stereotypes which accompany it. We do this for good pragmatic reasons. At the same time, the idealistic element (or as some say, the 'utopian moment') of such critique arrives when, like Luce Irigaray or Drucilla Cornell, we try to envisage alternative worlds, whether an alternative law of persons (Irigaray 1996, 50–51) or a protected 'imaginary domain' in which every human being can construct and live their own sexual identity (Cornell 1998). Such extensions beyond the present are generally regarded as contingent – they are merely points of departure for further dialogue.

Feminism can also be both pragmatic and idealistic when it comes to theorizing law. While reliance on institutions such as law may be necessary for pragmatic reasons, we also need to continue to think beyond law. This does not involve rejecting law as an instrument of change, but indicates that we need to continue to question law, to think about law differently, and to engage with the idea of law in both a practical and theoretical arena. Brown has made the following comment in relation to the need for feminists to think beyond present conditions, and I quote it at length here because I think it applies equally to the need to try to imagine a better law – not just better laws, but a better concept and understanding of law:

7 Brown uses the musical notion of counterpoint as an analogy for showing how the two poles of the contradiction – the resistant determinative concept of woman which shapes our lives, and the notion that gender/sex is unstable and not fixed in a duality – can be seen to exist together, without resolution or synthesis into a greater whole.

> If we underscore only what we take to be sexist and materialist constraints and we fail to practice living beyond these constraints in the present, we fail to build a bridge to another world with our feminist knowledge projects and everyday practices. At best, we leave the emancipation of gender, or from gender, to imagined better days. But if we do not strain in this moment toward another world, and especially toward pleasure and freedom, we live as if these constraints were total, which means that invention and possibility is not part of our politics. (Brown 2003, 367)

Building a bridge to another world of legal understanding is an important aspect of legal feminism and an essential project if we are to retain our optimism about the promise of feminist thought: if women and other marginalized groups are ever going to be able to identify with law, rather than struggle with its inadequate paradigms or simply reject it, then we need to re-imagine it.

To summarize then, reasons for optimism in feminism include the multiple potential 'pathways' for achieving change, the responsiveness of feminism to external and internal challenges, and the ability of feminist thought to encompass contradiction such as that between idealism and pragmatism. Feminism has become pluralistic in recent years in the sense that it encompasses a range of theoretical perspectives and political positions: these differences are irreconcilable – they cannot be reduced or abstracted in the name of a general feminism – and it is this heterogeneity, reflecting the demands of a complex and pluralistic social environment, which above all is a cause for optimism.

The Limits of Law: Beyond Unity

Law is commonly understood in a monistic or singular sense: the dominant conception of law sees it as derived wholly from state power, and having definite boundaries and some measure of internal coherence. Thus one of the basic limits of law which feminists have challenged is the defining limit of law itself – in the typical Western positivist conception, law is law only because it is limited, and in particular separated conceptually from the social context, including moral and religious norms, cultural norms, norms of ethnicity, gender identity, and sexuality. Law's identity is practically and conceptually separated from all of the other norms constituting human identity. This is the essential limit of a singular positivistic law, evident in both Nordic and Anglo legal cultures, (Svensson *et al.* 2004) and it is the one which accounts for some of the most fundamental deficiencies in law from the feminist point of view.

One way in which the law/non-law limit has traditionally been reflected in traditional liberal thought is through the reservation of law to the public sphere, while the 'private', including the domestic sphere and often the market (Thornton 1995a), is regarded as a space which ought to stay as free as possible from legal regulation. Every fact, norm, nuance, and relationship is either captured – and therefore reduced – by the legal structure or excluded from legal cognition. Most frequently excluded in liberal systems is the so-called sphere of private freedom – that place in which individuals are free to create their own lives, opinions and identities. The well-recognized negative consequences of the exclusion include the facts that the private sphere is also the area where power can be freely exercized and where non-hegemonic sexual orientations can be tolerated but concealed from a sanitized sphere of public regulation. The imperative against regulation is most extreme in relation to domestic life. Thus, as Catharina Calleman's chapter illustrates in relation to labour law, the frequent exclusion of the domestic zone from intrusive legal regulation operates against women's interests and against women's equality of treatment under the law (Calleman this volume). Typically, women are not well protected against 'private' or intra-familial harms such as domestic assault or underpaid employment in a family business or home, but the same types of harms are taken extremely seriously when they occur in the public and market domains. As we know, it is women who bear the brunt of the socially created and legally enforced discrimination between public and private.

The philosophy of legal unity also demands singularity in the model legal person around whom law is constructed: the legal subject is the rational individual fashioned in the image of various male role-models (worker, soldier, and property-owner, rather than parent or carer) and is devoid of real human content. In its emphasis on equality as sameness, law stops short of acknowledging the plurality of human beings and their very different social positions and contributions to the polity. The alleged boundary between law and the social, moral, and political realms also reinforces law's self-definition as objective and neutral, removing law from the lived subjectivity of human beings. This singularity is emphasized by Åsa Gunnarsson's analysis of social citizenship: as she argues, a more inclusive concept of citizenship needs to be devised which values a greater range of social contributions without necessarily dividing them according to sex.

In a general spirit of challenging the established dogmatic concept of law, all of the contributions to this project have identified some of law's limits, and considered the implications of those limits for feminism. Some of these limits relate to core conceptions about law in its abstract or theoretical state, for instance the institutional separation of law from the political and social/cultural sphere, (Persson this volume; Burman this volume; Mannelqvist this volume) and the basic paradigms for legal knowledge (Svensson this volume; Persson this volume). Others are limitations in fundamental legal constructs, for instance the limitations in the concepts of the citizen and subject of law (Gunnarsson this volume; Wennberg this volume; Granström this volume; Nilsson this volume) and manifestations of the public/private distinction (Calleman this volume). The presumption of legal singularity leads to the presumption that it can be understood by a single theory, a view criticized by Eva Nilsson (Nilsson this volume). Limits also exist between the spaces designated for legal decision-making as opposed to other forms of decision-making, such as that which exists in the medical or educational sphere or at the supra-national level under European policy. At the social level, there are limits on who can access law and under what conditions.

Although it is not necessarily the intention of all those who challenge the limits of law to promote legal pluralism, I see these challenges as symptomatic of a general movement towards a more pluralistic understanding of law. Pluralism can be understood in several ways. It can be seen as a definite theory or socio-legal approach to law based on empirical facts, or simply as an attitude critical of the limited conceptions of law and of legal subjects. Either way, the basic theme of legal pluralism is an approach which looks beyond the singular, state-derived, notion of positivist, dogmatic, and inherently limited law which has dominated the Western legal consciousness for the past century.

The movement towards a more pluralistic understanding of law is illustrated in several ways, all of which are reflected in the contributions to this book. Classical legal pluralism, developed originally by legal anthropologists, was based on the observation of two or more legal systems operating side by side in the one geographical space (Griffiths 1986; Merry 1988). This was most common in areas of the world where colonial law co-existed with pre-existing indigenous law and/or religious law. However, this form of legal pluralism (a multiplicity of 'legal' orders) may also now be said to characterize conditions in the European community, where European law exists alongside national law and international law, challenging the notion of defined territorial and jurisdictional limits of law. Whether the existence of such a pluralistic environment provides opportunities or further obstacles for feminists is not a question which admits of a definitive or general answer, as this will surely depend on local political, cultural, and legal factors. The liberalization/individualization of welfare policy which results from the confrontation of domestic and European law may seem to be a setback for Swedish feminists, but in other jurisdictions it may provide the opening for improving equality between women and men. Either way, the co-existence of different legal systems, each with their own approach and authority is an unavoidable fact of contemporary legal arrangements, and one which inevitably alters the terrain of feminist legal thought.

A second form of legal pluralism identified by the literature relies on the observation that society is ordered not just by formal law, but by multiple normative systems. These can consist of explicit systems of rules, such as the internal governance of a large organization, or the more embedded normative environments of culture and social values.

A third form of legal pluralism focuses on the positive law itself: for instance, Dalberg-Larsen identifies a number of forms of 'pluralism in official law' (Dalberg-Larsen 2000, 103-106)[8] such as its layered historical origins, the distinct locations of decision-making, and the complex and sometimes contradictory value systems and modes of reasoning upon which law relies. As indicated in the introduction, many of the chapters in this book represent a challenge to Swedish dogmatism insofar as they explore and exploit the internal contradictions in a legal system which is conventionally regarded as coherent.

In addition to the empirically-based observations of pluralism in legal systems, in quasi-legal systems or within positive law, debate has also surfaced over a 'critical legal pluralism' (Kleinhans and Macdonald 1997; Manderson 1996). This approach essentially rejects the objectification and compartmentalization of law and law-like entities, as though they were something different from the subjects who construct them in discourse. While some (systems) theorists have regarded normative environments as relatively autonomous, (see generally Teubner 1992) and therefore capable of self-definition and self-replication, in the critical view they are

8 Dalberg-Larsen is summarizing the work of Hans Petter Graver at this point.

not separate or autonomous, but inevitably inter-related. This is simply because all normative environments start with human agents and human language as the basis for their construction and interpretation. As Desmond Manderson has said:

> The human dimension of misreading is necessary to any genuine pluralism, for it rejects the reification of 'law', 'system', 'culture', or 'community', as a thing which can think or read. Law is not manufactured by a 'multiplicity of closed discourses' precisely because it is only realized through the actions of human beings who exist simultaneously in *several* discourses and who are, therefore, themselves plural. (Manderson 1996, 1064)

As Manderson says, human agents exist at once in several normative environments, and carry their language and conceptual apparatuses around with them: while we do have a remarkable ability to adapt to different contexts and alter our language games accordingly, we are also (as beings) entire entities with complex inter-relating capacities (see also Petersen 1997, 156). We are not compartmentalized machines, able to switch on and off different capacities depending on normative environment. Thus language, power, and cultural messages flow through quite different contexts: they are not strictly bound by the limits of legal doctrine, of academic disciplines, or of philosophy. It is therefore inevitable, and fortunate, that there is cross-fertilization between normative systems. It is also undeniable that an institution such as law only becomes an object, a singular entity, as a result of discourse and has no existence in itself.

In the case of the legal system, for example, it is clear that the daily interpretations and constructions of doctrinal law made by legal decision-makers, are inevitably influenced by prevailing social norms. As two chapters indicate in relation to criminal law, it is not possible to separate absolutely the doctrinal from the discursive: the idealized realm of doctrine cannot be sectioned off from some separate and inherently less organized social 'context' (Burman this volume; Niemi-Kiesiläinen *et al.* this volume). Any effort to effect such a separation is itself a contingent construction derived from a particular theory of law.

Conclusion

As I have indicated above, feminists and other critical theorists do not need to choose between accepting and rejecting the established limits of law. Pragmatism can be combined with idealism, critique with utopianism, and pluralism with monism, even though scholarly habits of thought ordinarily lead us to avoid any position involving contradiction, real or apparent. Thus, in order to come to an alternative understanding of law it is not necessary to begin by rejecting outright the conventional formalistic and doctrinally-defined notion of law. In fact, it is impossible to do so because the positivistic concept of law with which we are so familiar has a strong discursive influence, and is a paradigm for all manner of legally-oriented behaviours. Those who engage with or relate to the law act as if the positivistic conception of law is true, and therefore it is true as a discursive construct. However, its truth is limited to a specific context and instrumental purpose – the just regulation of society. Where it fails to do this, and where that failure is in part a consequence of the limits and limitations of law, feminists question and reformulate law on a general scale. Feminist legal scholarship therefore combines a pragmatic engagement with law, a critique of its limits and limitations, and an aspirational or utopian vision extending beyond the horizon of those limits (Armstrong 2004, 43). Such aspirations may never be realized in the form in which they were originally proposed, and they may even appear to be completely unrealistic, but they have a significant role in contributing to discursive change, which can lead to change in fundamental conceptions, and eventually transformation in institutional arrangements.

References

Literature

Armstrong, Susan (2004), 'Is Feminist Law Reform Flawed? Abstentionists vs Sceptics', 20 *The Australian Feminist Law Journal* 2004, 43–63.

Barron, Anne (2000), 'Feminism, Aestheticism, and the Limits of Law', 8 *Feminist Legal Studies* 2000, 275–317.

Brown, Wendy (2003), 'Gender in Counterpoint', 4 *Feminist Theory* 2003, 365–368.

Charlesworth, Hilary (2005), 'Not Waving but Drowning: Gender Mainstreaming and Human Rights in the United Nations', 18 *Harvard Human Rights Journal* 2005, 1–18.

Conaghan, Joanne (2000), 'Reassessing the Feminist Theoretical Project in Law', in 27:3 *Journal of Law and Society* 2000, 351–385.

Cooper, Davina (2001), 'Against the Current: Social Pathways and the Pursuit of Enduring Change', 9 *Feminist Legal Studies* 2001, 119–148.

Cornell, Drucilla (1998), *At the Heart of Freedom: Feminism, Sex and Equality* (Princeton: Princeton University Press).

Dalberg-Larsen, Jorgen (2000), *The Unity of Law: An Illusion? On Legal Pluralism in Theory and Practice* (Berlin: Galda and Wilch Verlag).

Feminist Legal Studies (2002), 'Special issue on gender mainstreaming in Europe', 10:3 *Feminist Legal Studies* 2002.

Goldman, Emma (1910) 'Woman Suffrage', in *Anarchism and Other Essays* (New York: Dover Publications, reprinted 1969).

Griffiths, John (1986) 'What is Legal Pluralism?', 24 *Journal of Legal Pluralism* 1986, 1–55.

Hawkesworth, Mary (2004), 'The Semiotics of Premature Burial: Feminism in a Postfeminist Age', 29 *Signs Journal of Women in Culture and Society* 2004, 961–985.

Hunter, Rosemary (2002), 'Talking Up Equality: Women Barristers and the Denial of Discrimination', 10 *Feminist Legal Studies* 2002, 113–130.

Irigaray, Luce (1996), *I Love to You* (Routledge: New York).

Kenny, Sally (2002), 'Breaking the Silence: Gender Mainstreaming and the Composition of the European Court of Justice', 10 *Feminist Legal Studies* 2002, 257–270.

Kleinhans, Martha-Marie and Macdonald, Roderick (1997), 'What is a Critical Legal Pluralism', 12 *Canadian Journal of Law and Society* 1997, 25–46.

Larcombe, Wendy (2002), 'The "Ideal" Victim v Successful Rape Complainant: Not What You Might Expect', 10 *Feminist Legal Studies* 2002, 131–148.

Liebert, Ulrike (2002), 'Europeanising Gender Mainstreaming: Constraints and Opportunities in the Multi-Level European Polity', 10 *Feminist Legal Studies* 2002, 241–256.

Mackinnon, Catharine (2000), 'Points Against Postmodernism', 75 *Chicago-Kent Law Review*, 687–712.

Malleson, Kate (2003), 'Justifying Gender Equality on the Bench: Why Difference Won't Do', 11 *Feminist Legal Studies* 2003, 1–24.

Manderson, Desmond (1996), 'Beyond the Provincial: Space, Aesthetics, and Modernist Legal Theory', 20 *Melbourne University Law Review* 1996, 1048–1071.

Mehdi, Rubya and Shahid, Farida (eds) (1997), *Women's Law in Legal Education and Practice in Pakistan* (Copenhagen: New Social Science Monographs).

Merry, Sally Engle (1988), 'Legal Pluralism', 22 *Law and Society Review* 1988, 869–896.

Nousiainen, Kevät (2001), 'Transforming Nordic Welfarism: Liberal and Communitarian Trends in Family and Market Law' in Nousiainen, Kevät, Gunnarsson, Åsa, Lundström, Karin and Niemi-Kiesiläinen (eds) (2001), *Responsible Selves: Women in the Nordic Legal Culture* (Aldershot: Ashgate Publishing).

Nousisinen, Kevät and Niemi-Kiesiläinen, Johanna (2001), 'Introductory Remarks on Nordic Law and Gender Identities' in Nousiainen, Kevät, Gunnarsson, Åsa, Lundström, Karin and Niemi-Kiesiläinen (eds) (2001), *Responsible Selves: Women in the Nordic Legal Culture* (Aldershot: Ashgate Publishing).

Nousiainen, Kevät, Gunnarsson, Åsa, Lundström, Karin and Niemi-Kiesiläinen, Johanna (eds) (2001), *Responsible Selves: Women in the Nordic Legal Culture* (Aldershot: Ashgate Publishing).

Petersen, Hanne (1997), 'Legal Pluralism, Legal Polycentricity, Legal Culture – Their Relevance for Women's Lives and Law', in Mehdi, Rubya and Shahid, Farida (eds) (1997), *Women's Law in Legal Education and Practice in Pakistan* (Copenhagen: New Social Science Monographs).

Smart, Carol (1989), *Feminism and the Power of Law* (London: Routledge).

Svensson, Eva-Maria and Pylkkänen, Anu (2004), 'Contemporary Challenges in Nordic Feminist Legal Studies' in Svensson, Eva-Maria, Pylkkänen, Anu and Niemi-Kiesilänen, Johanna (eds) (2004), *Nordic Equality at a Crossroads. Feminist legal studies coping with difference* (Aldershot: Ashgate).

Svensson, Eva-Maria, Pylkkänen, Anu and Niemi-Kiesiläinen, Johanna (2004), 'Introduction: Nordic Feminist Legal Studies at a Crossroads', in Svensson, Eva-Maria, Pylkkänen, Anu and Niemi-Kiesilänen, Johanna (eds) (2004), *Nordic Equality at a Crossroads. Feminist legal studies coping with difference* (Aldershot: Ashgate).

Teubner, Gunther (1992), 'The Two Faces of Janus: Rethinking Legal Pluralism', 13 *Cardozo Law Review* 1992, 1443–1462.

Thornton, Margaret (1995a), 'The Cartography of Public and Private', in Thornton, Margaret (ed.) (1995), *Public and Private: Feminist Legal Debates* (Melbourne: OUP).

Thornton, Margaret (ed.) (1995b), *Public and Private: Feminist Legal Debates* (Melbourne: OUP).

Thornton, Margaret (2004), 'Neoliberal Melancholia: The Case of Feminist Legal Scholarship', 20 *The Australian Feminist Law Journal* 2004, 7–22.

Young, Alison (1998), 'The Waste Land of the Law: The Wordless Song of the Rape Victim', 22 *Melbourne University Law Review* 1998, 442.

Young, Iris Marion (2003), 'The Logic of Masculinist Protection: Reflections on the Current Security State', 29 *Signs: Journal of Women in Culture and Society* 2003, 1–25.

Index